STATISTICS FOR LIBRARY
DECISION MAKING:
A HANDBOOK

D1714182

INFORMATION MANAGEMENT, POLICY, AND SERVICES

Charles R. McClure and Peter Hernon, Editors

Statistics for Library Decision Making: A Handbook

Peter Hernon

With

Pat K. Bryant, Maya De, Barbara D. Farah, Andrew J. Golub, Hae-young Rieh Hwang, and Li-ling Kuo

Graduate School of Library and Information Science
Simmons College, Boston

ABLEX PUBLISHING CORPORATION
NORWOOD, NEW JERSEY

Second Printing 1993

Printed in the United States of America.

Library of Congress Cataloging-in-Publication Data

Statistics for library decision making : a handbook / by Peter Hernon . . . [et al.].
    p. cm. — (Information management policy and services series)
  Bibliography: p.
  Includes index.
  ISBN (invalid) 0-9839158-6-6; 0-89391-605-6 (ppk)
  1. Library administration—Decision making—Statistical methods. 2. Library statistics. I. Hernon, Peter. II. Series.
Z678.S68   1989
025.1'021—dc20   89-6744
                                                CIP

Ablex Publishing Corporation
355 Chestnut Street
Norwood, New Jersey 07648

*To all Doctor of Arts Students at
Simmons College—Past, Present, and Future*

Contents

List of Figures

List of Tables

Foreword

Librarians have a love–hate relationship with statistics, those tools, those concepts, and those techniques which, when properly understood and utilized, could enable us to do a better job. On the one hand, we hold a fascination with the technology and its software, which provides a key to tests and measurements and facilitates the analysis of research. On the other hand, we collectively must often exhibit knowledge and skills relating to statistical applications. A certain unknown produces fear and skepticism.

Until relatively recent years, the application of statistics in addressing library problems seemed to be, at best, esoteric and, at worst, unnecessary for most professionals. Now, however, many recognize the advantage of sophistication in understanding statistical applications. This volume is for both the skeptic and the believer. It addresses key components and issues in the statistical processes and provides a conceptual, yet practical, understanding of statistical procedures. It directs one toward applying them in the decision-making process. Such an understanding is both admirable and challenging, yet long overdue.

Dr. Peter Hernon is no novice to research methodology. He is one of the bright forces in applying theory to library problems. His monographs, now numbering in the twenties, attest to his knowledge, perseverance, and interests in this arena. In addition, his enthusiasm and gentle coaching have affected his many students, particularly those in the doctoral program at Simmons College. His articulation of problems and needs has spawned numerous research projects which have found their way into the literature of librarianship and information studies. This present volume is a collaborative effort between Professor Hernon and six Simmons doctoral students. It should produce positive results by providing examples for practitioners to utilize and future students to follow.

The information in this compact handbook can be used by both students and practitioners toward understanding the role of statistics in our everyday library operations. The ultimate benefit is better application of management tools in our information centers. This book takes one giant step toward helping us understand the management of complex organizations called libraries.

Robert D. Stueart
Dean
Graduate School of Library
    and Information Science
Simmons College, Boston

Preface

Simmons College offers a Doctor of Arts degree in library management. Students in the program have a diverse management background and differing career aspirations. This handbook, written with six of the students, was intended to assist students in the program in better understanding statistics and the types of decisions that the selection of a test entails. At the same time, *Statistics for Library Decision Making* accomplishes nine objectives aimed at a wider audience:

- To review the research process
- To present fundamental statistical concepts and methods in clear prose
- To identify writings on library management using statistical analyses
- To discuss the utility and application of this literature to library management and decision making
- To enable library managers to become more informed consumers of research and statistics
- To encourage the application of critical judgment to the literature of library management involving the use of statistics
- To relate fundamental statistical concepts and methods to library managerial problems and the published literature
- To facilitate the comprehension of statistical tables and explanations in the published literature
- To familiarize library managers with statistical analysis and graphics software that operate on microcomputers.

This book is *not* intended as a textbook that identifies numerous statistical tests and merely details their computation. Rather, the book complements the pool of existing textbooks, by placing selected statistical applications in the context of the research process and library decision making. Library managers can use statistics for evaluating datasets and making interpretations and decisions based on their evaluation.

Library managers, as well as many library school students at both the master's and doctoral levels, may experience difficulties in reading professional literature that uses statistical applications. If they read such studies at all, it may be only the introduction and conclusion. They may bypass the analysis and presentation of the data. Complicating matters, published writings use, but do not explain, statistics. The purpose of this book is to supplement statistical textbooks and inform library managers and library school students about the application of selected statistical tests and the interpretation of statistical findings. Ideally, the ability of librarians and library school students to read, understand, and evaluate published research, in the area of library management, will improve as a direct result of consulting works such as *Statistics for Library Decision Making* and exploring the use of statistical analysis software (Hernon and Richardson, 1988).

It is our hope that more librarians will engage in action research and apply appropriate statistical analyses to the dataset. Such applications benefit library management, decision making, and the growth of library and information science as both a profession and a discipline.

"The terms statistics and research traditionally create a high level of anxiety . . . . This anxiety is simply unnecessary" (Huck, Cormier, and Bounds, 1974, p. x). Statistics, when properly used, characterize and make sense of numbers. In this book, we have tried to present *basic* statistical and research concepts clearly and to assist librarians and students in not only overcoming anxiety but also developing confidence related to research and the use of statistics.

Peter Hernon
February, 1989

Chapter One
Background—Research, Statistics, and Library Decision Making

RESEARCH

Research represents an investigation that is characterized by certain prescribed activities: (1) reflective inquiry (identification of a problem, conducting a literature search to place the problem in proper perspective, and formulation of a logical or theoretical framework, objectives, and hypotheses/research questions), (2) adoption of appropriate procedures (research design and methodologies), (3) the collection of data, (4) data analysis, and (5) presentation of findings and recommendations for future study. Presumably, attempts to address the issues of reliability (accuracy and consistency of response) and validity (measuring what is intended) guide the second and third steps.

Seldom do published studies include all five components. In fact, many studies lack a statement of the problem and any controls for reliability and validity, for example. For historical studies, some of the components (i.e., objectives and hypotheses/research questions) may be inappropriate. A weak link in any component may invalidate or negate the value of a particular study. Such a link might be the use of inappropriate statistical testing, failure to analyze data sufficiently, or misinterpreting the significance of a statistic.

This book neither examines the entire research process nor represents a textbook on research methods. Rather, it isolates on statistics and presents basic concepts for managers, regardless of library situation, wanting an introduction to statistics, with ample examples drawn from the literature of library science and from managerial problem areas (e.g., staffing, personnel, and collection development). These individuals might also profit from an examination of research methods and statistics textbooks (see Figure 1-1 for examples).

TYPES OF RESEARCH

In the social sciences, there are three types of research: basic, applied, and action. *Basic* research concerns the pursuit of knowledge for its own sake and

Figure 1-1.   Examples of Textbooks on Research Methods and Statistics

---

Ary, Donald, Lucy C. Jacobs, and Asghar Razavieh. *Introduction to Research in Education*. Second edition. New York: Holt, Rinehart and Winston, 1985.

Blalock, Hubert M., Jr. *Introduction to Social Research*. New York: McGraw-Hill, 1972.

Borg, Walter R. and Meredith D. Gall. *Educational Research*. New York: Longman, 1983.

Busha, Charles H. and Stephen P. Harter. *Research Methods in Librarianship*. New York: Academic Press, 1980.

Huck, Schuyler W., William H. Cormier, and William G. Bounds, Jr. *Reading Statistics and Research*. New York: Harper & Row, 1974.

Jaeger, Richard M. *Statistics: A Spectator Sport*. Beverly Hills, CA: Sage, 1983.

Langley, Russell. *Practical Statistics*. New York: Dover, 1970.

Martyn, John and F. Wilfrid Lancaster. *Investigative Methods in Library and Information Science*. Arlington, VA: Information Resources Press, 1981.

Nachmias, David and Chava Nachmias. *Research Methods in the Social Sciences*. Second edition. New York: St. Martin's Press, 1981.

Nie, N.H., C.H. Hull, and J.G. Jenkins. *SPSS: Statistical Package for the Social Sciences*. Second edition. New York: McGraw-Hill, 1975.

Powell, Ronald R. *Basic Research Methods for Librarians*. Norwood, NJ: Ablex Publishing Corp., 1985.

Roscoe, John T. *Fundamental Research Statistics for Behavioral Sciences*. New York: Holt, Rinehart and Winston, 1975.

Siegel, Sidney. *Nonparametric Statistics for the Behavioral Sciences*. New York: McGraw-Hill, 1956.

Swisher, Robert and Charles R. McClure. *Research for Decision Making: Methods for Librarians*. Chicago, IL: American Library Association, 1984.

Tuckman, Bruce W. *Conducting Educational Research*. Second edition. New York: Harcourt Brace Jovanovich, 1978.

---

may or may not immediately contribute to the theoretical base of a discipline or a profession. *Applied* research validates theory and leads to the revision of theory. *Action* research is usually applied research conducted with regard to an immediate problem by someone having a direct interest in that problem. Librarians often conduct *action* research and generate data to which they can apply judgments. In other words, they produce data useful for local decision making concerning library programs, collections, services, operations, staffing, and so forth. Specifically, the data address questions such as (Strain, 1982, p. 166):

- How much does the organization spend for information?
- How much do the potential users actually use the library?
- How productive is the library staff?
- Is the staff the right size for the service it has to provide?
- Are all potential users served equally? Do some get more service than others?
- What information will statistics give on a particular activity or problem?

To her list, we might append two additional questions:

• For what purposes do users consult the library?
• How effective and efficient is the library in meeting user needs?

LIBRARY MANAGEMENT

Library management "can refer to many levels of policy and responsibility" (Bruer, 1980, p. 339). It directs the organization to the successful achievement of its stated mission, goals, and objectives; and typically consists of seven basic elements. These are: planning, organizing, staffing, directing, coordinating, reporting, and budgeting (Gulick and Urwick, 1937, p. 13). Planning, i.e., strategic planning, balances aspirations against reality and involves making choices that presumably change and mature the organization.

It might be noted that strategic planning sets realistic (achievable) objectives. Constraints, in fact, may inhibit a library from accomplishing all that it might like. A law of diminishing returns leads to the notion of the 90% library (Bourne, 1965). Simply stated, the notion suggests that a library service might satisfy a large percentage—say 90%—of the demands effectively and efficiently. However, it might require a disproportionate amount of money, expertise, or effort to raise the percentage, even a few percentage points.

The 55% rule for reference service is a variation of the 90% library. This rule suggests that the staff of academic and public libraries correctly answer 55% of the factual and bibliographic questions (Hernon and McClure, 1987a). Libraries documenting "half-right" reference service might want to increase the level of accuracy, perhaps, another 10 percentage points by the next year. However, accomplishment of this objective might require the purchase of 300 new reference titles, further integration of database searching into reference service, extensive staff training, and so forth. Clearly, higher success rates require a disproportionate allocation of resources and staff commitment to reference service and the accuracy of question answering. It would seem that librarians can either satisfy the information needs of *all* users occasionally or meet the information needs of *some* users most of the time; they cannot meet the needs of all users every time.

As is evident, management involves making choices and selecting alternative strategies. Statistics can be helpful in evaluating datasets and drawing conclusions. Statistics can provide useful insights for all seven elements of management. Planning, however, serves as a focal point for placing statistics in the context of aspirations and objectives. The concept of the 90% library serves as a reminder that local constraints call for realistic planning—planning useful for decision making, change, and progress.

A library is a system in which individual parts are dependent on other parts, and the organization is more than just the sum of the parts. A system is a set of two or more interrelated elements, of any kind, that are coordinated for the accomplishment of certain goals. In short, the interaction among various system elements combine to produce an "essence" or attribute of the system that is not achievable by the individual parts alone. Planning pieces the parts together and guides the organization. Decision makers therefore must place departmental objectives and statistics in a larger context. The discussion of automation later in this chapter illustrates that libraries can develop and maintain systems that monitor diverse activities of the organization and permit the generation of statistics that have system-wide applications.

LIBRARY LITERATURE ON LIBRARY MANAGEMENT

The literature provides a wide assortment of published writings on library management. These writings present theories, philosophies, issues, the identification of problems and perhaps recommended solutions to those problems, managerial styles, "how to" manage, practices, and the historical development of practices, theories, and philosophies. These writings may also question the effectiveness (the meeting of goals and objectives) and efficiency (the allocation of resources) of library programs, services, and operations.

The overwhelming majority of this literature consists of treatises, essays, descriptions, and opinions. Some of the writings consist of research and the presentation of statistics for the purpose of addressing hypotheses and/or research questions. The base of pertinent research literature increases as library managers examine the writings covering particular activities, i.e., collection development, public and technical services, and bibliographic instruction.

Atkins (1988) analyzed the research studies published in nine journals, in library and information science, for 1975–1984. Library management comprised the largest percentage—5.7. However, other studies, such as action research on collection development and copyright, may have managerial implications. Surprisingly, the number of articles on library management, per se, has declined annually over the ten-year span. Atkins (p. 641) speculates that "articles on library management will continue to be the staple of library publishing, but, unless new management theories emerge from other disciplines, most of this research will be rehashing current library management theories." Furthermore (p. 656),

> Research in the library community is neither static nor volatile, but it has characteristics of both. A pendulum effect is in place as a few issues gain in popularity and another group diminishes in favor. While old standby subjects always appear, new issues force their way into the literature according to the needs of the library world at the time.

STATISTICS

Statistics comprise a method for making sense of data and numbers. Library managers can judge the significance, if any, of the data or numbers, and identify implications for decision making. A formal definition of statistics is:

> a set of procedures for organizing and summarizing data. These procedures aid in drawing inferences from data and in communicating research findings in a clear, concise, and meaningful manner.

Swisher and McClure (1984, p. 176) provide an excellent reminder. They note that "statistics *prove* nothing; they simply allow us to state that things *probably* are, or are not, the case in which the whole population from which a sample was drawn and computed." Statistics are not used in isolation. They must be viewed in a context—decision making, goals and objectives, specific research questions and/or hypotheses, and trends. Statistical analysis will not compensate for a faulty study design or plan.

The presentation of data and statistical applications can either assist in or detract from decision making. The presentation might include the use of statistical tests and concepts unfamiliar to library managers. Indeed, for action research to impact on decision making, the presentation may have to be aimed at the level of statistical knowledge already possessed by library decision makers.

For this reason, library researchers might consider the graphic presentation of data gathered from the use of *descriptive* (a set of procedures for merely organizing and describing observations) and *inferential* (a set of procedures for drawing inferences and generalizations from a sample) statistics. Such a presentation might take the form of histograms, bar charts, pie charts, and so forth.

"One sometimes gets the feeling that descriptive statistics have been made to play second fiddle to inferential statistics" (Davis, 1988). As Davis (Ibid.) notes,

> Descriptive and inferential statistics should be complementary, not mutually exclusive, and there are indeed cases where descriptive statistics (especially when accompanied by good graphics) can stand alone. For example, if an entire population is of reasonable size and has been used in its entirety, or if an appropriate representative sample has been taken, and cursory inspection reveals overwhelmingly substantial results, why bore everyone with an inferential statistic that shows the probability of error is less than .000001?

Library managers may experience problems with data interpretation and the application of statistical tests. One purpose of this book is to aid them in understanding different applications and to identify a body of articles using a particular test. This way, managers can engage in a process of self-education. Allen (1985, p. 217) inserts a caution that is worthy of re-emphasizing. He notes that:

. . . care must be taken, lest statistical information become the sole acceptable criterion for decision making, and a tyranny that would destroy the essence of professional judgment. Library management is not a science, least of all an exact one, but an art whose practitioners would still be wise to avail themselves of the assistance that statistical methods can, at times, afford.

Nonetheless, librarians have always had a "commitment to counting;" they "are great compilers of statistical data" (Ibid., p. 211).[1] Strain (1982, p. 165) regards them as "compulsive counters." They produce "a numerical record of the *greater part of the library staff's activities*" (Ibid., p. 167): the number of volumes/titles held and added annually, number of reference questions asked and answered, number of titles borrowed, and so forth. Such routine statistics are then added to monthly and annual reports, reports to accrediting bodies and government agencies, and so forth. In fact, the number of statistical sources on libraries—their collections, staffing, operations, and services—is staggering (Lynch, 1983). Of course, many of these statistics do not result from application of the research process. Rather, the statistics are intended for use "in the annual battle for resources" (Allen, 1985, p. 211).

Powell (1988) examined the importance of various knowledge bases to the performance of academic librarianship. Although his list does not place professional knowledge bases within a context (job position and responsibilities), it does provide a general indication of the overall importance of 56 different knowledge bases. Although librarians like to quantify and report the results, they did not rate "inferential statistics" as a highly prized knowledge base; inferential statistics ranked 54th, ahead of "history of libraries" and "collective bargaining."[2] Perhaps if descriptive statistics comprised one of the knowledge bases and if it were combined with inferential statistics, the ranking might have been higher.

Clearly, a dichotomy appears to exist. The library profession is statistics-oriented (numbers and percentages), but not fully committed to gathering data that lend themselves to inferential statistics. Library research, and the use of statistical analyses, have grown in sophistication over the years. This is "partly because of the availability of computer programs which can analyze large amounts of data in complex ways and solve complicated problems quickly and efficiently without enormous investments in manual labor" (Marchant, Smith, and Stirling, 1977, p. 1).

Many discussions of statistics, or the reading of a research article for that matter, seem to require "mathematical sophistication" on the part of the reader

---

[1] Futas (1984) and Lynch (1981) offer examples of data collection forms used by libraries. Association of Research Libraries (1987) discusses the necessity of "planning for management statistics."

[2] Powell and Creth (1986) had a similar ranking. "Inferential statistics" is not a highly prized knowledge base.

("The Usefulness of Fill Rates: Research and Debate," 1988). Statistics are often cast in terms of mathematics, the calculation of formidable appearing formulae, and a dry, and highly formal, writing style. Many research articles therefore reach only a limited audience, presumably one with a background in research and statistics.

An important question is "How much research and statistical competence should library managers and decision makers have?" This is a hard question to answer because so many factors must be taken into account. The larger and more complex the library and its environment, the greater the research and statistical skills that the library staff need for decision making and planning. As Swisher and McClure (1984, p. 20) suggest,

> by understanding basic research and statistical techniques, utilizing research to support decision making and planning, and encouraging the development of research competency in the librarians, the library will be better able to increase its effectiveness, respond to the information needs of its clientele, and assume a leadership role for accessing the information environment.

More librarians ought to become familiar with research and statistics, both as consumers and participants in the research process. To aid them, this book complements statistics textbooks and presents applications of statistical tests, supported by examples from the research literature on library management.

DECISION MAKING

Overview

Decisions are functional or may relate to a particular area (e.g., collection development or technical services). They also involve different organizational levels (see Figure 1-2). The categories depicted in the figure are not mutually exclusive; rather, they provide a framework for viewing information needs. Decisions might also be (Bommer and Chorba, 1982, p. 11):

> classified as structured or unstructured, depending upon the degree to which the decision process can be described in detail. Decisions are unstructured as a result of lack of knowledge, need for value judgments, complexity of the problem, uniqueness of the problem, etc.

As Bommer and Chorba (Ibid., p. 135) note,

> the decision-making process is often informal, with managers collecting ar.d piecing together information until patterns or mental models emerge as a result of using a trial-and-error sequential exploration approach. The experience and judgment of the manager can then be applied to develop effective alternatives and solutions.

Figure 1-2.   Decision Levels*

Level	Examples
Strategic Planning	Setting objectives; negotiating interlibrary agreements; adopting major technological innovations; expanding facilities.
Management Control	Allocating funds among subject areas; identifying staff development needs; assessing program performance with respect to strategic objectives; determining hours of library service; developing weeding policy; purchasing equipment and services; setting standards for operations.
Operational Control	Monitoring daily operations and activities with respect to standards, corrective actions, scheduling, response to complaints, coordinating special requests and projects. Decisions made in performing cataloging, shelving, acquisitions, weeding, circulation, reference, etc.

*Reprinted from Bommer and Chorba (1982), p. 11. Copyright 1982 and reprinted with permission of G. K. Hall & Co., Boston.

Decision making involves three stages: intelligence, design, and choice (see Figure 1-3). The decision maker need not proceed from stage to stage. For example, rejection of all courses of action might return the decision maker to the intelligence stage. The first stage places data collection and interpretation in a context, while the other stages may involve the use of statistics. Statistics therefore become a tool for evaluating choices and setting/maintaining a course of action.

Figure 1-3.   Stages of Decision Making*

Stage	Examples
Intelligence: Searching for Problems and Opportunities	Complaints; identifying documents which circulate infrequently; measuring adequacy of collection for specific programs; forecasting future needs; identifying potentially useful technological innovations; comparing performance to expectations.
Design: Defining and Analyzing Alternative Actions	Data gathering, modeling and parameter estimation to further understand problem structure; identifying contributing factors; creative generation of possible solutions; discovery of relationships between variables.
Choice: Selecting and Implementing a Course of Action	Forecasting implications of alternative actions; evaluating outcomes; dealing with behavioral and technical problems in implementation.

*Reprinted from Bommer and Chorba (1982), p. 12. Copyright 1982 and reprinted with the permission of G. K. Hall & Co., Boston.

Decision making usually involves three related topics: the decision-making process, the decision maker, and the decision itself. Within each of these areas, decision making attempts to influence value judgments that individuals hold. However, when decision making is equated with the process of converting information into action, then decision making is largely concerned with acquiring, analyzing, and reporting information (data) for the accomplishment of stated objectives (McClure, 1980, pp. 10–11). Library managers must be able to convert a broad range of information sources and the findings of research and evaluation studies into a coherent plan of action.

To make a decision concerning a library service or operation, managers may draw upon information sources such as oral information, printed/published information, or computer-stored information. Depending on the particular information need, its timeliness and complexity, and the information-gathering behavior of individual managers, the number of sources consulted varies significantly.

McClure (1980) offers insights into the number and type of sources used. He indicates that perceived value of information consists of different components: format, form, timeliness, physical availability ("law of least effort"), accuracy of source, expected benefits, and cost. Data collection and statistics, clearly, comprise a subset of information valued by library managers. Still, the value of data collection and statistics should not be discounted.

Research As a Tool Supporting Decision Making

Underlying the decision-making process is the need to collect, analyze, and integrate information and data resulting from research studies. Yet the time pressure for decision making may be intense and unrealistic. Decision makers rarely have time to gather all the information they might need. Therefore, they must plan and predetermine the types of information they might need for meeting various information needs.[3]

The decision-making process is weakened, and ineffective decisions may occur, unless research identifies, compares, evaluates, and selects alternative decisions; evaluates successes and failures resulting from a decision; or determines the impact of a decision on the environment (Janis and Mann, 1977).

The primary means for integrating research into library decision making and planning is to:

- Have clearly written missions, goals, and objectives
- Be able to relate research to specific decisions that are necessary or related to the library's goals and objectives
- Be able to demonstrate how the results from the research will assist the library in improving its overall effectiveness and efficiency.

---

[3] This chapter and book view data as a subset of information.

Addressing these three points before starting a research project is tantamount to asking "So what?" regarding the proposed study, before the research is conducted. If the research really does not matter and will not make an impact on either library effectiveness or efficiency, then another topic for investigation should be considered.

Data collection and the interpretation of statistics should come from librarians who have knowledge of the research process, who can relate that process to decision making and planning, and who are change-oriented. Without an interest in decision making, research, and measurement of the extent to which formal objectives are met, library staff will be unable to respond effectively to the changing environments affecting the library. Further, they will not be able to demonstrate accountability and to justify the existence of actual or planned programs and services. In effect, the staff might continue to do well (efficiently) activities that need not be done (ineffectiveness).

By understanding fundamental research and statistical techniques, utilizing research to support decision making and planning, and encouraging the development of research competencies in the professional staff, managers will be better able to increase the effectiveness of library collections and services, and to respond to the information needs of current and potential clientele.

AUTOMATION AS A STIMULANT TO DATA COLLECTION

The manual gathering, consolidation, processing, analysis, and reporting of data for use in decision making are often time-consuming and involve complex tasking. Automation, when firmly in place, has simplified completion of the tasks and offered increased opportunities to collect data and to simplify their reporting. As a consequence, "it is [now] easy to be swamped by the raw data from computerized systems" (Allen, 1985, p. 213). Still, with careful planning, the management information report generated from automated systems can provide "hard evidence" to support decision making.

Decision Support Systems

A decision support system (DSS) "provides the cognitive map of the operations of the library in a statistical framework" (Dowlin, 1982, p. 37). The primary reasons for developing and maintaining an information base useful for library decision making are to (McClure, 1984, p. 7):

- *Reduce ambiguity by providing an empirical basis for decision making*: there is a need to reduce uncertainty by validating assumptions without replacing creativity and the search for opportunities
- *Provide intelligence about the environment*: ignorance of the environment

perpetuates ignorance of opportunities, isolates the library, reduces knowledge of competitors, and confuses the "proper" role of the library
* *Assess historical, current, and future states*: various scenarios must be considered to deal with the future effectiveness of the library; past and present performance can assist in developing those scenarios
* *Evaluate process and monitor progress*: accomplishment of objectives cannot be determined, remedial action taken, resource allocations changed to meet changing contingencies, or planning for the development of new goals and objectives cannot occur without evaluation.

DSS may increase the centralization over whatever information the library collects and uses, the costs associated with information collection and analysis, and the percentage of librarian time spent in administrative activities. Such a system requires that library staff become more sophisticated users and consumers of statistical data.

As Dowlin (Ibid., p. 38) observes,

> With a decision support system, the impact is on decisions in which there is sufficient structure for computer and analytic aids to be of value and in which managers' judgment is essential.

A management information system, as he notes, provides "routine information on a regular basis." A decision support system, on the other hand, is more fine-tuned. It provides data in specific areas and "indicators of exceptions." Manipulation of the database enables managers "to find indicators that explain the exceptions" (Ibid., p. 46).[4]

Comparison of variables within a DSS affords opportunities for library managers to use different statistical tests highlighted in this book. They may also want to display the findings graphically so that a wide audience might quickly comprehend the significance of the findings.[5]

Statistical Analysis Software

Traditionally librarians, especially those working in academic libraries, have had access to mainframe computers that permit data analysis using the *Statistical Package for the Social Sciences* (SPSS) or *Statistical Analysis System* (SAS). Now spreadsheets, database management software, and special statistical analysis software (e.g., SPSS, SAS, StatPac, StatView 512+, and Minitab) provide a

---

[4] Hernon and Richardson (1988, pp. 4–6) provide examples of decision support systems.

[5] "The proper graphic representation of data can usually help in deciding which inferential statistics are needed or whether they are needed at all. Unfortunately, there is evidence that even the most prestigious journals publish articles by equally prestigious authors who take graphics all too lightly, thereby missing opportunities to make their cases more compelling" (Davis, 1988).

mechanism for microcomputer storage, retrieval, and manipulation of datasets, both large and small.[6] Such software is reliable and "versatile, available, relatively easy to use, not overly expensive" (Marchant, Smith, and Stirling, 1977, p. 2). For example, using dBASE III, one library developed a database for compiling bibliographic instruction statistics (Wells and Gadikian, 1987). Statistical analysis software offer an alternative to the manual preparation of online service reports and a means to calculating data on the use of computer-assisted instruction (Stakenas and Merrick, 1982). Further, library managers can "analyze vendor performance, monitor processing times, and provide other technical processing management reports" (Iehl and Kazlauskas, 1982, p. 141). They can also examine the financial standing of accounts (account and payment information, status of invoices, standing order renewals, and so forth). They can review the budget, the amount committed or encumbered, amount spent, and the remaining balance (Hawks, 1986).

Because librarians have access to affordable software—be it statistical analysis software, spreadsheets, or database management software—they have more opportunities to generate descriptive and inferential statistics. Analysis of percentages rarely provides sufficient insights into, and understanding of, datasets. Librarians often want to compare two, or more, variables and ascertain prevailing trends (see Hernon and Richardson, 1988). Reference librarians, for example, might not only monitor the number of reference questions asked, but also compare the type of question asked to the amount of time required to answer the question, patron type, subject, method of question asking (in person or telephone), and so forth (see Smith, 1984).

Because automation offers greater opportunities for more sophisticated data analysis to occur, library managers may turn more to books, such as this one, and continuing education for an understanding of different statistical tests. It is often important that they obtain as much information as possible from a dataset. Part of this information should include an understanding of the strengths and weaknesses of data collection, and how this information impacts on the selection of statistical tests.

ACTION RESEARCH, STATISTICS, AND PLANNING

Action research focuses on an immediate problem and is generally conducted by someone having direct interest in the resolution of that problem. Librarians conduct action research and generate data useful for local decision making. They focus on results and the evaluation of possible actions and options in terms of stated goals and objectives. Decision makers, as a result, identify significant

---

[6] Townley (1981) and White (1981) discuss the use of SPSS to analyze data related to the book collection and reference service.

problems that merit investigation and direct that action research be undertaken. That research, in turn, generates data requiring analysis and interpretation.

Statistics are a useful tool for library managers interested in planning and evaluation. Statistics provide a mechanism for imposing order and meaning on data. A library's mission, goals, and objectives, together with study hypotheses/ research questions, provide a context for data interpretation.

Planning and evaluation assume a philosophy of change and encourage the pursuit of library excellence. In some cases, they must be accompanied by a reorientation of attitudes regarding the importance of planning in an organization. As Taylor and Sparkes (1977, pp. 289–290) note, planning

> is not so much a battery of techniques and systems as a style of management, and the main benefits from planning derive from a continuing dialogue about the future of the organization. . . . But to start the dialogue involves a dramatic reorientation in management thinking—and a willingness to change.

Before a planning process can be implemented, the following conditions must prevail:

- The organization must be willing to change
- Existing management styles and assumptions must facilitate a planning process
- Adequate resources and staff must be available to support directly the planning process
- Both administrators and staff must have a basic understanding and competency about library planning, research, and statistics.

Library managers must recognize existing conditions and constraints in the library, assess their knowledge and competence about planning and evaluation, and monitor the overall willingness of the organization to change. Given these contingencies, they can develop administrative strategies supportive of an organizational climate that encourages planning and evaluation of library collections, services, programs, and operations.

Improved organizational decision making benefits from the production and maintenance of unique information that addresses various aspects of the library and its environment. That information includes data resulting from the research process and the application of statistical tests. "Indeed, it is the ubiquity of the computer that has made possible the relatively easy and universal invocation of statistics as a management tool" (Morton, 1987, p. 102).

Chapter Two
Value of Library Administration Literature Conveying Research Findings

ADMINISTRATION AND RESEARCH

Administration involves the coordination of both human and material resources for the accomplishment of stated objectives (Kast and Rosenzweig, 1985, p. 6). The administrative process in libraries includes four primary elements: (1) meeting individual objectives and organizational goals, (2) achieving a high degree of participation and productivity from each organizational member, (3) developing and implementing administrative strategies to fulfill goals and objectives, and (4) ensuring that information services and resources meet and resolve the information needs of library clientele. Library administration, which is not an end unto itself, strives to increase access to information resources and to improve services.

It might be noted that a number of textbooks and articles discuss the various administrative philosophies (see, for example, Koontz and O'Donnell, 1979, pp. 175–187; Wren, 1972; Argyris, 1973; Luthans, 1976; Kast and Rosenzweig, 1985). Each philosophy is based on specific assumptions—that are difficult to prove or disprove. But one's assumptions toward work and people affect the actual behaviors and administrative strategies that are used.[1,2]

Decision making is an administrative process of critical importance. Effective decision making cannot occur without the existence of organizational goals and objectives. The comparison and evaluation of alternative decisions enable administrators to consider a broad range of possible solutions, encourage creativity,

---

[1] The human relations school of thought (Argyris, 1973, pp. 257–269) sees workers valued as individuals and the group process of decision making and participation are, at least, as important as the task itself. Marchant (1976) is one of the few studies that takes a philosophy and scrutinizes it through applied research. Marchant examined the impact of management style on performance in libraries. He concluded that staff who were involved in library administration had greater job satisfaction. This satisfaction translated into "better libraries" (p. 164).

[2] *Library Literature* tends to treat management as a subset of administration. This chapter provides an overview of both management and administration, while subsequent chapters concentrate on the former.

and introduce a planning perspective into a decision-making process. Of course, a decision must be implemented; that is, specific steps must be identified and initiated. These steps or actions must be carried out by the appropriate individuals, at the appropriate time, and must meet previously agreed upon performance criteria. Both the outcome(s) of the decision, steps, and actions, as well as an analysis of additional or revised information derived from the environment, should be taken into account when reviewing organizational goals and objectives. When necessary, goals should be revised.

The decision-making process is inhibited unless library managers use the research process and the resulting data to identify, compare, evaluate, and select alternative decisions; to evaluate the consequences of a decision; or to measure the impact of the decision on the environment (Janis and Mann, 1977). A typical (and often ineffective) approach to decision making in some libraries is simply to define the situation in which a decision is necessary and to implement a decision. The presumption is that the decision produced the anticipated benefits and that any adverse consequences are insignificant.

Action research, which is intended to improve organizational effectiveness and efficiency, is the type of research needed in most library settings. Such research therefore focuses on the particular needs and problems of a library or information center. Swisher and McClure (1984) describe the process of action research.

As emphasized in Chapter 1, librarians need knowledge of the research process and how to relate that process to decision making and planning. Without such skills, librarians may be forced to accept traditional assumptions currently operating in the library. They may be unable to respond to the changing environments affecting the library, to demonstrate accountability, and to justify collections and services if asked to do so. Librarians need to ask questions such as:

- Do library patrons use some portions of the collection more than others; if so, which ones, and why?
- Do bibliographic instruction programs improve the patron's willingness to request reference assistance and gain access to information resources?
- How successful are public service staff in answering reference questions and making appropriate referrals?

Asking such questions is critical if libraries are to improve their services and increase access to resources.

In sum, without research, "there can hardly be any objective assessment of services, performance, or needs. . . . [Research] must also be seen as a significant element in the personal development of library staff and in the continuing evolution of librarianship as a profession" (Allen, 1986, p. 162). Allen (Ibid., p. 159) suggests that library managers have a responsibility to ensure the conduct of in-house library research, of the highest quality possible.

Planning and Evaluation

Planning is the process of setting goals and objectives, developing programs and activities to accomplish those objectives, and evaluating the effectiveness and efficiency of those programs in context of the goals and objectives.[3] Numerous planning theories and techniques have been developed but few implemented in library settings. With the appearance of practical manuals such as *Strategic Planning for Library Managers* (Riggs, 1984), *Planning and Role Setting for Public Libraries* (McClure et al., 1987), and *Output Measures for Public Libraries* (Van House et al., 1987), there are now guides that discuss the implementation of planning and evaluation techniques.

Evaluation accumulates "information for . . . decision making" (*Evaluating Bibliographic Instruction*, 1983, p. 9), is the accountability aspect of planning, and represents a measurement of library effectiveness in reaching a predetermined goal. Figure 2-1 illustrates the types of questions that decision makers and others would ask in one area of evaluation—bibliographic instruction. The figure serves as a reminder that evaluators query decision makers about what they want to know and how the data will be used (Ibid., pp. 10–11). The purpose is to ensure that having access to data not only *matters* but also leads to the accomplishment of objectives and improved library effectiveness or efficiency.

The complexity and uniqueness of existing administrative techniques, local situations, and the resources available in a particular library preclude "cookbook" recipes for how to prepare every organization for the implementation of every type of *formative* and *summative* evaluation. The purpose of summative evaluation is to determine the success or failure of a program or service, while formative evaluation seeks to improve an ongoing program or service. Both types of evaluation have a role in the planning process, and one is not necessarily better than the other.

Library managers must recognize existing conditions and constraints in the library, determine their knowledge and competency about planning and evaluation, and analyze the administrative assumptions under which libraries organize and service information resources. They should also assess the overall willingness of the organization to change. Recognizing and addressing these contingencies, librarians can develop administrative strategies to create an organizational climate that encourages the planning and evaluation of information collection and services.

Areas Amenable to Data Collection

Research can be conducted in almost all phases of library work. Hernon (1987), for example, illustrates the facets of reference service that lend themselves to the

---

[3] Goals are long-term directions for the library, while objectives are short-term, accomplishable, and measurable statements of action.

Figure 2-1.   Bibliographic Instruction: Who Wants to Know and What?*

Who Wants to Know?	Typical Evaluation Questions
Administrators	Does the program fit in with instructional goals?
	Does it have the support of students and faculty?
	How important are its objectives?
	Does it fit in with other institutional programs?
	How does it compare with programs at other institutions?
	What are the qualifications of those involved?
	Is the program operating smoothly in terms of time, cost, and resources?
	Is the program educationally sound?
Teaching Faculty	What good is this program educationally?
	Is it of any value to my students?
	Does it have the support of other faculty and students?
	Does it have the support of institutional administrators?
	What are the qualifications of those involved?
	Does program content coincide with my course objectives?
Students	Is this program worth my attention?
	What do I have to lose or gain from it?
	Is it interesting?
	Are the teachers any good?
	How does it fit in with my curricular requirements?
	Do other students find it interesting and/or useful?
	Do faculty recommend it?
Program Librarians	Is the program accomplishing what it is supposed to?
	Are students implementing what they learn?
	Do we have enough personnel, funding, and support?
	How much is our program growing or shrinking and why?
	Is the program having any adverse effects?
	Is the program running smoothly?
	Are we doing all we could be or should be doing?
	How can we improve our program?
Other Librarians	How does that program compare with ours?
	Is there something in the program that can help ours?
	Is there anything different or significant about it?
	Is the program run as it should be?
	Is the program accomplishing what it is supposed to?

*Reprinted with permission of the American Library Association, taken from *Evaluating Bibliographic Instruction: A Handbook*; copyright © 1983 by ALA.

development of performance measures. Librarians can evaluate both the *direct* (personal assistance, effectiveness and efficiency of bibliographic instruction, etc.) and *indirect* (collection development, etc.) aspects of reference service. Topical areas that they might examine include the:

• Staff themselves
• Clientele
• Library's capacity to provide service

- Reference questions asked
- Resources needed to answer questions
- Answers given.

Bommer and Chorba (1982, Chapter 1) identify specific performance or effectiveness measures for some of these aspects of reference service.

Methodologies Resulting in Data Collection Amenable to Statistical Analysis

Employing a variety of methodologies, librarians can collect data, reflective of different measurement scales, that can be subjected to statistical analyses using computer or hand calculation. Some of the methods for quantifiable data collection represented in library literature include:

- *Expert judgment.* For example, staff might evaluate the collection, according to written procedures, to gather data for the identification of strengths and weaknesses. Burr (1979) and McCartt (1983) are examples of this methodology
- *Retrieval of items from a database and evaluation of their usefulness and relevance.* Examples include Cooper (1968) and Robertson (1969)
- *Testing (standardized or locally developed tests).* Toifel and Davis (1983) is an example of a writing using this methodology
- *Self-rating of a project's impact from participants.* The success of numerous conferences and programs is often determined from the opinions of participants about sessions and the elements they either liked or disliked. Johnson and Mann (1980) provide examples of studies using a self-assessment procedure
- *Response to a questionnaire or interview.* Numerous studies have employed a survey methodology. For example, Rubin (1986) and Murfin and Gugelchuck (1987)
- *Observation of behavior and the impact of that behavior on programs and services.* For example, Kenney (1966) used a similar method to investigate the use of a card catalog
- *Unobtrusive evaluation* (the testing of staff members unaware that they are test subjects). Crowley and Childers (1971), as well as McClure and Hernon (1983) are two examples of this application
- *Obtrusive evaluation* (the testing of staff members who are fully aware that they are the test subjects, or an examination of how staff members work). Examples of studies using this methodology include Bunge (1967), Carlson (1964), and Orr and Olson (1968)
- *Content analysis.* Documents representative of an issue or topic are gathered and their contents classified and analyzed. One example might include taking

the arguments of all the stakeholders in the FBI Library Awareness Program and determine the frequency of each argument and which stakeholder advanced it. Then the researcher would verify the legitimacy of each argument. Another example is Wilson (1982)

* *Analysis of historical and current records.* Studying statistical or other records for patterns may be simplified by placing such information onto diskette, magnetic tape, and so forth, for computer manipulation. Wiegand and Steffens (1988) analyzed 100 ALA presidents according to variables such as gender, race, martial status, political affiliation, religion, and highest nonlibrary degree earned. They reported data by percentages and did not use more sophisticated means of analysis. Based on their findings, they raised a series of questions such as "Why doesn't the [ALA] membership elect people from the West in greater numbers?"
* *Queuing* (or the monitoring of traffic patterns, e.g., observing the flow of traffic at reference, periodical, and circulation desks). For a discussion of queuing theory and its application, see Halperin (1977) and Lee (1966)
* *Transactional analysis* (e.g., analysis of circulation records or records resulting from participants' use of online catalogs). Technology captures each transaction (or use), and researchers analyze patterns in the records. Examples include Borgman (1983) and Tolle (1983)
* *Bibliometrics and citation analysis.* Bibliometrics studies investigate the structure of published literature and its usage: patterns in "authorship, publication, reading, and citation." Bibliometrics includes studies relating to "the growth of the literature on a given subject," "patterns in the distribution of publishing productivity by individual authors," "how articles on any subject are dispersed across journals," "the 'obsolescence' of literature," "the epidemiology of ideas as reflected in scholarship as evidenced by analyses of who cites whom" (Buckland, 1983, p. 166). Broadus (1977) reviews various studies using citation analysis; many of the studies listed in the appendix of Hernon (1984) used citation analysis.

Lancaster (1977, 1988) identifies and describes a number of studies that have used the above mentioned methodologies and that have produced data amenable to analysis on microcomputers.

Citation Analysis

Citation analysis, one of the methodologies highlighted in the previous section, can generate data useful for collection planning and management. The staff of academic and special libraries, as well as researchers in the discipline of library and information science, may examine—through citations—patterns among the works cited in articles, books, conference papers, etc., as to their:

- Form (monograph, periodical, dissertation, map, government publication, etc.)
- Class of material (primary, secondary, or tertiary)
- Language (English, etc.)
- Subject
- Age of cited sources.

Citation studies might also probe the reasons for citing works. Although authors cite works for many reasons, i.e., noting shortcomings to cited works and refuting interpretations, some relationship between citing and cited works presumably exists. Studies might also gauge the *impact factor*, number of citations received by a periodical or conference proceedings in comparison to the number of articles contained in that source (see Lancaster, 1988, p. 61).

The number of citation studies conducted in the social sciences varies significantly from discipline to discipline, and field to field.[4] These studies may have some utility to library decision makers because they provide one indicator of use of information resources. The studies may suggest published forms, and the language in which they are written, that scientists or social scientists prefer and use most frequently. In addition, these studies reveal age patterns to the resources used. Using such information (together with circulation and other information), library managers might conclude that, for example, academic economists are most likely to use periodicals and government publications, generally from among a core of titles not over three years. It might be possible to factor such information in a library's selection profile, retention decision making, and decisions concerning on-site versus remote storage. Less useful (however defined) titles would obviously be likely candidates for discarding, remote storage, or microforming.

RESISTANCE TO DATA COLLECTION

The library director might favor data collection and decision making based on "hard evidence." This person might also assume that the staff share his/her enthusiasm. In fact, other managers might not be supportive. They might believe in their intuitive ability to recognize "poor quality" and "inefficiency" and resist data collection because the data might conceivably be used against the library— to argue against a program or service favored by the library. Staff might view data collection as a distraction; research takes them away from the provision of services and programs. McClure's discussion (1986) of the use (or, more correctly, nonuse) of performance measure data illustrates internal resistance to data collection and distrust of the utility of such data. Further, the "identification of

---

[4] Hernon (1984, pp. 421–429) provides a list of studies on the information needs of those in different social science disciplines. The list is not comprehensive; rather it is suggestive.

'poor' performance on a specific service would require a remedial action and would represent a change in the status quo" (p. 329).

Performance measures represent a broad managerial concept that encompasses both *input* (indicators of those resources essential to library services) and *output* (indicators of the services resulting from library activities) measures. Such measures depict the extent, effectiveness, and efficiency of library operations, services, and programs. Yet, even middle management might have little understanding of such measures—their purpose and relationship to planning (Ibid., p. 326). They might also surmise that performance measure data will not alter the decision-making process and that a complex and time-consuming data-collection process far exceeds the value of the resulting data (Ibid.). McClure discovered instances in which department heads kept two sets of records: one for submission to the director and the other for internal use (p. 327).

Clearly, books such as our handbook can identify the benefits of conducting research and engaging in the planning process. At the same time, researchers can develop, improve, and refine research designs and methodologies. Such activities, however, do not guarantee that libraries will engage in the conduct of action research. The McClure essay indicates that organizational change must be acceptable throughout the library. There must be a strong commitment to change, a sense of purpose, and a willingness to conduct research that impacts local decision making and the profession, and improves the quality of library collections, operations, programs, and services.

THE RESEARCH LITERATURE ON LIBRARY MANAGEMENT AND DECISION MAKING

Both management and decision making are complex topics that contain many facets. The literature on management and decision making, which is often a subset of the administration literature, is enormous, especially if writings from disciplines other than library and information science are included. Focusing on the one discipline—library and information science—the literature is still sizable (see Chapter 1). Many other articles, speeches, and monographs have implications for management and decision making. Research obviously comprises a subset of the literature on management and decision making.

Utility of the Research Literature

The literature offers good examples of practice and methods for studying a problem. Managers obtain an understanding of different research plans (research designs and methodologies) and can consider the replication of these studies locally. If feasible, they might have staff conduct case studies employing different data collection methodologies (e.g., interviewing, survey questionnaires, unobtrusive testing, and the completion of logs). With consensus among the findings reported from the use of the different instruments, staff can assume greater validity in study findings. Case studies are especially relevant for studying knowledge utilization because "the topic covers a phenomenon that seems to be inseparable from its context" (Yin, 1984, p. 99). Case studies offer excellent opportunities to understand local circumstances and determine the reliability and validity of datasets.

The literature also illustrates what can be evaluated and how evaluation can occur. For example, managers interested in studying the 55% rule (see Chapter 1) locally but not wanting to use unobtrusive testing will discover alternatives (e.g., Benham and Powell, 1987; Murfin and Gugelchuck, 1987). They might develop a form demonstrating high degrees of validity and administer it to users of reference service (Murfin and Gugelchuck, 1987).

In many libraries, reference departments frequently record the number of reference questions asked and identify questions that they were unable to answer or that proved difficult to answer correctly. However, the recording and counting of hash marks has limited utility for decision making related to the physical location of reference desks and to staffing patterns. A detailed analysis of questions asked might suggest reference titles meriting purchase, or removal from the general collection and inclusion in the reference collection. Hallman (1981) discusses "designing optical mark forms for reference statistics." Using such an article, library staff could develop a reference question evaluation form that could be coded for data input into a microcomputer for analysis by a statistical analysis software package.

The literature might discuss issues or topics not previously known and offer insights into how such research might be conducted. For example, in recent years, writings have focused on *burnout*, an inability to cope with one's work on a daily basis. Those suffering from burnout display both physical symptoms and emotional conditions. The literature suggests methods for diagnosing and treating burnout. However, it merits mention that selection of the instrument to document burnout must be done carefully, testing must occur, over time, on a test–retest basis, and managers should be careful in their interpretation of the findings. Here they might prefer to rely on outside consultants, in particular, ones from psychology or medicine.

Another topic might be the introduction of information technologies into the library. Managers, for example, should be sensitive to ergonomics studies that view people in their work environment for the purpose of designing environments supportive of improved job performance and increased staff comfort. Specifically, ergonomics addresses topics such as eye strain, physical discomfort, and the impact of screen glare in relationship to the amount of time staff spend at microcomputer workstations. Ergonomics studies suggest that workstations should have adjustable lighting and comfortable chairs, and support staff should receive periodic breaks from data coding, entry, and editing.

Of course, librarians engaged in proposal writing should be aware of the research literature. Needless to say, such writings place a problem in context of what others have done, identify variables for inclusion or exclusion, forewarn researchers of problems that they might encounter, and so forth.

One final topical area merits mention. The literature might assist with staffing decisions in different library departments. Should, for example, the reference department place nonprofessional staff at public service desks and under what circumstances will they refer questions to professional staff? Managers should determine how well that referral process operates. They might also want to reorganize departments on the presumption that computerization either reduces the need for separate departments or necessitates the creation of additional departments.

The literature contains writings useful to decision makers and decision making. We must look at the literature in terms of not only what it is now but also what it could be. Librarians, together with publishers and editors of journals and monograph series, should strive to improve the quality of the research base and to incorporate new topical areas, ideas, and approaches to problem solving into the professional literature. We should not leave the writing and research to others; instead, we should all be involved in the process. Only through its literature does a discipline, field, or profession mature.

Awareness of the role of research and the relationship between theory and practice will enable librarians to better adapt to new environments and situations. At the same time, existing values, beliefs, and practices will be reviewed, evaluated, and challenged. Research must also expand into the development and testing of models. Such studies depend on prior conducting of descriptive research and on gathering information on the current status of phenomena. Further, these studies document a situation as it exists at the time of the study, so that accurate and valid data can be used in model construction and testing. The profession needs to be aware of, and to consider, a variety of models so that those most appropriate to a given situation, level of funding, political climate, etc., are identified and implemented.

Is the Research Literature Underutilized?

To what extent do managers use the research literature? McClure (1980) suggests that it is not as frequently used as might be expected. Clearly, managers turn to the literature in only certain circumstances (see Ibid.) and then probably discover that the writings vary substantially in quality. They may have to sort through a variety of writings to find those relevant to their information need.

Availability of a literature is not synonymous with *use*, and *use* is not the same as *impact*. A central question becomes "How to gain ready access to those writings that will be used and have an impact on decision making?" Impact is difficult to operationalize and measure, because researchers cannot easily isolate a particular variable and remove competing or confounding variables.[5] Furthermore, no single methodology adequately captures impact, and a source that has been used might much later be recognized for producing an impact.

It would seem that the literature is also underutilized because writings are redundant (rehash a topic or problem). A particular writing may be difficult to locate or comprehend. If the source sought is not contained in the collection and a decision must be made soon, will the manager consult interlibrary loan or directly contact another library? The use of statistics and the formal and prescribed writing style associated with scholarly writings may inhibit use of an article or book. Research may be contained in local reports that do not receive national visibility, and published writings are not always sufficiently indexed. In addition, managers may not be aware that the literature has covered a particular topic. An excellent research topic for someone to pursue would be "How much of the research literature is action research having local application and demonstrating utility?"

Statistics Used in the Research Literature

In preparation of this book, we examined an enormous number of writings in order to select those for discussion in the following chapters. As might be expected, the majority of writings use elementary statistics such as descriptive statistics, in particular percentages. The next greatest number of writings employed lower-ordered statistics, meaning correlations, chi-square test of independence, etc. The smallest number used more complex statistics such as analysis of variance, regression analysis, and factor analysis.

Given the literature base, this book will concentrate on the first two types of statistics (descriptive and lower-ordered), with brief attention given to more complex statistics. The purpose is to get managers to think of the literature and to expect the use of statistical analyses in the datasets presented to them. From the modest base being presented in this book, others can expand their knowledge of statistics and the application of statistics to library decision making.

INCREASING USE OF STATISTICS

As has been stressed in this and the previous chapter, librarians collect large amounts of data, which might be digested into monthly and annual reports, or reports to accrediting bodies. At the same time, they might conduct online database searching or have online catalogs and circulation systems. They might

---

[5] For a discussion of impact assessment, see Rossi and Freeman (1985), Chapter 5, "Strategies for Impact Assessment," pp. 185–227.

also be developing an automated decision support system (see Chapter 1). Where computers automatically capture transactions or are programmed to record the types of information sought by decision makers, there are increased opportunities for compiling data subject to statistical analysis.

In addition, many libraries conduct community analyses and surveys. It would seem that managers should reassess how they want the data reported. Do they want staff to incorporate statistical analyses and the graphic presentation of data in internal reports and formal studies? It is our hope that this book will encourage an affirmative response to the question.

Chapter Three
Microcomputer Applications

Microcomputers can play an important role in planning and monitoring decision-making processes. They can be used to gather and evaluate information relevant to the organization's mission, goals, and objectives. They also make available larger quantities of information for the decision maker than is possible in a manual data or record-keeping system. That person has an opportunity to identify the types of information useful to him/her, and the methods by which that information is more easily consumed. The decision maker may prefer the graphic display of information for a quick identification of trends and issues.

The proliferation of microcomputers, and their increased capabilities and reasonable purchase price, has been nothing short of incredible. Microcomputers can be used to acquire, organize, control, and increase access to bibliographic and managerial information in many library settings. The implementation of in-house automated systems for serials control, circulation, reference services, and more is now possible with relatively little capital outlay.

Researchers and decision makers can also use microcomputers throughout the research process, including the drafting of a proposal, data analysis, and polishing the final version of a report. This chapter provides a brief overview of microcomputer applications throughout the research process, and highlights examples of statistical analysis and graphics software. In so doing, the chapter provides a foundation for the tutorials contained in subsequent chapters and the appendices.

COST OF MICROCOMPUTER HARDWARE AND SOFTWARE

As of the winter of 1988, an IBM compatible microcomputer with 80286 CPU turbo speed, 640K RAM expandable 1 MB, 2 hard/2 floppy controller, 1.2 hi-density drive, 20MB Seagate hard drive, Hercules graphics adapter, parallel print port, AT style keyboard, monitor, and real time clock (battery backup) costs $1,295. A 1200/300 modem costs another $75.00. A good quality printer and interface can be obtained for approximately $500.00. Thus, an extremely powerful, sophisticated, and speedy microcomputer can be obtained for approximately $2,000.

Depending on the number and types of software selected from Figure 3-1, as well as the cost of individual packages, researchers and librarians could easily spend, at least, another $1,500–$3,000. As this chapter illustrates, librarians have choices and the completion of many data collection projects may require the purchase of software that their library does not already possess. To assist users of particular software packages, some commercial companies are creating packages intended to piggy-back on already existing programs. For example, a library might obtain a template for Lotus 1–2–3 that permits the calculation of selected statistical tests (such as chi-square) on a routine basis.

Figure 3-2, which identifies cost components, indicates that hardware and maintenance costs are higher for large organizations starting to use microcomputers system-wide. "The system costs start at the time the procurement is initiated and continue throughout its life" (Hecht, Hecht, and Press, 1984, p. 92). "Major cost components include hardware, software, procurement, site preparation, installation and implementation, training, supplies, maintenance, and communications" (Ibid.).

Use of microcomputers for research need not involve all these costs. However, it would be rare that a library would dedicate a microcomputer solely for research purposes. Research would comprise but one application. Librarians undoubtedly would use a microcomputer for *administrative* (document prepara-

Figure 3-1.   Summary of Types of Microcomputer Software*

Software	Purpose
Wordprocessing	Create, edit, and print reports, etc.
Writing Aids	Spelling checkers and analysis of writing style
Database Management	Organize, store, manipulate, and retrieve data
Financial Management	Perform calculations and formatting for tabular reports, e.g., budget forecasting
Graphics	Presentation of data graphs and preparation of diagrams and illustrations
Communication	Data transfer to and from other systems
Project Managers	Produce time schedules for project completion
Research Aids	Questionnaire preparation and the input of questionnaire data into machine-readable form
Statistical Analysis	Process data and perform statistical analyses
Miscellaneous	Simulation, etc.

*Adapted from Hecht, Hecht, and Press (1984), p.x.

Figure 3-2.   Microcomputer Cost Factors*

Class	Items
Procurement	Requirements specification
	Consultations
	Purchasing process (include preparation of RFP and evaluation of bids if relevant)
Hardware	Basic system (CPU, memory, disk drives)
	CRT terminal(s)
	Additional disk drives (e.g., hard disk)
	Printer(s) (dot matrix and letter quality)
	Modem
	Attachments and accessories (additional RAM, interfaces, cables, etc.)
	Additional peripherals (plotters, joy-sticks, digitizers, etc.)
	Specialized interfacing costs (consider when adding any serial device)
Furniture	CRT tables, chairs, printing stands, etc.
	Noise hoods
	Electrical power conditioning equipment and battery backup units (as required)
Software	Operating system(s)
	Purchased application software
	Software installation and modification
	Custom developed packages
	Cost of updates
	Ongoing software support costs
Site Preparation	Air conditioning
	Electrical work
	Installation of cables
	Alteration of offices and work areas (including carpentry work)
	Lighting changes (desk lights, curtain, etc.)
	Lost production time during site preparation
Conversion	Inputting data to new system
	Modifying (or rewriting) programs
	Setting up files
	Managing conversion effort
Implementation and Installation	Lost production time during installation
	Cost of running parallel operations
	Planning and supervising costs
	Freight charges
	Keeping track of the location of all hardware and software components
Training	Cost of training and supplemental materials not included with package purchases
	Lost production during training
	Cost of providing space for on-site training
	"Refresher" courses and ongoing training for new employees
Supplies	Disks
	Paper
	Ribbons

Figure 3-2.   (*Continued*)

Class	Items
	Anti-static mats and sprays
	Cleaning supplies
	Glare screens
	Paper stands
Maintenance	Cost of maintenance contracts (if available)
	Cost of transporting systems to repair depot (if on site service is not provided)
	Cost of spare units
	Lost production time
	Lost production data
Communications	Telephone charges
	Cost of components (cable, interfaces, software)
	Cost of network installation
	Outside network charges

*Reprinted from Hecht, Hecht, and Press (1984), pp. 92–93.

tion, planning and budgeting, contracts and personnel administration, etc.), *professional* (document and bibliography preparation, data management, statistical calculations, the generation of graphics for reports and presentations, and other specialized applications), and *clerical* (document preparation, data entry, and preparation of routine budget and fiscal reports) purposes (Hecht, Hecht, and Press, 1984, p. 91).

Prior to purchase or dedication of a microcomputer for research purposes, library decision makers and researchers should review proposed uses of the hardware and software. The more frequently that they engage in data collection and produce large datasets, the more they would benefit from access to a hard disk drive and software tailored to use on such equipment.

USES OF MICROCOMPUTERS FOR RESEARCH

Researchers might use microcomputers at different stages of the research process. Drafts, as well as the final version, of a proposal might be wordprocessed. The spelling of words contained in a proposal might be reviewed with software that contains a spelling checker. Researchers might also use an electronic thesaurus to vary word or phrase choices and either RightWriter or Grammatik to check for errors in grammar, writing style, word usage, and punctuation.

RightWriter, a product of RightSoft, Inc. (4545 Samuel Street, Sarasota, FL 34233) supports wordprocessing software such as WordPerfect, WordStar, pfs: First Choice, and MultiMate. Version 3.0 contains over 4,000 rules governing business writing. As shown in chapter 11 and Hernon and Richardson (1988, pp.

182–184), researchers can use this writing aid to measure the strength, readability, and other qualities of their writing. They can adjust (lower or raise) the readability level of their writing depending on the audience for which a proposal, report, or manuscript is intended.

Grammatik III, sold by MicroPro (33 San Pablo Avenue, San Rafael, CA 94903), recognizes parts of speech and evaluates writing in context. It highlights jargon, sexist terms, redundant phrases, neologisms, misused or overused phrases, and improper use of homonyms (e.g., they're, their, and there), possessives (e.g., its and it's), and transposition (e.g., form and from). It also indicates any disagreement between subject and verb, redundant comparatives, incomplete sentences, double negatives, split infinitives, and so forth; incidentally, RightWriter performs many of these same functions.

After preparing the proposal, researchers might use a spreadsheet to organize the budget and project managers to develop a GANTT chart or time schedule for the completion of all tasks. Once set, these software programs can be adjusted as necessary; in other words, the researchers can manage the budget and time schedule.

Concerning data collection, some software focuses on note-taking and enables researchers to piece the notes together into a text. Some researchers might wordprocess questionnaires or other data collection forms, which can then be either xeroxed or printed. In other cases, they might use interactive software. For example, FormTool, which is published by BLOC Development Corp. (1301 Dade Blvd., Miami Beach, FL 33939), constructs business forms. Using it, researchers can develop either simple or complex data collection forms with different lettering, borders, graphic symbols, check-off squares, bar codes, and so forth.

Ci2 System 100, Version 2, a product of Sawtooth Software Inc. (208 Spruce North, Ketchum, ID 83340), is a microcomputer-interactive, interviewing system for the IBM PC, and compatibles, that can produce a survey from questionnaire composition to administration and data analysis. (That survey, however, must be used for personal interviewing; either the respondent or a telephone interviewer sits at the microcomputer.) Based on the answers to questions posed by Ci2, researchers develop questionnaires that are reviewed for design logic, skip patterns (do survey subjects complete all the questions or skip from one section to another), word and phrase choices, and the types of categories to use for closed-ended questions. Using Ci2, researchers enter responses to completed questionnaires into a machine-readable form and generate tallies.[1] Such software

---

[1] Researchers can use the Field program in Ci2 to create field disks for interviewing purposes. The Setnum program preassigns respondent numbers to field disks and prints the numbering on the field labels. Upon completion of field interviewing, the Cum program accumulates data from the field disks into a single file for analysis. The Data program examines the responses and generates marginal tabulations, including frequencies and measures of central tendency.

is not as sophisticated as statistical analysis software (e.g., Minitab and StatPac). However, researchers can produce ASCII files that can be read on spreadsheet and statistical analysis software. For data analysis and manipulation, therefore, researchers have choices; they can select from among statistical analysis software, spreadsheets, and database management software. The next section of the chapter will briefly highlight each of these. However, readers interested in a detailed discussion of each, with illustrations and examples, should consult Hernon and Richardson (1988).

In preparing the research report, wordprocessing software—together with RightWriter, Grammatik, and the other software discussed with proposal preparation—become useful. With wordprocessing software (depending on the package), researchers can also insert bibliographic information into a separate bibliography and generate an automatic table of contents, lists of tables and figures, and indexes.

Researchers might want to use graphics software to summarize large quantities of data and visually display trends (see Hernon and Richardson, 1988, pp. 153–156, 163–165, 185–187). They can produce bar graphs, histograms, pie charts, and so forth, on software such as Harvard Graphics, a product of Software Publishing Corp. (1901 Landings Drive, Mt. View, CA 94039–7210).[2]

Research has shown that the format in which information is presented has an independent effect on the facilitation of decision making (Bybee, 1981, p. 364). The reprinting of computer printout, the reporting of numerous statistical tables in a report or oral presentation, or a question-by-question presentation of data do not lend themselves to easy readability and the quick comprehension of statistical relationships. Designing the formats of oral presentations and written reports to meet the needs of specific audiences will make any summary of findings more useful (the utility of findings is an important consideration for action research) and enable managers to include the data in their decision making.

Using interactive software, researchers and/or managers could merge graphic presentations, data reporting, and wordprocessed text into an eye-catching report that is the result of desktop publishing. They can lay out individual pages of an internal report and produce both a table of contents and index. Such a report might appeal to boards of trustees, accrediting bodies, and so forth.

STATISTICAL SOFTWARE

As highlighted in this section, different types of microcomputer software perform statistical calculations. Developments in the marketplace are making it

---

[2] Harvard Graphics 2.1 has a spelling checker, over 200 new symbols, and improved editing capabilities. Published comparisons of different graphics software generally comment on the high quality output and ease of use associated with Harvard Graphics (see "Buyer's Guide," 1989, pp. 121-176).

easier for librarians and others to obtain software that interfaces with other types of packages. For example, SPSS/PC+ is a fully integrated package that enables users to enter and edit data; analyze the data using statistical procedures; generate graphics, charts, and maps; produce presentation-ready tables instantly; and identify trends (forecasting or time series analysis). Having access to such software, researchers and others can readily produce reports and manuscripts. Clearly, from existing software, librarians have opportunities to analyze and manipulate datasets. The technology is in place; now they must learn to use and apply it to the datasets that they are already collecting and maintaining. At the same time, there are increased opportunities to create new datasets and use appropriate statistical analyses for hypothesis testing, answering questions, and examining trends and patterns.

Spreadsheet Software

Library decision makers can use spreadsheet software for budgeting, project monitoring, financial and manpower projections, and planning. They can perform simple parametric analyses (see next chapter), generate descriptive statistics, and produce calculations amenable to presentation in tabular form. Chapter 6 of Hernon and Richardson (1988) discusses "data analysis using spreadsheets." That chapter identifies procedures for treating spreadsheets as more than calculators that simply add or subtract rows of figures.

It might be noted that some statistical analysis software operates with spreadsheets or that a spreadsheet file can be converted to ASCII format for loading into a statistical analysis package. Spreadsheets, by themselves, do not perform the range of statistical analyses that more specialized software will. Further, statistical analysis software handles larger datasets. A disadvantage of using spreadsheets for statistical analysis is that library staff may have to "write the formulas and create a series of worksheet commands for the statistical procedure" (Ibid., p. 111). In addition, "unlike some microcomputer statistical analysis programs . . ., spreadsheet programs operate in interactive rather than batch mode. Thus, users cannot easily run multiple [and different] statistical procedures one after another" (Ibid.). Indeed, "statistical analysis packages are a better choice for applications where large datasets, data validation, data transformation, and complex or batch statistical procedures are needed" (Ibid., p. 120).

Analytical Databases

Analytical databases combine features of spreadsheets and database managers. Reflex (available from Borland/Analytica Inc., 4585 Scotts Valley Drive, Scotts Valley, CA 95066) is one such example. It performs basic statistical functions; however, similar to spreadsheets, library staff might have to write formulas. Reflex "can sort, manipulate, categorize, and perform computations of data in surprisingly sophisticated fashion" (Hernon and Richardson, 1988, p. 146). Further, "in comparison to dedicated statistical analysis packages, it does not offer the array of built-in statistical tests that those packages offer. However, for typical descriptive statistical computation it is quite powerful" (Ibid.). An added advantage of such software is its low cost.

Special Statistical Software

Using such software, librarians can produce financial and manpower projections, and analyze research and other data using simple and complex parametric and non-parametric routines. Depending on the particular package, they might determine sample sizes and generate a list of random numbers. They might also be able to evaluate the reliability of a dataset (see Appendix B).

For the purposes of discussion and comparison, this book emphasizes two statistical analysis software packages, StatPac (Walonick Associates, Inc., 6500 Nicollet Avenue South, Minneapolis, MN 55423) and Minitab (Minitab Data Analysis Software, 3081 Enterprise Drive, State College, PA 16801).[3] Both are well known and widely used programs that operate on IBM and IBM compatible microcomputers. Minitab resembles a spreadsheet on which researchers issue commands or data analysis instructions. StatPac is menu-driven; however, Stat-Pac Gold, its counterpart for hard disk drives, can be either menu- or command-driven. Figure 3-3 compares both versions and highlights differences.

StatPac, a batch system written in compiled BASIC, needs only 128K Random Access Memory (RAM) and can handle a maximum of 5,000 cases, the equivalent of 255 card columns, and 500 categories per variable, in either a fixed or free format. This package handles a wide assortment of statistical tests but has only rudimentary graphics capabilities.

StatPac Gold, on the other hand, offers presentation-quality graphics, interactive and batch processing, and can handle up to 500 variables and 32,767 cases. It provides descriptive statistics, frequency counts, crosstabs, t-tests, correlations, linear and non-linear regression, stepwise multiple regression, probit regression, principal components analysis, factor analysis, analysis of variance, and quality control and forecasting.

Minitab, another general purpose statistical analysis package, is easy to use, powerful, and flexible. It consists of a worksheet of rows and columns in which researchers store, analyze, and manipulate data using approximately 180 commands. These commands permit the reading, editing, and printing of data, statistical calculations, and the preparation of plots and histograms. The maximum size of a dataset is 16,000 elements, with a 50 column or variable maximum.

---

[3] Hernon and Richardson (1988) identify over 70 statistical analysis packages for microcomputers. Their book offers two tutorials on the use of StatPac.

Figure 3-3.   Comparison between StatPac and StatPac Gold

StatPac	StatPac Gold
Functions on a microcomputer with two floppy disk drives or a hard disk	Operates only on a hard disk
Operates in batch mode	Has both batch and interactive processing
Offers fewer statistical analyses	Offers more statistical analyses (more options under analysis of variance and interactive prediction capabilities for regression analyses)
Requires less time to master	Requires more time to master; however, the programming language is more powerful and versatile
Designing the analyses is quick; however, execution of the analyses can be slow	Designing and running the analyses are faster
Ideal for occasional research projects, requiring smaller datasets (the data file limits are 5,000 records, 254 variables, and 254 bytes of information per record)	Useful for larger datasets (32,767 records, 500 variables, and 5,000 bytes of information per record)
Low-resolution character graphics	Presentation-quality graphics. Produces both low and high resolution graphics

Criteria for Evaluating Statistics Software

The commercial sector is constantly improving the sophistication of statistical software programs. Still, such software varies greatly in the ease of its use, its ability to interact with other computer systems, and the data analysis techniques that it can perform. In addition, supporting documentation varies in quality and complexity; software documentation may claim that the program performs a routine but does so clumsily; the documentation might identify the formula used in the statistical calculations but not document the source from which it was taken or derived; software may malfunction and need to be returned to the vendor; files may be difficult to utilize for the production of the desired output; and programs may offer different types of statistical analyses but not always the exact ones needed.

In some instances, a vendor will make an abbreviated version of the package available for a trial demonstration or will provide a tutorial diskette. Many vendors are perhaps fearful that if they supply the entire package for perusal, the recipient would copy the documentation and software, and return the original, without making a purchase.

Some questions to keep in mind when evaluating a software program for possible purchase include:

- What uses will be made of it?
- How large will the datasets be?

- How much experience do the staff have with statistics and microcomputers?
- Do the staff prefer a menu- or command-driven program?
- How much does the program cost?
- Is the potential package compatible with microcomputer hardware and software (such as the version of DOS) that the library already has?
- Which statistical computations do the staff need?
- How many variables will the program handle and how many values can be assigned to a variable?
- Does the package offer extras, such as a random number generator?
- Does the statistical software interface with a spreadsheet, wordprocessor, data management system, or mainframe computer?

Of all these evaluation criteria, five are perhaps the most important. These are: ease of use, compatibility with existing hardware and software, preferences for statistical analysis techniques, the ability to use datasets with other software or on a mainframe computer, and the quality of available documentation. Given the extensive verification of the accuracy and speed of different programs, this criterion should not be one of the five (see Chapter 4 and appendix of Hernon and Richardson, 1988, for a discussion and comparison of 23 evaluation criteria). Cost is also not one of the five because many good programs have a list price of under $600. In some instances, the vendor might lower the price and offer the software at an educational discount.

PLANNING FOR THE USE OF STATISTICAL SOFTWARE

A library planning to incorporate statistical software programs into its decision-making process should take a few simple steps to ensure that the staff settle on the program most appropriate to their particular needs and level of statistical sophistication. First, the library should review its goals and objectives, as well as its expectations from such software. Second, decision makers should examine the data elements that they want to collect and then review these with consultants or other library personnel knowledgeable of research and statistical methods. Third, they might encourage staff members to take a research methods and statistics course. Fourth, decision makers should identify their current and long-term expectations from the use of statistical software programs. Fifth, staff could preview some of the software programs identified in Hernon and Richardson (1988). In addition to exploring the previously mentioned questions, they should:

- Review copyright restrictions on the software and consider purchasing site licensing agreements
- Review technical requirements and specifications
- Investigate the opportunities for staff members to receive training.

Staff members should develop a list of questions to guide their evaluation of software. They can then query colleagues who have used different software and obtain some packages for examination. They should compare different programs and identify the one(s) most appropriate for their needs. The key point is to experiment with different software. Some librarians might prefer menu- to command-driven software because menu-driven software requires less time for staff training. The more that library staff become accustomed to microcomputer software for data input and analysis, the greater should be their use of such software.

Librarians ought to constantly challenge themselves and attempt to improve the effectiveness and efficiency of the library's information services, operations, and management. As more libraries acquire microcomputers, they have greater opportunities to explore the various uses that they can make of these machines. By emphasizing the need for the collection and reporting of data that address library goals and objectives, and that have compatibility and comparability across library departments and libraries themselves, librarians have established the framework for another use of a microcomputer—basic and sophisticated data analysis applicable for library decision making.

Chapter Four
Basic Definitions and Concepts

MEASUREMENT

Measurement, a specialized form of description, provides a means for quantifying variables and making comparisons among them. It "is the process through which observations are translated into numbers" (Ary, Jacobs, and Razavieh, 1985, p. 95). A measurement scale is a set of rules for assigning numerical scores to a variable. There are four types of measurement scales: nominal, ordinal, interval, and ratio.[1]

Nominal measurement, which is the lowest level, classifies observations, objects, or individuals into different or mutually exclusive categories; no relationship between the categories exists. Categories "are qualitatively rather than quantitatively different" (Ary, Jacobs, and Razavieh, 1985, p. 96). Numbers may be assigned to the categories to distinguish one from the other. The numbers, however, are arbitrary; they do not have intrinsic value.

Figure 4-1 includes six questions from a hypothetical questionnaire. The first question, on gender, is an example of nominal scale. In tabulating responses, the researchers would be determining how many people were of each gender. They are *not* assuming that one category has more value or worth than the other.

With ordinal or the second type of measurement, librarians place observations, objects, or individuals in ascending or descending order, without either specifying or knowing the magnitude of the difference between them. In other words, an ordinal scale will rank order things, according to *a more or less than* categorization. Consequently, library decision makers "know more about a variable than that it is present . . . as one of the mutually exclusive categories of the variable" (Swisher and McClure, 1984, p. 76).

Returning to Figure 4-1, questions 2, 3, 5, and 6 are all examples of ordinal scale. Status of the respondent (question 2) treats each category, or value label, as having equal significance. However, for some studies and decision making, librarians might accord greater significance to the responses of perhaps faculty members than they would college students and local community members.

---

[1] Swisher and McClure (1984, pp. 74–80) offer an excellent discussion of measurement scales, with examples drawn from librarianship.

Figure 4-1.   Sample Questions from a Survey

| 1. | Gender: | | Female____ | Male____ |

2. Are you a:

		Yes	No
a.	College student	____	____
b.	Faculty member	____	____
c.	Staff member of school	____	____
d.	Local community member	____	____
e.	Other (Please specify)	____	____

3. What level of schooling have you completed?
   (Only check the category for the highest level completed)

a.	Some or all of elementary school	____
b.	Some or all of junior high school	____
c.	Some or all of high school	____
d.	Vocational education degree	____
e.	Some or all of college	____
f.	Master's degree or doctorate	____

4. As of your last birthday, how old are you? _____

5. For what purpose(s) did you use the library today:

		Yes	No
a.	Browsing current periodicals and newspapers	____	____
b.	Conducting research	____	____
c.	Reserve room reading	____	____
d.	Study hall	____	____
e.	Other (Please specify)	____	____

6. In using a library, are you hesitant to approach a reference librarian to ask for assistance?

a.	Never ____	c.	Frequently ____
b.	Sometimes ____	d.	Always ____

For question 6, there is a progression in response from "never" to "always." However, distinctions between "never" and "sometimes," or between "frequently" and "always" are imprecise. Ultimately, it might be beneficial to treat "never" and "sometimes" as one category and "frequently" and "always" as a second category, and to compare responses between the two groupings. Interval measurement classifies observations, objects, or individuals on an ordered series of points that are equally spaced. There is "some sort of physical unit of measurement which can be agreed upon as a common standard and which is replicable, i.e., can be applied over and over again with the same results"

(Blalock, 1972, p. 18). With interval measurement, library staff can "determine amounts or quantities much more precisely" (Ibid.). However, there is no absolute value for zero; rather, the zero is arbitrary. The Fahrenheit scale of temperature is an example of interval measurement.

Question 3 (see Figure 4-1), at first glance, appears to be cast in the context of interval measurement. However, there is a definitional problem; does junior high school include grades 7, 8, and 9, while high school comprises grades 10, 11, and 12? Depending on the survey population, the phrases summarizing educational level may or may not present a problem. Some people attended education programs where grade 9 was part of high school. Elementary school may or may not include sixth grade, and how does vocational education fit into the progression from less to more education?

If decision makers want to convert question 3 into an interval scale, they might ask:

3.   How many years of schooling have you completed since high school?____

Grade level, as a unit of measurement ("StatPac Gold—Statistical Analysis Package for the IBM: Manual," 1988, p. 49),

is considered interval scaled because the intervals between grade levels are equal. A response of zero would indicate that the respondent has not completed a year of school beyond high school. This "zero-point" is not an absolute number. That is, a zero on this scale does not indicate the "absence of education."

Ratio measurement has all the properties of an interval scale and adds an absolute (not arbitrary) zero point. This zero value is a point on the scale that represents a complete absence of the characteristics involved. As a result, it can be determined "that object A possesses twice as much of some property as object B, because the ratio has an absolute zero point. Weight and height are examples of ratio scaling" (Swisher and McClure, 1984, p. 78).

If one library has 500,000 books and another library has 1,000,000 books, the second library has twice as many as the first. However, to ensure ratio measurement, library decision makers must be certain that the basis for the comparison is identical. In other words, is the comparison based on a title or volume count, or a mixture of both?

Question 4 (see Figure 4-1) is an example of ratio measurement. A response of 60 is twice as much as one of 30. If question 3 "had been worded 'How many years of school have you completed?,' it would have been considered ratio type data" ("StatPac Gold—Statistical Analysis Package for the IBM: Manual," 1988, p. 49).

As shown in the figure, and the above discussion, whether a variable is to be considered as nominal, ordinal, interval, or ratio depends on the conceptual underpinnings of the variable. Before deciding on measurement scales, library researchers and decision makers need information about the conceptual variable that the numbers will index or reference. They must also understand the rules of measurement employed in assigning the numbers.

As this section has illustrated, a data collection form may include questions representing more than one type of measurement. Researchers and decision makers have choices and options in the wording of a question. Their decision will determine the measure of central tendency (see next chapter) that will be used and the statistical test(s) that will be applied (Siegel, 1956, pp. 1–5; Swisher and McClure, 1984, p. 79). Their decision must be made prior to data collection; researchers make study decisions based on their information needs and study framework (objectives, hypotheses/research questions, research design, etc.) not the database resulting from actual data collection. Researchers should not generate and test hypotheses from the same dataset. If they want to engage in hypothesis testing, they should formulate hypotheses in advance, using the literature and perhaps data gathered from previous studies.

In the debate between D'Elia and Van House in *Public Libraries* over the utility of fill rates as performance measures, Van House (1988) discusses the limitations of the chi-square test and encourages the application of higher powered statistical analyses. However, as D'Elia (1988, p. 29) observes, "given the nature of the fill rate data (nominal level data that are the lowest and weakest level of measurement), the chi-square test is the only appropriate test for differences." He concludes that "the problem is not the statistical test but rather the inherent weakness of the fill rate data that mandated the chi-square test." Clearly, libraries may experience problems in collecting data beyond the ordinal level of measurement. Still, librarians should select that measurement scale (or scales) that produces data most appropriate to decision making.

LEVELS OF SIGNIFICANCE

The level of significance is the predetermined level at which a null hypothesis is rejected.[2] The level is an arbitrarily chosen probability that is used to decide whether a given sample is likely to have come from a given population. The most commonly used levels are .05 and .01. When librarians collect management data—action research—they might increase the margin of error and accept, e.g., the .10 level.

The .05 level of significance corresponds to the .95 level of confidence. The .01 level is the same as the .99 level of confidence, while the .10 level equals the .90 level of confidence.

---

[2] A null hypothesis states that no difference exists between the populations being compared.

Decision makers either support or reject a null hypothesis on the basis of the level selected. For example, by setting the level at .05, librarians reject a null hypothesis if the probability is less than .05. The probability level may be reported as $p < .05$, with p meaning probability and the symbol $<$ standing for "less than."

Librarians should select a level of significance prior to data collection after evaluating the consequences of making a Type I error (rejecting a true null hypothesis) or Type II error (accepting a false null hypothesis as true). The final determination should also reflect the purpose for data collection—action research, publication, and so forth—and the margin of error that decision makers are willing to accept.

Suppose that library decision makers would like to determine the number of titles that circulated in the science collection and the frequency of the circulation of these titles. They might want to determine how many titles circulated in the last year or last couple of years. Further, suppose that this collection contained 12,000 titles and that decision makers only need impressionistic data—they are willing to tolerate a lack of precision in study findings. The decision makers therefore decide not to have student employees examine every title; rather, they want a random sample of titles drawn and examined.

The decision makers will determine the sample size on the basis of answers to questions such as:

- How much confidence do they want to place in the data collected?
- How important is the decision that they intend to make?
- How costly would a mistake be?
- How soon do they need the results?
- How feasible is it to collect more precise data?
- Do they intend to seek publication of the study process and findings?

Using StatPac, similar microcomputer software, or a textbook on statistics, they calculate that a:

- 90% confidence level, ± 5 = 264 titles
- 95% confidence level, ± 5 = 372 titles
- 99% confidence level, ± 5 = 628 titles
- 99% confidence level, ± 3 = 1,596 titles.

They select the first option and have the students examine 264 titles drawn from a random number generator, such as that available with StatPac (see Table 6-1). The purpose of the sampling process is to give all 12,000 titles an equal chance of inclusion in the sample. Examination of 264 titles might be feasible for the staff within a short time and provide decision makers with clues about the circulation of science books.

ERRORS OF MEASUREMENT AND CLASSIFICATION

Social science research and measurement are susceptible to error. In the case of some surveys, measurement and classification error may be insignificant, while, in other instances, they might seriously jeopardize the conclusions drawn from the dataset. Although errors of measurement and classification are never entirely eliminated, researchers try to minimize them and to limit their impact on hypothesis testing.

This section highlights some of the errors that might emerge in the conduct of a study. The purpose is to be suggestive, not comprehensive. The point is that research findings cannot compensate for a "silly question" or one that is ill-defined, vague, and open to interpretation (see Hernon, McClure, and Purcell, 1985, Chapter 6). Statistics and statistical tests should not be viewed in isolation; researchers and decision makers should place them in the context of the entire research process (see Chapter 1).

Errors in Data Processing

As discussed in Hernon and Richardson (1988, Chapter 5 and 9), problems might arise in the transcribing, coding, and scoring of data for statistical analysis. Moreover, researchers might have to interpret responses. Having written documentation that guides processing, together with the development of procedures to monitor the accuracy of data input, will reduce processing errors. Still, some errors in processing are likely to remain, and it may be too time-consuming and expensive to eliminate them.

Sampling Errors

Sampling is a process by which researchers select part of a population, according to rules of probability. From measurement of the sample, they then estimate values of the entire population. Different types of sampling errors (the difference between a sample estimate and the result that would have been obtained had the entire population been used with the same methodological procedures) can be classified into three categories: coverage, measurement, and sampling errors.

Coverage errors result from inadequate sampling frames and low response rates. Measurement errors are due to faulty data collection instruments, poor quality interviewing, poor respondent recall, and mistakes in editing, coding, data entry, and analysis. Sampling error is basically a function of sample size, and in the case of small populations, the relationship of the sample size to the population.

In some surveys, non-sampling errors may exceed sampling errors because of the complexity of the questions asked. Unfortunately, non-sampling errors are not measurable unless a follow-up study of the non-respondents and the validity of the survey instruments and procedures is determined, often at high cost (see Hernon and Pastine, 1977).

Response, Observer, and Instrument Error

Response variation may produce measurement errors. Respondents, for example, might guess or attempt to reconstruct events of long ago. Memory lapses compound the problem of trying to get people to recall childhood use of the library (see Bradburn, Rips, and Shevell, 1987). For such reasons, researchers might ask respondents to remember *critical incidents* around which use might be more vividly recalled.

Data generated from observation might reflect measurement and classification error. The observer generally does not see everything that is occurring. To minimize observer error, researchers extensively train those involved in data collection and monitor completed data collection forms in order to identify problems that interviewers might experience (see Chen and Hernon, 1982). Measurement and classification error might be associated with data collection forms and instructions guiding data collected and tabulation. Researchers want to ensure that people do not interpret the instructions or questions differently.

Misrepresentation as Error

Misrepresentation might be intentional or not. Clearly, falsified records contribute to measurement error. Exaggeration might also be a source of error. The graphic display of the data used by other researchers has, at times, disclosed patterns clearly indicative of falsified data (Tufte, 1983; Cleveland, 1985). There is no easily applied procedure, however, for identifying misinformation and leading to its correction.

The Reliability and Validity of Measures and Classification

Reliability suggests stability and consistency of measurement—accuracy and replication. A replication may involve *test–retest reliability*, the application of the same measurement to the same cases at different times; *inter-scorer reliability* the application of the same measurement to the same cases by different observers (see Hernon and Pastine, 1977); or *split-half reliability* or *equivalent-test reliability*, the application to the same cases of different measures that purport to measure the same characteristic in those cases. If the replications produce highly correlated measures, the measurement or classification has high reliability.

Validity is viewed in two contexts—either external or internal. The former suggests the extent to which the data are generalizable to a large setting, while the latter examines the extent to which the data measure what they purport to measure. "One validates not the measuring instrument itself but the measuring instrument in relation to the purposes for which it is being tested" (Carmines and Zeller, 1979, p. 17).

Determining the validity of measures, and improving measures with low validity, presents complex problems for social science researchers. Readers interested in the application of reliability and validity might examine Hernon and McClure (1987b), which discusses quality of data issues in the context of the unobtrusive testing of library reference service.

Summary

As this section has illustrated, the thoughtful and careful interpretation of data requires consideration of how measurement and classification error might impact the study and data analysis. The prudent interpreter of numbers examines probable sources of measurement error and the magnitude of that error. In cases where action research is conducted for use by local decision makers, the issue of utility merits consideration. For data to have utility, the data also ought to demonstrate some degree of reliability and validity—assuming that library decision makers need more than impressionistic data. The utility issue asks (Paisley, 1969):

- What are the findings good for?
- What decision in the real world do the findings impact?
- What insights will the study provide, and can the study be dismissed with the comment "so what?"

Utility involves applications, impacts, and usefulness of the findings. It presupposes that one of the broader purposes for data collection is to affect library policies or decision making.

FUNCTION OF STATISTICS

Descriptive Statistics

Descriptive statistics provide a useful and convenient means for summarizing datasets. Librarians might collect, say, 500 completed questionnaires and then need to digest or summarize the information. By computing percentages, measures of central tendency, and correlation coefficients—and by displaying the results graphically—librarians reduce the data to manageable proportions. In the process of describing and summarizing data, information is lost and the results might be misleading or insufficiently interpreted. Therefore, the limitations of any measure should be noted.

Inferential Statistics

Inferential statistics is a set of procedures used in drawing inferences and generalizations based on a sample of cases from a population. These procedures are derived from the principles of probability theory. Many populations (such as the student body of a university or residents of a community) are too large to permit the investigation of every case. Sampling distribution serves as a means for characterizing the population. It might be noted that there would be little need for statistical inferences if researchers could observe directly all the cases in the population.

There are two types of statistical inference: estimation and hypothesis testing. Statistical estimation is the equivalent of an educated guess about a parameter (a characteristic of a population), given a sample statistic (a sample characteristic) and an appropriate sampling distribution. Using statistical estimation, it is possible to identify the range of values within which the parameter probably falls. Statistical hypothesis testing, of which more will be stated in subsequent chapters, addresses any differences in the means of populations and whether a sample is likely to come from a population. On the basis of sample data, researchers can decide whether an hypothesis about a population is likely to be true or false.

PARAMETRIC AND NONPARAMETRIC STATISTICS

Parametric statistics make certain assumptions about population parameters. A parameter is a population score, whereas a statistic is a score for a sample randomly drawn from a population. One assumption is that population scores are normally distributed about the mean, and another is that the population variances of comparison groups in a study are similar. When research data deviate substantially from these assumptions, parametric statistics are not appropriate. Instead, researchers should use nonparametric statistics that do not make assumptions about the shape or variance of population scores.[3]

Parametric statistical tests generally require interval or ratio level data, and meet the assumption, for example, that "the scores were drawn from a normally distributed population" or that "both sets of scores were drawn from populations having the same variance . . . or spread of score" (Siegel, 1956, pp. 2–3). When scores are dichotomous or in the form of either categories or ranks, nonparametric statistics are more appropriate.

---

[3] Harwell (1988) offers an excellent discussion about choosing "between parametric and nonparametric tests."

Nonparametric statistics are generally less powerful and "require fewer qualifications" (Siegel, 1956, p. 3); they need larger samples to produce statistical significance. Using such statistics, researchers propose that "regardless of the shape of the population(s), we may conclude that . . ." (Ibid., p. 3). Nonparametric procedures may result in the "loss of information." However, researchers may have no alternative to their use (Swisher and McClure, 1984, p. 79). The chi-square test, for example, is a nonparametric test that is used for research data in the form of frequency counts. These frequency counts are grouped into two or more categories.

SUMMARY

As this chapter has indicated, statistics must be viewed in a context—the entire research process, including the methodology(ies) employed. Survey research, for example, involves more than just the development of an instrument and its completion by respondents. Librarians must be aware of types of error and whether they want "research" or "management" data.

In many instances, library managers must make timely decisions based on no or limited data. Management data therefore have great appeal, but also present threats to reliability and validity, such as those noted by D'Elia elsewhere in the chapter. Clearly, managers should collect the types of data they need/want and any statistical test employed should recognize the constraints inherent in the dataset. (The availability of data to support decision making has become a significant issue, in particular, as a climate of fiscal constraint and accountability prevails.) Data, however, should not dictate managerial decisions; rather, managers impose a framework in which they interpret the data. That framework includes, for example, study hypotheses and research questions.

Chapter Five
The Descriptive Presentation of Data

Descriptive statistics convert raw data into indices that summarize or characterize datasets. In effect, they provide a means of "making numbers make sense" (Jaeger, 1983, pp. 11–42) and "transform large groups of numbers into more manageable form" (Huck, Cormier, and Bounds, 1974, p. 19). Descriptive statistics include measures of central tendency (averages) and dispersion. They also depict the *shape* of a distribution. This chapter provides an overview of descriptive statistics and encourages the display of frequency counts and percentages in graphic form, such as through bar and line graphs. Figure 5-1 contains a brief synopsis of the key terms discussed in this chapter.

FREQUENCY DISTRIBUTION

A frequency distribution is a straightforward method of summarizing a dataset, displaying the frequency of occurrence, and highlighting patterns in the distribution of scores. A frequency distribution groups data into predetermined categories and reports numbers and percentages for individual questions. Such a distribution arranges responses from lowest to highest (or vice-versa) in relation to a quantifiable characteristic.[1]

Microcomputer statistical analysis software, such as StatPac and Minitab, of course, generate frequency distributions and percentages. Spreadsheets and database management software will also perform such calculations (Hernon and Richardson, 1988). Using such software, researchers might determine that a reference department received a total of 600 reference questions during the month of September; 400 of these questions were asked in-person, 150 by telephone, and the remaining 50 by mail. The percentage of questions received in-person was 66.7; that percentage was determined by dividing 400 by 600, and multiplying that number by 100.

---

[1] In a normal distribution, most of the scores fall in the middle of the frequency distribution. When scores concentrate at either end of the distribution, the distribution is skewed. The latter part of this chapter discusses normal and skewed distributions.

Figure 5-1. Description of Terms for Descriptive Statistics

Statistics	Description
Dispersion	It indicates the extent of scatter around the average.
Mean	The arithmetic average is the sum of all the values in a distribution divided by the number of cases.
Median	This measure of central tendency is the midpoint in the distribution below which half of the cases reside.
Mode	This measure of central tendency is the most frequently occurring value in the distribution.
Normal Curve	It is a distribution that is perfectly symmetrical about its mean. In other words, the curve is bell shaped.
Range	It is the difference between the highest and lowest scores in a distribution. The smallest value is subtracted from the highest.
Standard Deviation	This statistic indicates the spread of scores in a distribution. The greater the scatter of scores, the larger is the standard deviation.
T-score	It is a standard score that places the mean raw score at 50 and the raw score standard deviation at 10 T-score points. Thus, a score one deviation above the mean would have a T-score of 60, that is, 50 plus 10.
Variance	It is an indicator of the spread of scores in a distribution. The greater the scatter of scores, the larger is the variance.
Z-score	It is a raw score converted to standard deviation units. Because standard deviations are measured from the mean, Z-scores begin at the mean and range up and down the scale.

When the percentage of questions received in-person (66.7) is added to the percentage of telephone questions (25), the *cumulative percentage* becomes 91.7. Inclusion of the mail questions (8.3) accounts for all the reference questions. At times, researchers might *round off* decimals to the nearest hundredth or whole number. In such cases, they should indicate that the reported data were subject to rounding.

Table 5-1 offers another example. Suppose that the staff of an academic library studied student use of the library and that respondents encompassed five class levels. In this case, the cumulative percentage is determined by adding the

Table 5-1. Depiction of Percentage and Cumulative Percentage

Category	Frequency Distribution	Percentage	Cumulative Percentage
Freshmen	68	17.0	17.0
Sophomores	45	11.2	28.2
Juniors	90	22.5	50.7
Seniors	73	18.2	68.9
Graduate Students	124	31.0	99.9
Total:	400	99.9*	

*Percentages subject to rounding.

percentage at a given grade level to the percentages below it. For example, 22.5% of student library users were juniors, and 50.7% of the users were juniors or a lesser class level.

Researchers can group *percentiles*, score points in a distribution, and thereby identify the relative position of one score to the other scores. To identify that position, they might, for example, use *cumulative percentages, quartiles*, or *deciles*. A cumulative frequency distribution might be converted into cumulative percentages. If the categories are numerical ranges, both the cumulative frequency and the cumulative percentage describe a given interval in a distribution in terms of the number of cases that have appeared up to and including that interval. Given the frequency distribution shown in Table 5-2, the cumulative frequency for the category 40–54 is 82 (that is, 82 observations are less than or equal to that category) and the cumulative percentage at the value 40–54 is 41% (that is, 41% of all observations are less than or equal to 40–54).

Deciles divide the distribution of raw scores into units of 10%, while quartiles divide the distribution into segments of 25%. Both deciles and quartiles are points along a scale, not segments of that scale. The advantage of reducing the number of percentiles is that patterns may become more readily apparent when fewer categories are present. However, the reduction of categories should be accomplished in such a way that data are not grossly distorted and incorrect inferences drawn.

Table 5-1 reported the frequencies by class level as 45, 68, 73, 90, and 124. The frequencies could be characterized by the median (73), the number that divides the scores into two equal halves. The median therefore is the 50th percentile. A dataset might be characterized in other ways. Researchers might also report the 25th and 75th percentile. By so doing, they have identified the quartiles—the 25th percentile (the lower or first quartile), the 50th percentile (the median), and the 75th percentile (the upper or 3rd quartile). Salary scales are often reported in terms of quartiles. For example, *The ALA Survey of Librarian Salaries* (1988) reports the first quartile, median, and third quartile for salaries paid by library type and geographical region. The document also provides the mean and range.

Frequency distributions and percentages are not a sophisticated or complex

Table 5-2. Cumulative Frequency and Cumulative Percentage

Category	Frequency Distribution	Cumulative Frequency	Percentage	Cumulative Percentage
1–24	15	15	7.5	7.5
25–39	25	40	12.5	20.0
40–54	42	82	21.0	41.0
55–69	50	132	25.0	66.0
70–84	38	170	19.0	85.0
85–99	30	200	15.0	100.0

method of data analysis. Rather, they are a concise way of presenting and communicating study results. The straightforwardness and simplicity of frequency distributions and percentages are both a strength and a weakness. Due to their simplicity, such descriptive statistics are often utilized, even when statistical tests might be more appropriate.

The literature of library and information science contains numerous examples of studies that have used frequency distributions and percentages. Wong and Zubatsky (1985), for instance, surveyed 189 academic library chief administrators to determine both their tenure status and the rate of turnover in directorships. The authors present survey results in a variety of easy to read tables.

AVERAGES

Averages, or measures of central tendency, comprise a type of descriptive statistic that indicates "the most typical or representative score in the group" (Huck, Cormier, and Bounds, 1974, p. 22). Averages "describe a large group of scores" or responses (Ibid., p. 25). There are three types of averages: the *mode*, *median*, and *mean*. The mode, the point(s) at which the largest number of scores fall, is the most frequently occurring score or the largest frequency in a distribution. When scores are tied or data are grouped into classes, more than one mode may emerge. The mode, as a result, is the least stable of the measures of central tendency. The mode is most likely to change from one sample of a population to another. This measure of central tendency is associated with nominal measurement.

The median is the midpoint of a distribution or the point below which half of the scores fall. The median, which only identifies the value of the middlemost case, can be used with ordinal, interval, or ratio measurement. If there are a few extreme scores in one direction, the median provides the best or most representative measure of central tendency. It is not as sensitive to extreme scores as is the mean.

When people add a list of scores and divide the total by the number of scores, they have calculated the arithmetic mean. The mean is appropriate for interval or ratio, but not for nominal or ordinal data. The mean is a more precise measure than either the mode or median, because the position of every score in a distribution assists in determining the location of the mean. Metz (1979) used the mean to characterize the roles and functions of the academic library director, based on responses to a mailed questionnaire. He reported the roles and functions of directors in both small private colleges and large public, graduate institutions.

MEASURES OF VARIABILITY

Library managers frequently consider staffing, budget, and other differences among units within the organization. They might also be interested in variation between their library and other libraries locally, regionally, or nationally. Variation, or variability, indicates dispersion, spread, or the scatter of scores around a measure of central tendency.

Measures of dispersion, sometimes referred to as scatter, indicate variations between/among values represented in a dataset. For example, two libraries might record the number of online database searches performed during a two-week period. The number of searches conducted at one library might be more widely dispersed throughout the study period than the number at the other library. Measures of central tendency may provide insufficient information to describe the dataset. The mean and median offer a single value that represents all the cases in the distribution. If the dataset contains tied values, there could be more than one mode. Additional insights emerge from an examination of dispersion. The measures of dispersion discussed in this chapter are the *range*, *variance*, and *standard deviation*.

Range

The range, the difference between the highest and lowest values, uses an ordinal measurement scale. The values are arranged in ascending or descending order; one value is greater, equal to, or less than another value in the distribution. For example, suppose that the salaries of the lowest paid and highest paid librarians in a corporate library are $16,000 and $66,000 per year. The range of salaries in the library becomes $66,000–$16,000, or $50,000.

Librarians often report ranges of values; these ranges serve as indicators of the scope of a library's collections, operations, programs, and services. Ranges might also compare one library to another in areas such as salaries, budgets, and collection and staff size. When reporting ranges, librarians might compress or collapse daily or weekly data into a larger unit—perhaps monthly.

When librarians survey students about their frequency of library use, one item on their questionnaire might be:

Estimate how many times you used the resources of the college library last semester.

a. More than 20_____   d. 6–10_____
b. 16–20_____   e. 1–5_____
c. 11–15_____   f. 0_____

Librarians could tally the number for each response category. Depending on the distribution of responses, they might be able to develop a scheme whereby they characterize students as *heavy*, *moderate*, and *limited* users, and as *nonusers*.

Managers might use the range in establishing guidelines for staff procedures. For example, from an examination of use records, a circulation manager may make decisions concerning the number of copies of a title to place on reserve. That person might decide that if a reserve item is used 1–10 times per day, the library should make one copy available. Usage of 11–20 times a day would necessitate two copies, and so forth.

As the examples illustrate, the range is a quick but informative measure of the scope of an operation, service, or resource. Although the range may highlight potential areas where problems might exist, it is not a precise measure of accuracy. This is so because the range measures only two values in a distribution, the high and the low. The range indicates neither variations in between those two values nor the nature of the spread around any measure of central tendency. The range also does not take into account the number of cases in a distribution.

The assumption may be that a range of figures represents a typical case or situation. In fact, the range may represent an atypical situation, such as a low budget year or a very small sample. In addition, the range is extremely sensitive to skewness (see note 6) at either end of the scale because it is directly affected by an abnormally high or low value at either end of the distribution. Skewness is likely to occur if any one distribution tapers to zero. This might occur in reserve room statistics where a certain course, although required for departmental majors, is offered only every other year.

Using another example, a manager might compare the budget that his/her library allocated to media services with that allocated by other regional libraries. Yet, unknown to this manager, several of these regional libraries may be sharply reducing their media budgets for the fiscal year under review in order to install new computer capabilities linking their libraries. The installation might be reflected in the systems' budgets of those libraries, but the manager may not take this shift in priorities into account in comparing budget ranges. A similar example would be a state library mandating that all public libraries compute fill rates and other performance measures. State library funding might then be allocated solely on the basis of fill rate values. As is evident, a single value, or a range of values, may not reflect the entire picture. A range, like other statistics, must be placed in a context—what is actually occurring in the libraries reporting the data and the mission, goals, and objectives of these libraries.

Variance

Measurement, such as the range, is useful mainly for cursory examination or estimation. The range does not indicate the number of values between the high and low, what their significance is, or how they are grouped or scattered about the mean. Variance measures the amount of dispersion of a value from the mean of an interval-level variable (Swisher and McClure, 1984, p. 65). Whereas measures of central tendency compress different values for a given variable into one value that represents a generalization about all the values, variance places a numerical value on the dispersion of each of a property's values in a dataset. Knowledge of the dispersion assists somewhat in making predictions about what might occur. If demand for services increases or decreases during a specified time period with some predictability, managers might adjust staffing levels accordingly.

The degree of dispersion or variability is both observable and measurable. Variation and standard deviation are two valuable methods for measuring the degree of dispersion (Ary, Jacobs, and Razavieh, 1985, p. 110). Returning to the earlier example about the distribution of online searching in two branch libraries, Library A has less dispersion or scatter around the mean than does Library B (see Table 5-3):

Library A: 50   100   50   50   100   200   150   (Mean = 100).
Library B: 100   100   200   50   150   95   5   (Mean = 100).

To measure variability, we use a formula based on the deviation score. The deviation score is a calculation of each score deviation from the mean score calculated for a certain distribution. Each library has a set of seven raw scores. The deviation score, sometimes referred to as the deviate score, is the difference between the raw score and the sample mean: $x = X - \bar{X}$, where x is the deviation score, X the raw score, and $\bar{X}$ the sample mean.

The variance is calculated from the distribution of raw scores. It is the sum of the squared deviation of each score from the mean and the division of that sum by the number of raw scores minus 1 ($N - 1$). Deviation scores are squared because, by definition, their sum is always equal to zero (Ary, Jacobs, and Razavieh, 1985, p. 112). Scores below the mean are represented as negative values and scores above the mean are positive values. In order to eliminate negative scores, that is, those that fall below the mean ($\bar{X}$), the deviation score (x) is squared. Mathematically, the variance, called s^2, is written as:

$$s^2 = \Sigma (X - \bar{X})^2/N - 1 = \Sigma x^2/N - 1.$$

S^2 is variance, Σ is sum of, x is deviation of each score from the mean ($X - \bar{X}$), and $N - 1$ is the number of cases or scores in the distribution minus 1. The calculation is based on a sample rather than the population, and $N - 1$ indicates the number of deviations about the mean that vary.

If we have measurements of 2, 4, and 6, the mean is 4 and the deviations about the mean are -2, 0, and $+2$ respectively. If any two of the deviations are known, the third is fixed and does not vary. Hence, the degrees of freedom (df) is $N - 1$.[2] Most statistics textbooks will offer several examples of the calculation of variance. To clarify the concept of variance, consultation of these additional examples would be helpful.

There are two items of importance to note. First, because variance is calcu-

---

[2] Degrees of freedom varies with the number of rows and columns in a table. The probability of obtaining a statistically significant value depends on the number of cells in a table. Degrees of freedom takes the number of cells into account in determining statistical significance.

lated from the mean, the level of measurement is interval or ratio. Because it is higher-level measurement, variance is suitable for parametric statistics that assume a normal distribution (see Chapter 4). Because the test of variance measures the extent to which one case or object differs from another, it is useful in extracting the item or individual that exhibits characteristics that deviate widely from the mean. As such, the test indicates sampling error.

Table 5-3 summarizes the calculation of the variance for the online search statistics of libraries A and B. There is more variability in the scores for Library B, although the mean for both libraries is identical. The variation score, s^2, for Library B is higher—the scores are more spread out. The smaller value of s^2 for Library A indicates that there is less variation in the search statistics than there is in Library B. As the variation increases, the scores deviate from the mean. If all values or observations in a distribution were the same, the variance equals zero.

Instead of analyzing online searching, Table 5-3 might have considered the number of special seminars given in Group A, a liberal arts college, and Group B, an engineering college of a major university, for different weeks of an academic term. As an alternative, the table might have depicted use of the print *Science Citation Index* in comparison to the CD-ROM *Science Citation Index* over a seven-day period.

Returning to the table once more, managers might discover that the days when librarian X is scheduled for online searching are the days when faculty members request the most searches. Managers might assume therefore that this librarian's time should be concentrated on the one service. Of course, other explanations might account for the wide variation in searches performed in Library A. The temptation is to read too much into one descriptive statistic. The fact that task assignment, the criterion variable in one variation test, overlaps the criterion variable of searches performed, should not signify that there is a causal relationship between task assignment of librarian X in Library A and the number of searches performed on certain days.[3]

These examples demonstrate the utility of variance to place a numeric value on the amount of dispersion in a sample. Library managers usually use variance as a basis for the calculation of standard deviation. In addition, the variance test is used when there are insufficient values to perform a chi-square test of independence. Cochran (1954) found the variance test to have significance when chi-square did not. The fact that the variance test uses interval or ratio levels of measurement gives it more power than a test that examines nominal or ordinal level data.

Patterns of book and journal use in libraries have been the subject of numerous studies and applications of statistical tests. Lazorick (1979) used the variance test to distinguish between two types of distribution—a negative binomial and a

---

[3] Swisher and McClure (1984, pp. 57–72) provide an excellent discussion of causal associations and inferences on covariation.

Table 5-3. Calculation of Variance

Daily Raw Score X	Library A: Search Statistics Variation from Daily Mean $x = (X - \bar{X})$	Variation Squared x^2
50	− 50	2500
100	0	0
50	− 50	2500
50	− 50	2500
100	0	0
200	+100	10000
150	+ 50	2500
700		Σx^2 = 20000

$\bar{X}$ = 700/7 = 100 N = 7 $N - 1$ = 6

$s^2 = \Sigma x^2 / N - 1 = 20000/6 = 3333.33$

Daily Raw Score X	Library B: Search Statistics Variation from Daily Mean $x = (X - \bar{X})$	Variation Squared x^2
100	0	0
100	0	0
200	+100	10000
50	− 50	2500
150	+ 50	2500
95	− 5	25
5	− 95	9025
700		Σx^2 = 24050

$\bar{X}$ = 700/7 = 100 N = 7 $N - 1$ = 6

$s^2 = \Sigma x^2 / N - 1 = 24050/6 = 4008.33$

Poisson distribution.[4,5] Because negative binomially distributed, random variables have a variance greater than the mean, the variance test may have indicated that a negative binomial distribution was possible; however, the evidence was

[4] Binomial distribution refers to the probability (p) that an event will happen in a single trial. The number of trials (n) is usually fixed and the number of events (s) is observed. In a negative binomial distribution, the number of occurrences of the events (r) is fixed and the number of failures (x) is the

inconclusive. The variance test did suggest that the data were not Poisson distributed, that is, they were probably negative binomial distributions. The implications derived from the application of the variance test were that if demand for collections of books is negatively binomially distributed, the use of individual books would be Poisson distributed and queuing models could be developed to help ensure better accessibility to items in a library's collections (see Lee, 1966).

Finally, it might be useful to note limitations of the variance test. The variance test does not indicate trends. It is strictly a measure of units of analysis that exist in the present or in the past. While variance can be used for predictions, it is not a measure of statistical inference or probability. Further, like any results calculated on a sample, rather than the population, sampling error may occur.

Standard Deviation

There are several methods by which a numerical value can be attached to the amount of dispersion of a distribution. The variance test is one method and standard deviation is another. The standard deviation measures the dispersion of scores around the mean. The greater the scatter of scores, the larger is the standard deviation. Because standard deviation is computed using the values of each individual raw score, researchers can assess similarities or differences between one individual or object's value and the dispersion or set of values.

The standard deviation, which uses interval or ratio data, is the square root of the variance. It takes into account the deviation of each score from the mean value of the dataset. To calculate the standard deviation, square the differences, sum the results, and subtract one from the number of cases in the dataset. The formula for the variance, as was already noted, is:

$$s^2 = (X - \bar{X})^2 / N - 1.$$

---

random variable where $x = n - r$. For a detailed explanation of the form of the negative binomial distribution, see Lazorick (1979) and Spiegel (1961).

[5] Poisson distribution is distinguished from the negative binomial distribution by comparing the magnitude of the variance (s^2). In the Poisson distribution, the variance equals the mean. The variance is greater than the mean in a negative binomial distribution. (A binomial distribution has a variance that is always less than the mean.) The variance test is used to determine which distribution formula to use for estimating the probability that an event will occur. A distribution where the frequencies of occurrence are given by the formula

$$\frac{e^{-np}(Np)^x}{1.2.3 \ldots x} \qquad x = 0,1,2,3, \ldots .$$

where $e = 2.71828$
N = random sample of individuals or things
p = proportion of N with a particular trait

is called Poisson distribution. For a detailed explanation see Busha and Harter (1980, pp. 132–138), Lazorick (1979), and Molina (1942).

To find the standard deviation (*sd*), we take the square root of the variance, or:

$$sd = \sqrt{(X - \bar{X})^2 / N - 1}$$

If either the mean or score values are uneven (say, the mean is 5.256), computation is more complex. In such cases, readers should consult a statistics textbook.

The standard deviation applies to both parametric and nonparametric tests. Because it is calculated from the mean (and used in conjunction with the mean), the standard deviation applies to interval or ratio measurement. If all the scores in a distribution were identical, both the variance and standard deviation are zero. The standard deviation can range from zero to a small or large number. Jaeger (1983, p. 61) assists in the interpretation of standard deviation units and determining whether a deviation is large or small.

Table 5-3 illustrated the calculation of the variance score for libraries A and B. For Library A the score was 3333.33 and for Library B it was 4008.33. Calculating the standard deviation involves taking the square root of the variance, or:

$$s^2 = 3333.33, \text{ and } sd = 57.73 \text{ (Library A)}$$
$$s^2 = 4008.33, \text{ and } sd = 63.31 \text{ (Library B)}.$$

Even from the small sample displayed in the table, it is evident that Library A, which exhibited less scatter or dispersion in the raw score data has a smaller standard deviation than does Library B.

For a normal distribution (one identified by a bell shaped, symmetrical curve), researchers interpret the standard deviation as the distance measured from the midpoint or center of the bell shaped curve to a point along the baseline. The baseline is divided into standard deviation units. Plus or minus one standard deviation from the center of the curve represents approximately 68% of the cases in a sample; plus or minus two standard deviation units accounts for 95% of the cases. Knowing how many standard deviation units a groups falls above or below the center points of the curve offers a useful means for comparing different groups, provided the groups compared are measured under similar conditions or with like variables. A further assumption is that the distribution adheres to a normal curve or distribution (see subsequent discussion in this chapter).

Perhaps two examples might assist in clarifying the discussion of standard deviation. Suppose school librarians obtained the scores of elementary school children assigned to two contrasting learning groups. The first group met once a week for a presentation on strategies for using the library effectively, while the other group visited the library once a week for a tour and to check out books. The second group did not receive the formal presentation. The number of books each group checks out over a ten-week period are as follows:

| First group: | 29 | 35 | 37 | 42 | 49 | 58 | 62 | 63 | 69 | 70 |
| Second group: | 5 | 7 | 17 | 31 | 45 | 47 | 68 | 85 | 96 | 99. |

The mean of the first group is 51.5 and that of the second group is 50. The initial impression might be that the presentation did not have a direct impact on the number of books borrowed. However, the standard deviation for the first group was 14.86 and 35.63 for the second group. The fact that the one group had less deviation in its scores may be important. However, before drawing conclusions, managers should be aware of *statistical inference* and the use of statistical tests such as the *t*-test (see Chapters 6, 7, and 8).

Popa, Metzer, and Singleton (1988) used standard deviations as part of their data analysis. They wanted to assess any differences that might have occurred in the scores of college students taught search strategies using both online public access terminals (OPAC) and the traditional card catalog. A question central to their study was "Would teaching search strategies on the OPAC system result in higher posttest scores than teaching card catalog search strategies?" Calculation of the standard deviation played a significant role in determining that there was insufficient evidence to conclude that OPAC training was more effective— produced higher posttest scores.

A comparison of standard deviations alone can lead to inaccurate and incorrect interpretation. A correction coefficient, the coefficient of variation, guards against some incorrect interpretation of the standard deviation (Carpenter and Vasu, 1978, p. 19). The standard deviation is a stable form of measurement and a more accurate measure of the population parameter than other measures of variation (Ferguson, 1981, p. 71). As a statistical tool, the standard deviation forms the basis for many other calculations and is widely employed to measure error. This descriptive statistic serves as a benchmark for comparing similarities or differences in comparative subjects or objects.

NORMAL CURVE

A normal distribution is actually a family of distributions that assumes the shape of a symmetrical, bell shaped curve. Figure 5-2 is a graph of the normal distribution. This bell shaped curve extends infinitely in both directions in a continuum close to the horizontal axis or baseline, but never touching it. The fact that the tails of the curve do not actually touch the baseline is not important because the area under the extreme ends or tails is negligible. The most important feature of the curve is that it is symmetrical about its mean or central point. This signifies that if a normal curve were folded along its central line, the two halves of the curve would coincide.

Normal curves can have different shapes depending on the mean; however, there is only one normal distribution for any given mean and standard deviation

Figure 5-2.   An Example of A Normal Curve

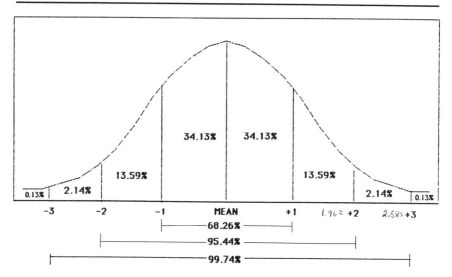

The percentage of cases falling between successive standard deviations in a normal distribution.

(Freund, 1976, p. 156). In a normal curve, the mean, mode, and median in the population are the same: 50% of the cases fall above the central point and 50% fall below it. If the measures of central tendency are not equal, the distribution is distorted.[6]

An examination of Figure 5-2 indicates that most of the cases in the normal distribution fall close to the mean. The actual areas under the curve are described in standard deviation units. Knowing what proportion of the area is under the curve at any point from the mean, or a proportion of the total area above or below any point on the baseline, can be important because that knowledge provides a reference point for interpreting both individual and group attributes.

The figure gives the area represented by 1, 2, and 3 standard deviations. A score of one standard deviation to the right of the mean represents approximately 34% of all cases in a normal distribution. A score of minus one standard deviation indicates a score one standard deviation to the left of the mean of approximately 34%. Therefore, a standard deviation of plus and minus one standard

---

[6] There are two ways that a distribution is distorted: skewness and kurtosis. With skewness, the tail of the curve is either top or bottom heavy—the largest part of the tail goes to the right (top heavy) or the left (negatively skewed). A value of zero for skewness indicates a symmetrical distribution.

A curve with kurtosis might be platykurtic (flat) or leptokurtic (very peaked). The Kolmorgorov-Smirnov statistic is a convenient means to determine the degree of normality in a dataset. As the value deviates from zero, the dataset does not approximate a normal distribution.

deviation is equal to 68%. The area between one and two standard deviations equals approximately 14% on each side of the mean, thereby adding an additional 28% to the total area under the curve. Plus or minus two standard deviations accounts for approximately 96% of the area. And, 99.7% of the scores in a distribution fall within the range of plus or minus three standard deviations.

The advantages of displaying the normal curve graphically, either hand- or computer-calculated, is that, for a symmetrical normal distribution, the approximate percentage of cases that fall within a certain range is visualized. The fact that the areas under the curve are given in standard deviation units associated with a percentage of the population that fall within that range enables researchers to place a random value obtained from a normal distribution in context of the population.

The normal curve is almost always described in terms of a standard score, a score expressed as a deviation from the mean in terms of multiples of the standard deviation. *Z-scores* and *T-scores* are two types of standard scores.

Z-SCORES

In research, data may not lend themselves to display in terms of full standard deviation units. Instead, action research may produce fractional parts of these units. The Z-score is a systematic approach for dealing with such instances. The Z-score is a raw score converted to standard deviation units. Because standard deviations are measured from the mean, Z-scores begin at that point and proceed up and down the scale. The mean assumes a value of zero and deviations to the right of the mean are positive; those to the left are negative.

To calculate the Z-score, the deviate score $(X - \bar{X})$ is divided by the standard deviation of the real distribution. The formula is:

$$Z = (X - \bar{X})/sd.$$

This formula merely converts the score of one normal distribution to that of another normal distribution—the Z-score whose mean is zero and whose standard deviation is one. However, researchers can only convert the standard deviation score to a Z-score if there is a normal distribution, a bell shaped symmetrical curve when plotted on a graph. The values of the area under the curve can be located from a "table for Z-scores" and need not be calculated.

By converting two sets of scores from the same population to Z-scores, researchers have produced a common scale: a Z-score unit in one normally distributed variable for a set of data is the same as a Z-score unit in another normally distributed variable for the same population. As a result, researchers might compare intelligence test results with achievement scores, or grade point average with performance on a library skills test.

The comparison between the two sets of scores can be accomplished without changing the general shape of the normal distribution. In effect, researchers subtract a constant from the score and divide by the standard deviation. This procedure is also known as a linear transformation because although it may shift the curve to the left along the baseline (by subtracting) and reduce the dimensions of the distribution (by dividing), the shape of the curve does not change.

Statistics textbooks frequently contain tables that provide values for measuring Z-scores up to four decimal places. Any measure of variance or standard deviation used where the distribution is thought to be normal can be converted to Z-scores. Both Z-scores and areas under the normal curve are based on the population. Hence, a comparison of one score places that score in the context of the population, not a sample.

It might be useful to illustrate the use of the normal curve and Z-scores. The proportion of the area under the curve in Figure 5-2 falling above the mean and Z = +1 is .3413 in a table for Z-scores. For practical purposes, let us convert this to a percentage and round off to 34% (.3413 × 100 = 34.13%). Because the curve is symmetrical, the portion between plus and minus $1Z$ = 34% plus 34%, or roughly 68%. The proportion below + $1Z$ is 34% plus 50% (all the area to the left of the mean of zero) or a total of 84%.

If we compare our own salary with the national average, we first assume that salaries approximate a normal distribution. We then place our salary in the formula for finding a Z-score: $Z = (X - \bar{X})/sd$. If our salary was $50,000 and the national average for librarians was $40,000, with a standard deviation of $5,000, then $Z = (\$50,000 - \$40,000)/\$5,000 = 2$. Two standard deviation units above the mean is .4772 in a Z-score table. Because the two standard deviation units are positive, we know it is greater than 50—the midpoint of a bell shaped curve. Conversion of .4772 produces a percentage of 48. This is 48% greater than the mean. Therefore, we add 50% to this percentage and discover that our salary is in the upper 98%. In other words, only 2% of the national salaries are higher than ours.

O'Conner (1982) offers an example of library applications of both normal curves and Z-scores. He gathered survey data from 96 public libraries in New Jersey and converted the data to ratio scores and Z-scores. The Z-score was then converted to a Library Quotient (LQ) score, a linear score with a mean of 100 and a standard deviation of 15. The standard score method developed by O'Conner was intended to serve as a model for assessing one library's performance in the context of that for other libraries.

It merits repeating that the area under the normal curve, between two or more scores, applies only to a normal distribution. Other types of distributions necessitate the use of different statistical applications, ones of greater complexity. Skewness or kurtosis (non-normal distributions) renders Z-score findings spurious (see note 6). As is evident, it is important to examine the shape of the distribution before applying the Z-score conversion.

T-SCORES

It is common practice to standardize scores, particularly in education and psychology. Knowing a score or a single value does not provide information on the standing of that score or value, in a comparative sense. There should be a reference point from which to evaluate a score, rating, or value. Yet some people find it inconvenient to use Z-scores because the scale has zero in the middle and minus values.

Once researchers have selected a value from a known distribution, they might want to determine whether that value is high, moderate, or low. Using the normal curve, for example, they can plot which values fall above or below the selected value. Even by making a graph of the normal curve, they might find it difficult to view an entire distribution and to know whether the selected value is comparatively small or large. Z-scores perform this function to a certain extent. If a Z-score is 70 for instance, we know it is, by definition, 2 standard deviation units above the mean, but we do not know exactly how many scores are greater than 70. This indicates a need for a normalized Z-score. Such a score is known as a *T*-score.

The *T*-scale places the mean raw score at $T = 50$ and equates the raw-score standard deviation at 10 *T*-score points. Thus, a score one standard deviation above the mean (Z-score of 1) has a *T*-score of 60: $T = 10Z + 50$. A score of two standard deviations below the mean (a Z-score of 2) would have a *T*-score of 30.

T-scores are normally distributed. Every point on the baseline of the normal curve corresponds to a percentile rank. Table 5-4 shows points on the baseline of the normal curve corresponding to these percentile ranks. These points are readily available from almost any textbook that gives areas under the normal curve.

Conversion to percentile ranks has applications in library and information science. Academic reference librarians, for example, may teach classes. As such, they are accountable as both librarians and classroom teachers charged with making students skilled in information retrieval and computer literacy. Reporting their effectiveness in the context of *T*-scores makes it possible to represent scores documenting their performance as percentile points and percentile ranks. Percentile points are the scores above or below a particular value. For instance, if 70% of a class have scores less than a certain value, that value is the 70th percentile point (Ferguson, 1981, p. 450). On a class examination, if 90% of the students score less than 80, then 80 is the 90th percentile point. The percentage rank, on the other hand, is the value in the normalized score, the *T*-score in this case, corresponding to the percentile point. For example, to convert a Z-score to a *T*-score, given a Z-value of 4,

$$T = 10 (4) + 50, \text{ or } 40 + 50 = 90.$$

Percentile points and percentile ranks are not meaningful for small samples. Both Z-scores and *T*-scores are useful for test scores but are valid only with

Table 5-4. Points on the Baseline of the
Unit Normal Curve Corresponding to
Selected Percentile Ranks*

Percentile Rank	Standard Deviation
99	+2.33
95	+1.65
90	+1.28
80	+ .84
70	+ .52
60	+ .25
50	.00
40	− .25
30	− .52
20	− .84
10	−1.28
5	−1.65
1	−2.33

*Reprinted from Ferguson (1981, p. 456).

normal distributions. Where the ranking of scores is important, tables for converting any score value to percentile ranks are helpful. An advantage of using either Z-scores or T-scores is that each can easily be depicted graphically, especially with statistical analysis software such as StatPac and Minitab.

The disadvantages of using the T-score are that if the sample is small, the points on the graph may reflect a high degree of irregularity and a normal curve is unobtainable. When librarians discover that a variable is not normally distributed, they might normalize the distribution, in some cases, by performing special statistical manipulations on the data. If researchers measure the population, they might compute T-scores to normalize the population; use of this procedure, however, is not always recommended. The conditions essential for statistical manipulations and the transformations are beyond the scope of this introductory handbook.

GRAPHIC PRESENTATION OF DATA

The graphic presentation of data serves as a reminder that "a picture is worth a thousand words—and at least ten thousand numbers" (Jaeger, 1983, p. 23). As Tufte (1983, p. 13) observes, the graphical presentation of data should:

- Depict the data
- Induce the audience to reflect on substance—the meaning of the data
- Avoid distorting that meaning
- Present many numbers in a small space

- Summarize large datasets and make them coherent
- Encourage visual comparisons among data
- Reveal the data at different levels of detail, from a broad overview to the fine structure
- Serve a reasonably clear purpose: description, exploration, tabulation, or decoration
- Be closely integrated with the statistical and verbal descriptions of a dataset.

People cannot always visualize patterns among data presented in a table. The table might contain too much data or be incorrectly set up. Readers might also experience problems in transferring numbers into proportional groupings that summarize the patterns. For such reasons, librarians might present data in graphic form such as in a pie chart or histogram (bar graph or chart).

This section of the chapter discusses some of the options for presenting hypothetical circulation data (see Table 5-5) as a graph. The graphs reproduced here were prepared with the use of either CHART-MASTER, Version 6.21 (Ashton-Tate, 20101 Hamilton Avenue, Torrance, CA 90502–1319) or Harvard Graphics (Software Publishing Corp., 1901 Landings Drive, Mt. View, CA 94039–7210). The graphs were printed on a Hewlett-Packard Laserjet printer.

Histograms are basically bars representing the frequency with which different values of a variable occur. In constructing a histogram, librarians should exercise careful judgment in marking off the scale. The key to the creation of a good histogram is to find the intervals that reflect changes, yet group the data in a meaningful way.

Table 5-5.   Monthly Circulation Statistics for 1988

Month	Number of Titles Borrowed by	
	Students	Faculty
January	156	112
February	313	72
March	258	81
April	279	84
May	213	56
June	103	123
July	98	82
August	52	36
September	221	158
October	386	92
November	268	74
December	113	41
Total:	2460	1011

Bar charts may take several forms. Figure 5-3, for example, depicts a *clustered bar chart*: two variables (students and faculty) are compared over a twelve-month period. This graph shows the variations in circulation for each group over time, as well as compares both groups. As Figures 5-3 and 5-4 illustrate, the bars can be either vertical or horizontal. Figure 5-5 displays a *stacked bar chart* showing the overall total per month, how one group compares to the other for that month, and how one month compares to the others.

The *frequency polygon* is another type of graphing technique for frequency distributions. The coordinates of the variables under study are plotted and then connected with straight lines. The end points of a frequency polygon are placed on the horizontal axis. This type of graph reflects changes over time. A *line graph* is similar to the frequency polygon (see Figure 5-6). In this instance, each line represents a different variable. An *area chart* takes the line graph but shades each group in a different color.

A frequency polygon that represents cumulative frequency distributions is called an *ogive*. The vertical axis indicates frequencies or percentages. The scores of the variable (interval level data) are placed along the horizontal axis. The form of an ogive on a graph always rises or falls, depending on whether the cumulative data increase or decrease. An S-shaped ogive illustrates a rapid increase, followed by a levelling-off period and more rapid increase.

Figure 5-3. Clustered Bar Chart

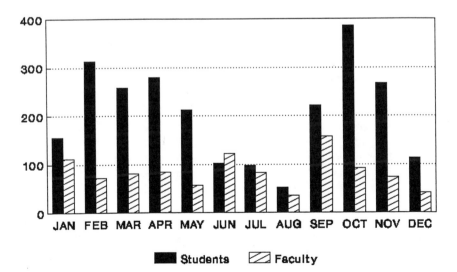

BAR CHART
Circulation Statistics for 1988

Figure 5-4.   Horizontal Bar Chart

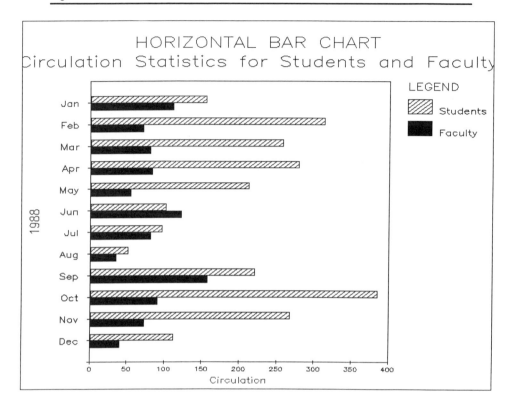

The *pie chart* is another common form for graphing data. Pie charts show the proportion of each variable to the whole. That proportion is expressed in terms of percentages. Figure 5-7 indicates the proportion of faculty and student circulation for the year, while Figure 5-8 displays student use by month. Figures 5-9 and 5-10 *explode* or separate a part of the chart. The purpose of explosion is to call attention to a particular part and its relationship to the whole.

The *scattergram*, or scatter chart, portrays the distribution of the findings. Perusal of Figure 5-11 indicates that scattergrams illustrate patterns or the presence of linear relationships. Both correlation coefficients (see Chapter 8) and regression analysis (see Chapter 9) draw upon scattergrams. Statistical analysis software, such as StatPac, produces scattergrams as part of the calculation of both correlation coefficients and regression analysis.

It is possible to mix types of graphs. Figure 5-12, which shows a line graph superimposed on a bar graph, clearly illustrates how one variable compares to the other.

Figure 5-5.   Stacked Bar Chart

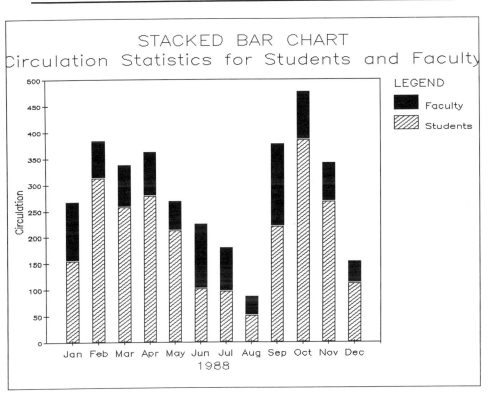

As Cleveland (1985) notes, and as examination of the various figures presented here reveals, everything on a graph should be explained. Different symbols should be easily distinguishable from each other, and both the lettering and
shading should be distinctive and true to form. A pie chart should be circular, not
oval-shaped.

The research literature of library and information science contains examples
of the use of graphs. Nelson (1973), in his article on faculty awareness of library
services, provides an excellent illustration of the use of a horizontal bar graph.
He charted the percentage of faculty aware of various services. Sanders, O'Neill,
and Weibel (1988) used stacked bars and clustered bar graphs to illustrate library
holdings in specific subjects by university. They also compared library holdings
in a network in the context of the total number of titles held by type of network
member.

Kelly, Andre, and Morrison (1988) used stacked bars in their analysis of
delivery methods for agricultural information. They compared user preferences

Figure 5-6. Line Chart

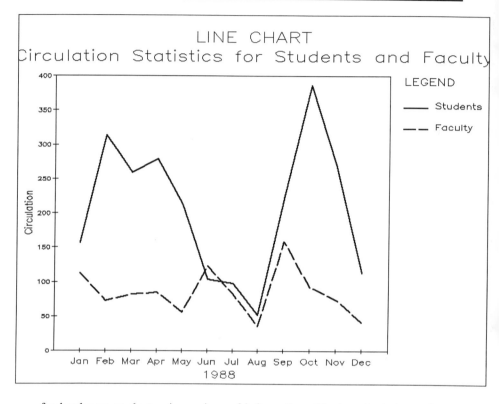

LINE CHART
Circulation Statistics for Students and Faculty

LEGEND

——— Students

— — Faculty

1988

for hardcopy or electronic versions of information. The bars in their graphs are three-dimensional, making quite attractive graphs.

Clack and Williams (1983) used a different type of bar graph. To indicate the annual percentage of change from one index to another, they used a bar graph with zero percentage change as the horizontal axis. To reflect increases, the bars went up from the axis; bars going down the axis represented decreases. Both the increases and decreases were easily discernible.

In his work on participative management, Marchant (1976) made effective use of a line graph. The staff and top management of a library, as well as the faculty of the college, rated certain aspects of the library, such as resources, services, and facilities. In his chart, the lines depicting each group were vertical. As a consequence, it is easy to see how highly the respondent groups scored certain areas and how the scores compared across the three groups.

As these examples and the figures depicted here indicate, graphics may enhance a written or oral presentation. With the wide variety of software packages now on the market at a reasonable price, the task of producing graphs and charts is easier. Researchers can experiment with different types of graphs and ways to capture, retain, and stimulate audience interest in study findings.

Figure 5-7.   Pie Chart

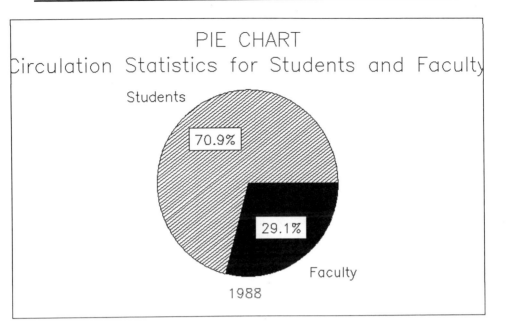

PIE CHART
Circulation Statistics for Students and Faculty

Students

70.9%

29.1%

Faculty

1988

Figure 5-8.   Pie Chart

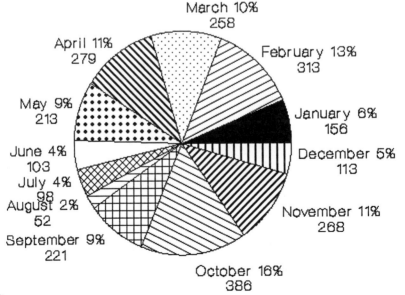

PIE CHART
Circulation Statistics for Students

March 10%
258

April 11%
279

February 13%
313

May 9%
213

January 6%
156

June 4%
103

December 5%
113

July 4%
98

August 2%
52

November 11%
268

September 9%
221

October 16%
386

1988

Figure 5-9. Exploded Pie Chart

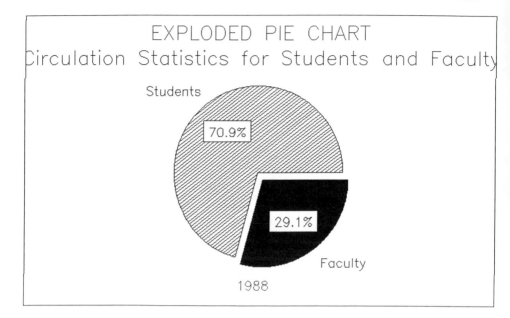

Figure 5-10. Exploded Pie Chart

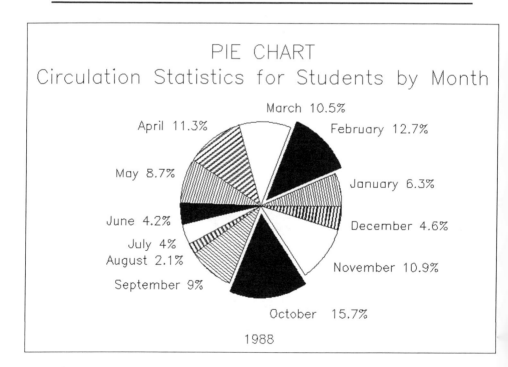

Figure 5-11. Scattergram

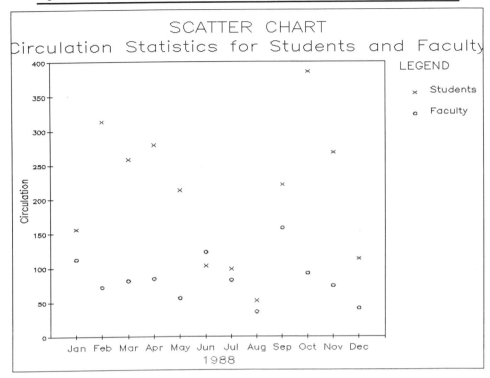

Figure 5-12. Mixed-Type Chart

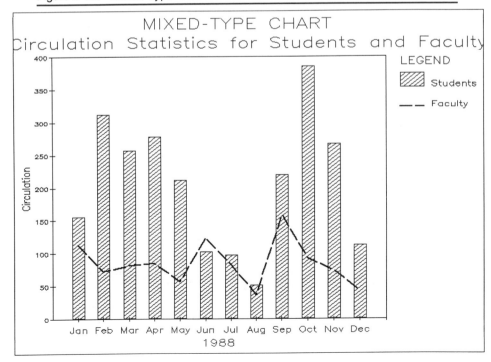

SUMMARY QUESTIONS (BASED ON THE CHAPTER)

A particular university identifies its students as attending one of three colleges: Arts and Sciences (CAS), Health Sciences (CHS), or Medicine (COM). From a sample of students observed borrowing library materials, it was discovered that:

Student A was from CAS.	Student G was from COM.
Student B was from CHS.	Student H was from CHS.
Student C was from CHS.	Student I was from COM.
Student D was from COM.	Student J was from CHS.
Student E was from CHS.	Student K was from CAS.
Student F was from COM.	Student L was from CHS.

1. How would you summarize these data using a frequency distribution?
2. How would you summarize these data using percentages?

In a library instruction class, library staff members recorded the following frequency distribution for student test scores:

Score	Frequency	Percentage	Cumulative Frequency	Cumulative Percentage
56–60	1	3.6		
61–65	1	3.6		
66–70	3	10.7		
71–75	2	7.1		
76–80	4	14.3		
81–85	5	17.9		
86–90	8	28.6		
91–95	3	10.7		
96–100	1	3.6		

3. How would you report these data using a cumulative frequency distribution?
4. How would you report these data using cumulative percentages?
5. In this frequency distribution, determine the category ("score") that represents the 50th percentile (the median), the lower quartile, and the upper quartile.
6. Three branch libraries have circulated the following number of titles for a six month period:

Library X:	1200	1100	1200	1350	1200	1150
Library Y:	800	1000	900	400	200	150
Library Z:	900	950	900	900	950	850.

Calculate the range, variance, and standard deviation for each library. How would you interpret the results?

7. A sample of 20 faculty members—10 instructors and 10 professors—completed a library survey about their knowledge of the library and effective search strategies. The staff then scored the results thusly:

Instructors: 60 50 85 30 50 70 20 40 80 70
Professors: 70 80 80 90 75 85 85 90 85 85

Which descriptive statistics would best characterize the dataset? How would you interpret the results?

8. Below are the pretest scores for a bibliographic instruction class. Calculate the Z-scores and the T-scores to two decimal places.

$$
\begin{array}{ccccc}
41 & 29 & 33 & 46 & 52 \\
52 & 48 & 30 & 39 & 41 \\
28 & 51 & 27 & 47 & 36 \\
46 & 45 & 45 & 51 & 39 \\
48 & 30 & 49 & 52 & 33 \\
\end{array}
$$

9. Assume the Z-scores in the previous question were obtained from a normal distribution of pretest scores. What percentage of scores falls above a raw score of 49 in a normal distribution? (You will need to consult a "table for Z-scores" in a statistics textbook).

10. The following values represent the proportion of the budget that 10 libraries spent on print materials. Assuming a normal distribution, calculate the mean, the standard deviation, the Z-scores, and the T-scores for these 10 libraries.

$$
\begin{array}{cc}
.270 & .340 \\
.245 & .310 \\
.280 & .280 \\
.300 & .275 \\
.290 & .270 \\
\end{array}
$$

Appendix A provides the answers to the questions

Chapter Six
Statistical Inference and Hypothesis Testing

The previous chapter presented descriptive statistics as a means to describe a group of data. By discussing statistical inference, this chapter serves as a foundation for subsequent chapters. Inferential statistics enable researchers to characterize a population based on a sample(s) drawn from the population. This chapter briefly highlights sampling and the context for interpreting data. That context for applied research studies will be hypothesis testing. However, in the case of action research conducted to impact managerial decision making, research questions may serve as a substitute for hypothesis testing. Regardless of whether researchers use hypotheses or research questions, a study should formulate objectives and examine these through the use of hypotheses and/or questions.

PROBABILITY AND STATISTICAL INFERENCE

Often librarians would like to draw conclusions about a population, but lack the time, resources, and so forth, to study such a large group. Instead, they sample the population and then attempt to draw inferences about that population. Inferential statistics is a set of formalized procedures for making generalizations beyond the sample data.

No sample probably represents a true or complete picture of the population. If many samples from a population are randomly drawn, the means (see Chapter 5) would resemble the population parameters. Yet, in spite of our best efforts, the samples might still differ from the population.[1]

A population, in inferential statistics, denotes all possible cases of something,

---

[1] Permut, Michel, and Joseph (1976) developed four criteria to determine the extent to which a sample of articles in marketing research meet the criteria of population validity. First, there must be a clear description of the population. Second, the sampling procedure should be specified so that others could replicate it. Third, the sampling frame, its strengths and weaknesses, merit identification. And, finally, the return rate, as well as a comparison of respondents to nonrespondents, should be provided. The purpose is to test whether nonrespondents, as a group, differ from the pool of respondents.

while a sample is a set of cases drawn from a population for the purpose of making inferences about that population. A parameter is a measure that describes a characteristic of a population. Both the mean and standard deviation (see Chapter 5) are parameters; the mean is a measure of central tendency and the standard deviation indicates the degree of dispersion for the population. A sample statistic describes a sample characteristic. From this brief definition of terms, it becomes clear that statistical inference is the process of drawing inferences about a parameter from a statistic.

Sampling a population raises two fundamental questions: (1) "Will different samples disclose the same characteristics?" and (2) "What is the range for the population value?" In the first question, librarians investigating a bibliographic instruction program might draw five random samples of college freshmen from a particular academic institution. The librarians would want to know if each sample will produce a different *mean* grade point average. For the second question, they might not be able to speculate about the *mean* grade point average of freshmen within the state university system of Indiana. Nonetheless, they want to hypothesize about the value of this mean. They could draw a random sample of freshmen from the university system and compute the mean for the sample. Because the mean of a sample will only occasionally differ substantially from that of the population, they could speculate about the range within which the population value falls.

The answers to both questions involve probabilities associated with various outcomes. Sometimes, researchers reach incorrect conclusions; however, with knowledge of the frequency of possible outcomes, they can estimate how often they are likely to be wrong. Probability, the key to the success of our estimation, is the proportion of times that the event occurs if the chances for occurrence were infinite. By tossing a coin that has both a heads and a tails, we can determine the probability of getting four tails from a toss of twelve coins; the probability of no heads or tails; and so forth.

Let's say that we surveyed a random sample of all academic libraries in New England and have a return rate of 65%. A key question is "To what extent do the sample and the actual respondents represent (or characterize) the population?" By maintaining a database on all New England libraries whereby we insert information on variables such as highest degree offered, budget and volume size, and number of professional staff, we could compare responding and nonresponding libraries. Where no differences emerge, we obtain evidence that the sample reflects the population. If differences emerge, however, we know those categories where we should seek additional survey participation (e.g., public master's-level institutions with volume counts between 75,000 and 150,000).

Another example is in order. For the past month, library staff members have conducted a study into the success of their bibliographic instruction program. They want to classify students according to whether the program improved or did not change their library skills (this is similar to counting the frequency of heads and tails in coin tosses). The probability for improvement is the ratio of improved cases to the number of students exposed to the program.

Sampling

Sampling, the process of selecting cases from a population, permits researchers to gather information more quickly and conveniently, and at a lesser cost. In research studies, the sample should be large enough so that investigators can assume that if they drew another sample of similar size and using the same procedure they would obtain approximately the same findings.[2]

Surprisingly, a carefully designed sample survey may collect more reliable data than a population survey because certain sources of error can be controlled when only a small number of items are examined. The decennial Census of Population and Housing conducted by the U.S. Bureau of the Census is less accurate than the various sampling studies conducted by the Bureau. The population survey touches so many people, not all of whom report data fully and accurately. Further, interviewers may be inexperienced and the number of non-sampling errors (i.e., mechanical and clerical) typically exceed the number of sampling errors. (Powell, 1985, pp. 82–86, discusses causes of sampling error.)

While developing the research project and setting the study design, librarians must decide on the sampling frame, or the best representation of the population. The sampling frame might be a list of libraries or networks, students at the college, and so forth. Some sampling frames are incomplete or outdated. For example, a list of libraries might have been compiled five years ago and be incomplete. Telephone directories do not include all households.[3]

When researchers draw a sample, the sample statistic is probably not exactly the same as the corresponding population parameter. Almost any value, within a range of values, present in the population could be obtained from a sample statistic. How, then, can a decision about a population be made from sample data? The next section addresses this question and illustrates options that researchers have in the selection of a sampling method.

Examples of Sampling Methods

Sampling involves the selection of a part of a population as representative of that population. Library researchers will have to decide on the most appropriate sampling method for their sampling frame. Part of the decision will depend on study constraints (e.g., time and money). In some cases, they make the decision based on convenience. It may be easier to conduct the study using a particular

---

[2] For an excellent introduction to sampling, see Slonim (1960).
[3] For an excellent discussion of sampling frames, see Swisher and McClure (1984), pp. 104–106.

method. Still, some methods generate more generalizable findings than do others.

Random sampling becomes one method for drawing inferences. Random sampling is a procedure for selecting cases from a population in such a way that every member of the population has an equal and independent chance of inclusion in the study. Such sampling ensures that the sample statistic is representative of the population parameter. By using random sampling, researchers can determine the amount of difference between a statistic and parameter.

The difference between the characteristics of a sample and those of the population from which the sample was taken is called *sampling error*. For random samples, researchers can estimate this error. Sampling error is a function of the size of the sample; the error is largest when the sample size is small.

Stratified random sampling divides the population into subgroups and selects representatives from each subgroup. The subgroups may be selected in proportion to their numbers in the population itself. In some instances, researchers might use *disproportional* stratified sampling. For example, only three public, baccalaureate institutions might be included in the population. Random sampling, or a proportional stratified sample, would underrepresent this category. The researchers therefore might include all three institutions in the study. With disproportionate sampling, researchers could adopt a weighting procedure to correct for the disproportionate representation of a stratum or strata. Many statistical analysis software packages make provisions for weighting.

Systematic sampling does not chose each member of the population independently. Once the first member of the population has been chosen, other members of the sample are automatically determined. For example, researchers might decide to select every 15th page from the telephone book and every 20th name on that page. Using this procedure they go through the telephone book until they have chosen all the names needed.

If librarians want to draw a sample of 50 cards from a shelflist of 5,000 cards, they would select every 100th card [(5,000/50)=100]. They would select the first element at random from one of the first 1000 cards and then each 100th card thereafter. If they took, for example, the 10th card, the next would be the 110th, then the 210th, and so forth, until the 50 cards were identified. The procedure might entail going through the shelflist a second time until the entire sample had been drawn.

Cluster sampling focuses on a naturally occurring group of individuals. Researchers divide the population into subdivisions, clusters of smaller units. Some of these subdivisions, or clusters, are randomly selected for inclusion in the study. If the clusters are geographic subdivisions, this kind of sampling is known as *area sampling*. Librarians planning a community analysis might want to concentrate data collection in neighborhoods known for their ethnicity. Cluster, or area, sampling divides the population into clusters or groups, within which researchers might random sample households (see Powell, 1985, pp. 76–79).

Quota sampling recognizes that researchers want to select a proportion of the population according to certain characteristics. For example, academic librarians might decide to base their sampling on class level and to take a proportion of freshmen, sophomores, and so forth. For convenience, they might conduct the study in the student union and select participants according to their class level. Once the quota for each class level has been filled, and respondents have answered the questions, the researchers terminate data collection. From such a study, researchers would not label study participants as representative of the population; rather, they would only discuss responding quotas.

Common Sampling Mistakes

A common mistake is to assume that all types of sampling equally reflect the population. Random sampling is essential for studies involving an experiment and the use of control and intervention groups. The purpose is to give every person an equal and independent chance of inclusion in a particular group. Random sampling raises the fewest threats to internal validity.

Another mistake is to investigate people from a population simply because they are available. For example, the population might be those in attendance at a particular conference. Yet the investigators might assume that those hearing a particular presentation reflect the population. Research results cannot be applied with sufficient confidence to those people not attending the one presentation.

Another mistake would be to select people from another population and assume that they reflect the population that the researchers want to investigate. Other commonly made mistakes include failure to define the population and to describe it adequately. Researchers might also select too small a sample size or draw incorrect conclusions based on study findings.

A common mistake is that researchers may not adequately consider the different types of sampling procedures and, select the one most appropriate to them. Stratified random sampling is a powerful procedure and may involve more than one sampling unit. For example, researchers could select, as the primary sampling unit, academic institutions and sample them according to highest degree. A secondary sampling unit could be academic departments, and a third unit might be whether faculty members are full- or part-time. The sample size will increase with the more sampling units included. Therefore, researchers must be realistic about the procedure selected.

Determination of Sample Size

The determination of sample size is obviously important. Most statistics textbooks identify an appropriate formula and discuss computation of the sample size. (Figure 1-1 offers examples of such textbooks.) Statistical analysis software, such as StatPac, contain a program for determining sample size. Please note, however, that the use of stratified random sampling and other specialized sampling methods may require consultation with a statistician to set the exact sample size.

In stratified sampling, researchers often maintain the same proportionality on stratification parameters in the sample as occur in the population. If gender, for example, were a stratification parameter, and the population contained an equal proportion of males and females, the researchers would retain the equal proportionality in their sample. The representativeness of the sample, in terms of the population, addresses sampling error, the confidence level, and distribution of a stratification parameter.

For research studies, the confidence level may be set at 95% (the .05 level), meaning that there is a 95% chance that the sample is distributed in the same way as the population. Management studies may accept a less stringent level e.g., (90% or .10).

To repeat, sampling error is the extent to which the sample means of repeatedly drawn random samples deviate from one another and presumably the population mean. By minimizing sampling error, researchers increase the likelihood that the sample represents the population. Larger samples tend to reduce the sampling error. "Yet there is no point in utilizing a sample that is larger than necessary; doing so unnecessarily increases the time and money needed for a study" (Powell, 1985, p. 79). However, "samples that are quite small place significant limitations on the types of statistical analyses that can be employed" (Ibid., p. 80).

Let's clarify the discussion with an example. Assume that the researchers at a university with 1,500 full-time faculty members want to draw a random sample of the faculty and to survey them about their information needs and use of the library. The researchers have access to a current and accurate directory of the faculty and do not want to sample the faculty based on academic rank, department, or college. For the purposes of the study, they will accept a random sample of the population.

The researchers number the faculty in the directory from 1 to 1,500. Next they turn to StatPac and program 4, on the utility menu, entitled "Determine Sample Size and Generate Random Numbers." They then calculate that 305 faculty yield a confidence level of 95%, ± 5. They also quickly see that 459 faculty correspond to 99%, ± 5; 500 faculty for 90%, ± 3; and 623 faculty for 95%, ± 3.

Upon reviewing study objectives and constraints, as well as managerial needs, the researchers decide on a random generation of 305 faculty so that all 1,500 names have an equal and independent chance of inclusion in the study. Using the same StatPac program, they generate a random number list (see Table 6-1) and check off the corresponding names in the telephone directory. They now have the sample and could compare the sample to the population on certain

Table 6-1.   Random Number Table

1139	1367	0941	0675	0220	0931	1127	0537	1207	0269	0182
0822	1000	0426	1369	0826	1442	0031	0183	1349	1318	0425
1237	1384	0658	0980	0719	1266	1104	1412	1475	1431	0269
0771	0185	1436	1059	0781	0863	0562	0807	0727	1295	0810
1465	0457	0968	1282	0828	1303	1084	0492	0710	0971	1455
0140	0633	0660	0218	0426	1182	0862	1485	1173	0942	1163
0183	0485	0537	1206	1296	0659	1254	0861	0751	1418	1205
1221	1187	0676	1023	0241	0506	0451	1029	0798	0356	1343
1368	0046	1377	0859	1291	0172	1431	0174	0734	0096	1496
0051	0477	0501	0363	1054	0899	1441	0518	0989	1292	0154
1104	1155	1336	0270	0543	0038	1116	0441	1492	0741	0568
1487	1236	0853	0285	1131	0316	0573	1417	1372	1338	1395
1416	1272	1240	0876	1464	0372	0914	0761	1294	0188	0902
0223	1276	1357	0258	0482	1498	0667	0262	0265	0412	0774
0378	0553	1363	0793	1348	1346	1382	0922	0784	1038	0612
0281	1149	0194	1238	1083	1291	0774	1302	1205	1302	0624
1233	1326	1175	0980	0814	0964	0232	0196	0534	1177	1029
0181	1495	0006	1180	0744	1003	0889	0261	1447	1376	1468
0013	0377	0455	1457	1417	1438	0195	1131	0045	0717	0555
0782	1178	0311	0501	1189	0281	1407	1345	1441	1270	0726
0451	0188	1040	1229	1490	0579	0677	1404	0672	0933	1159
0672	0064	1348	1105	1083	0803	0854	0672	0363	1375	0872
1207	1421	0269	0966	0819	1000	0501	1498	0110	1134	1186
0635	0891	0812	1353	1176	1265	0158	0179	0974	0449	0736
1177	0634	1343	0784	1228	0065	0814	1185	0983	1262	1027
1118	1409	0264	1147	0076	1229	0088	1416	0782	0026	0798
0753	1197	0257	0806	0188	0685	0774	0253	0082	0611	1420
1469	1149	1397	0745	0693	0244	0880	0571			

characteristics. The better the match, the greater the confidence that the sample is, indeed, representative of the population.

Examples

Drott (1969) offers three examples where librarians could engage in random sampling. First, they might select a subset of holding records to check the degree of inaccuracies and determine if an inventory of all records is necessary. Second, they might survey a random sample of patrons as they enter the library and solicit their opinions about library services. And, third, librarians might determine how much shelf space would be gained from the removal of lesser-used titles from the collection. Drott shows how to compute the sample size for each example.

As another example, suppose that library managers at a university with an enrollment of 35,000 have decided to conduct a study of student use and nonuse of the library. Clearly, they have options to consider. First, they must decide whether to investigate the population or a sample and the time frame for completion of the study. They might set, as their goal, a completion date of ten years. By so doing, they could concentrate on particular colleges or departments each year. Complicating matters, they would have to realize that comparisons among colleges and departments become difficult as time progresses. The student population will change; the central questions become "How much?" and "What types of changes have resulted?"

Let's say that the managers decide to draw a sample of students from the population of full-time students. What type of sample should they use? They might consider a random sample of students or classes. The university may or may not have an accurate and up-to-date list of all students. As an alternative, there would be a list of all classes offered for each term, from which a random sample of classes could be drawn. Of course, such an approach would require faculty cooperation in the distribution and presumably collection of a questionnaire during class sessions.

Another option would be to draw a systematic sample of classes or students. Again, the same type of problems, as previously mentioned, emerge. The managers might take a systematic sample of students entering or leaving the library. However, this approach would not get at the nonuser. Therefore, they might conduct a study at the student union and draw a systematic sample of those present during certain times of the day. Managers might also consider the use of a quota sample that takes into account so many students per class level or college. As this example illustrates, managers must explore different options and determine the one most applicable to their situation, information needs, budget, and time frame for decision making.

OBJECTIVES

Research objectives provide a narrowing of the statement of the problem and illustrate the aspects of the problem that will be investigated. The statement of the problem identifies a problem and its significance. Study objectives clarify the aspects of the problem that will be probed. Choices must be made and the specification of these choices constitutes the study objectives. The basis for making the choices might be convenience, interests of library staff and managers, utility to decision making, and social or professional significance.

Research objectives provide the conceptual framework for formulating and testing hypotheses and questions. Basic research involves the conceptualization of theory or models, while applied research tests theory and may lead to the refinement of theory. Action research, which serves as the basis for this book, generates two types of objectives. The first *depicts* or *identifies* something, while the second *relates* or *compares* key variables.

Every objective has two aspects: (1) the verb (action) and (2) intent (content). For example, an evaluation study might pose the objective, "to determine the reasons for faculty nonuse of the library." The verb indicates the action component, while the remaining clause identifies the content component. Perhaps another illustration might be useful. Unobtrusive testing of library reference personnel might have as its objective, "to identify the accuracy with which staff members from academic and public libraries answer questions of a factual and bibliographic nature." Researchers might also want "to compare the number of correct answers by library type (academic and public) and department (general reference and government publications)."

HYPOTHESES/RESEARCH QUESTIONS

Hypothesis testing, a type of statistical inference, offers direction to the research. Hypotheses provide a framework for viewing and reporting study findings. Hypotheses are expectations about the nature of things based on generalizations about the assumed relationship between variables. Hypotheses enable researchers, on the basis of sample data, to determine whether or not something about the population is likely to be true or false. Since it is difficult to obtain unequivocal support for a hypothesis or disprove that statement absolutely, researchers tend to be cautious and to emphasize that they are supporting (not proving) or rejecting (not disproving) that hypothesis.

As Powell (1985, p. 159) observes,

> a single statistical "acceptance" of a hypothesis does not prove it to be true with absolute certainty. It is seldom if ever possible to accept a hypothesis outright as the single correct one, since there are a larger number of additional hypotheses which also could be accepted. One simply decides, based on the statistical results that a hypothesis should not be rejected. This does provide, of course, some support for the hypothesis.

Hypotheses do not explain the reasons behind a relationship or enable researchers to make causal inferences.

Researchers may explore alternative hypotheses and eliminate the less viable ones (see subsequent discussion of one- and two-tailed tests). "Social science researchers frequently have to settle for . . . hypotheses which state a correlational but not causal relationship between two or more variables" (Ibid., p. 32).[4]

Hypotheses might be framed as null, directional, nondirectional, and so forth. The null hypothesis, the "no difference" or "no effect" statement, suggests that small (neither significant nor substantial) differences could result due to chance variation; there is no relationship between the variables. Directional hypotheses identify the relationship between the variables studied, while nondirectional hypotheses presuppose a relationship but the researcher is unsure of what that relationship is.

---

[4] Powell (1985, pp. 28–36) provides a succinct discussion of hypotheses.

Consider the following three hypotheses related to bibliographic instruction:

1. Workbooks are a more effective learning tool than classroom lectures.
2. Workbooks and classroom lectures are equally as effective as learning tools.
3. There is no statistically significant difference between workbooks and class-room lectures (at 0.05 level) as learning tools.

The third hypothesis is cast in the null form. The null hypothesis is rejected if the differences are large and real. As already noted, in the social sciences, the 95% level (or $p < .05$) is an acceptable level of confidence to reject a null hypothesis. The .05 level is an arbitrary decision point. In cases of managerial studies, researchers might use, e.g., the 10% level ($p < .10$); however, they should exercise extreme caution in data interpretation.

Formulation of hypotheses and questions involves a three-step process that (1) includes the selection of key questions appropriate to the objectives, (2) defines major components of study variables, and (3) identifies relationships, if appropriate, between variables. Hypotheses reflect a highly sophisticated conceptual framework for the study, while questions indicate a less sophisticated and rigorous framework.

Any hypothesis should:

*   Be stated succinctly and clearly
*   Express the relationship between variables
*   Be testable and explicitly stated—a person is unable to draw inferences from it
*   Be value neutral, not value laden
*   Have explanatory power
*   Be supported by (and consistent with) theory, previous research, or, at times, experience.

As an alternative to hypothesis testing, researchers conducting a descriptive survey or evaluating library programs, services, or operations might formulate research questions. The purpose of the data collection therefore is to address these questions. Note, however, that researchers do not answer the questions definitely. Neither do they demonstrate cause–effect nor assume that additional samples from the population would automatically yield the same findings.

Sometimes, it is easier to write a question than to develop a hypothesis. As a general rule of thumb, librarians might consider that they have two hats from which they can make appropriate selections. In one hat, there are hypotheses. To oversimplify matters, they could select either a directional or another type of hypothesis. Selection of a directional hypothesis should be done with extreme caution. If the findings do not support the directional hypothesis, researchers should attempt to discover the reason(s). Further, researchers do not want readers of the final report to question the logic, subjectivity, or bias of the direction indicated. For example, a directional hypothesis might be that "males are better fundraisers than females; better is equated with raising more money." The legitimacy of such a hypothesis can (and should) be questioned. A body of theory, practice, or research must indicate the possible direction. Researchers do not want data collection to be guided by subjectivity or guesses. They want to rely on a clear and defensible rationale.

The other hat contains research questions. From which of the two hats will the researcher select? The answer depends on factors such as the level of difficulty associated with writing a clearly understood hypothesis, the conceptual framework of the study, and the needs of decision makers. Some decision makers may understand a question better than they would a hypothesis. Researchers might even select from both hats and take a mixture of hypotheses and questions. When they use hypotheses, these hypotheses will probably be cast in the null form.

ONE- AND TWO-TAILED TESTS

In estimating the value of the population mean, researchers might believe that the population mean can only be on one side of the sample mean. In such cases, they are dealing with only one tail of the sampling distribution. Researchers use one-tailed tests when a hypothesis suggests the direction of the deviation. In some cases, the hypothesis does not predict the direction of the difference. Instead, researchers only discover that the sample results differ from the null hypothesis. With a two-tailed test, researchers locate a *critical region* in both ends (tails) of

Figure 6-1. One- and Two-Tailed Tests

A. One-Tailed Test (Critical region for .05—upper end of the sampling distribution)

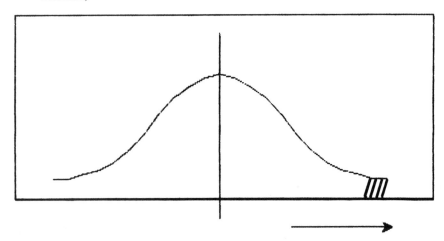

B. One-Tailed Test (Critical region for .05—lower end of the sampling distribution)

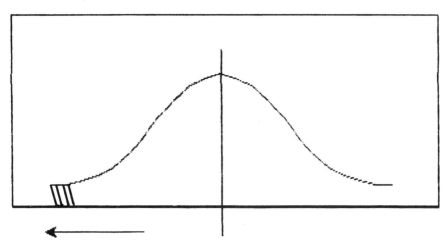

C. Two-Tailed Test (Critical region(s) at 0.05)

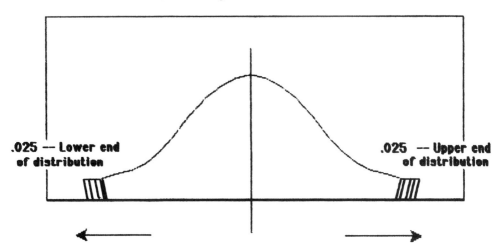

.025 — Lower end
of distribution

.025 — Upper end
of distribution

the sampling distribution. As a result, the statistical test is sensitive to departures, in either direction, from the null hypothesis. Figure 6-1 clarifies the distinction between one- and two-tailed tests. In the case of the two-tailed test, the critical region is divided into equal parts in each tail of the sampling distribution.

Theory and substantive knowledge guide the formulation of directional predictions and the use of a one-tailed test. A one-tailed test is more sensitive in detecting departures from the null hypothesis, assuming that the direction was correctly predicted. The two-tailed test is better to use when the direction cannot be predicted with any confidence. However, such a test is *weaker*, since it lacks the theoretical justification of a one-tailed test. As should be evident, one- and two-tailed tests can lead to different statistical decisions regarding the acceptance or rejection of a null hypothesis.

Perhaps an illustration might be helpful. Researchers cannot always speculate about the impact of an experimental treatment—student skills in using the library, for example, may or may not improve. In such circumstances, researchers might consider the use of a two-tailed test. However, when they have good evidence that the treatment (or intervention) will produce an effect only in one direction, a one-tailed test is appropriate.

The selection of either a one- or two-tailed test depends on available theory and knowledge, the proposed alternative hypothesis, and the problem under investigation. An alternative hypothesis offers a different, but plausible, explanation. This rival hypothesis is a statement that the same population parameter differs in value from that specified in the null hypothesis.

TYPE I AND TYPE II ERRORS

Researchers should select a level of significance prior to data collection after evaluating the consequences of making two possible, incorrect decisions: a Type I or Type II error. A Type I error is the possibility of rejecting a true null hypothesis. Some randomly drawn samples from other populations may resemble samples from the population actually under investigation. Although these samples should be rejected, they might be accepted as being from the study population. When this occurs, the researchers have made a Type II error.

The probability of committing a Type I error is known as the confidence level. As already discussed, it is generally set, in the social sciences, at .05 or .01. The decision to use either level depends on the consequences of committing a Type I error. The probability of a Type II error is difficult to determine because such error can occur whenever the true parameter differs from that stated in the hypothesis, and the probability varies with the magnitude of that difference.

Figure 6-2.   Type I and Type II Error*

Conclusion		Hypothesis Stated Is	
		True	False
Sample indicates	Reject hypothesis	Type I error	Correct conclusion
	Accept hypothesis	Correct conclusion	Type II error

*Reprinted with permission from *Introduction to Probability and Statistics*, 6th edition, by Henry L. Alder and Edward B. Roessler. Copyright © 1960, 1977 W. H. Freeman and Co.

As Alder and Roessler (1977, p. 156) illustrate, "depending upon whether the stated hypothesis is true or false, and depending upon the conclusion reached from the sample, there are four different possibilities . . ." (see Figure 6-2).

A Type I error leads to misinterpretation. The consequences of such error therefore are often more serious than those of a Type II error. When researchers conduct management studies that test at the .10 level of significance, they are taking only moderate precautions against a Type I error. They are not taking a large risk, however, of a Type II error.

CHOOSING THE APPROPRIATE STATISTICAL TEST

Statistical tests aid in data interpretation. Researchers use statistical testing to compare data and to determine the probability that differences between groups of data are based on chance. "And the final interpretation of the analysis must be done by the investigator; statistics can only facilitate the process" (Powell, 1985, p. 161).

To decide on the appropriate statistical test, library researchers must determine the number of independent (the experimental or predictor variable that the researcher manipulates and that presumably produces change) and dependent (influenced by the independent variable) variables, whether they are willing to risk a Type I or Type II error, whether the distribution has one- or two-tails, as well as the measurement scale.[5] They must also decide whether parametric and nonparametric tests are more appropriate. To repeat, nonparametric tests make fewer assumptions about the distributions, do not require a normal distribution (or population) or equal group variance, and are based on nominal or ordinal measurement. They are useful for large samples not meeting the assumptions of parametric tests.

Other considerations include whether researchers are analyzing one group, or two or more groups. Further, the researchers must decide if they want to characterize respondents or cases (provide descriptive statistics) or draw inferences to the population (inferential statistics).

The selection of statistical tests, and the interpretation of the results, should be done after careful review of the conceptual underpinnings of the objectives and hypotheses, as well as other steps in the research process (see Chapter 1). It is important to remember that (Powell, 1985, p. 159):

a statistically significant result is not necessarily socially or practically significant. Differences of a few thousand volumes between two university library collections could produce significant statistical differences, but in terms of multi-million volume collections, such difference holds little if any practical significance.

---

[5] Many libraries only collect data at the nominal and ordinal levels. For example, many performance measures report nominal measurement. In addition, surveys that solicit the purpose for using the library and the types of sources used during the visit report nominal measurement.

Researchers should also exercise caution when dealing with "weighted data, small sample sizes, complex sample designs, and capitalization on chance in fitting a statistical model . . ." (Andrews et al., 1974, p. 2).

The discussion in subsequent chapters will introduce readers to different statistical tests and offer actual examples of the application of these tests. The examples are both hypothetical and drawn from the literature of library and information science. The selection of readings concentrates on studies subjectively judged by us as having *value* to library managers and decision makers. The selection does not include all the readings using a particular test. Rather, the purpose is to encourage readers to review the literature and obtain a practical understanding of the tests and their application. One final caveat is in order. This book is not a substitute for studying a textbook(s) on statistics. Our book, though, complements such textbooks and provides examples from the discipline of library and information science.

The t-test, Mann-Whitney U Test, Chi-square Test of Independence, and Phi Coefficient*

In effect, this chapter is divided into four parts. The first one covers the parametric *t*-test and one of its nonparametric equivalents, the Mann-Whitney U Test. The second part of the chapter discusses the chi-square test of independence, which is perhaps the most frequently used inferential statistical application in library and information science. The third part introduces correlation, the topic of the next chapter, by discussing the Phi coefficient. This statistic is presented here because it is often associated with chi-square. We might consider the Phi coefficent as a companion to interpretation of the chi-square value. The final part of the chapter serves as a reminder that inferential statistics should be used in a context and that such statistics either compare populations or determine the likelihood that a sample is part of a particular population. Figure 7-1 identifies the major statistical tests that are discussed in this chapter, while Figure 7-2 offers examples of writings that have used a particular test.

t-TEST

The *t*-test, which is used to compare the means of two groups, addresses the question "Does the performance of one group differ significantly from the performance of another?" The test is frequently used for the evaluation of bibliographic instruction programs, where librarians want to measure the impact of interventions on student learning and information-gathering behavior. Librarians compare pretest and posttest scores to measure if there is a statistically significant difference between the two.

The t-distribution depends on sample size. With small sample sizes, the distribution is leptokurtic (a very peaked curve). For samples over 30, the distribution approaches a normal distribution.

There are two basic kinds of parametric *t*-tests: one for matched pairs and the

---

* Portions of this chapter are reprinted from Hernon and Richardson (1988, Chapter 5).

Figure 7-1.   Brief Descriptions of the Tests Discussed in This Chapter

Test	Description
t-test	It tests the difference between means of two samples for interval or ratio-type data.
Mann-Whitney U Test	It is the nonparametric equivalent of the t-test for independent groups. The test is used to evaluate the difference between two population distributions.
Chi-square Test	It is used in tests of statistical independence of two variables. The chi-square test applies to nominal and ordinal level data.
Fisher's Exact Test	This test gives exact, not approximate, probabilities for 2 × 2 tables.
Yates' Correction	It applies to the chi-square test for 2 × 2 tables where the degrees of freedom equal one.
Phi Coefficient	This coefficient measures the strength of the relationship between two variables. It also compares two crosstabs with unequal Ns.
Cramer's V	It is a slightly modified version of the Phi coefficient that is used with contingency tables larger than 2 × 2.

Figure 7-2.   Examples of Writings Using the Tests Discussed in This Chapter

t-test

D'Elia, George P. "The Determinants of Job Satisfaction among Beginning Librarians," *Library Quarterly*, 49 (1979): 283–302.

Hardesty, Larry, Jamie Hastreiter, and David Henderson. "Development of College Library Mission Statements," *Journal of Library Administration*, 9 (1988): 11–34.

Hardesty, Larry, Nicholas P. Lovrich, Jr., and James Mannon. "Evaluating Library Use Instruction," *College & Research Libraries*, 40 (July 1979): 309–317.

Harter, Stephen P. and Mary Alice S. Fields. "Circulation, Reference, and the Evaluation of Public Library Service," *RQ*, 18 (Winter 1978): 147–152.

Hernon, Peter and Charles R. McClure. "Experimental Approach," in *Unobtrusive Testing and Library Reference Service*. Norwood, NJ: Ablex, 1987, pp. 78–103.

Hert, Carol Anne. "Predictors of Interlibrary Loan Turnaround Times," *Library and Information Science Research*, 9 (1987): 213–234.

Hobson, Charles J., Robert F. Moran, Jr., and Arena L. Stevens. "Circulation/Reserve Desk Personnel Effectiveness," *Journal of Academic Librarianship*, 13 (May 1987): 93–98.

Kesselman, Martin and Sarah Barbara Watstein. "The Measurement of Reference and Information Services," *Journal of Academic Librarianship*, 13 (March 1987): 24–30.

Pungitore, Verna L. "Perceptions of Change and Public Library Directors in Indiana: An Exploratory Study," *Library and Information Science Research*, 9 (October/December 1987): 247–264.

Saunders, Carol Stoak and Russell Saunders. "Effects of Flexitime on Sick Leave, Vacation Leave, Anxiety, Performance, and Satisfaction in a Library Setting," *Library Quarterly*, 55 (January 1985): 71–88.

Scamell, Richard W. and Bette Ann Stead. "A Study of Age and Tenure As It Pertains to Job Satisfaction," *Journal of Library Administration*, 1 (Spring 1980): 3–18.

Figure 7-1. *(Continued)*

Mann Whitney U Test

Hernon, Peter and Maureen Pastine. "Student Perceptions of Academic Librarians," *College & Research Libraries*, 38 (March 1977): 129–139.

Chi-square Test of Independence

Davis, Jinnie Y. and Stella Bentley. "Factors Affecting Faculty Perceptions of Academic Libraries," *College & Research Libraries*, 40 (November 1979): 527–532.

Evans, G. Edward and Claudia White Argyres. "Approval Plans and Collection Development in Academic Libraries," *Library Resources and Technical Services*, 18 (Winter 1974): 35–50.

Gothberg, Helen M. and Donald E. Riggs. "Time Management in Academic Libraries," *College & Research Libraries*, 49 (March 1988): 131–140.

Hert, Carol Anne. "Predictors of Interlibrary Loan Turnaround Times," *Library and Information Science Research*, 9 (1987): 213–234.

Luyben, Paul D., Leonard Cohen, Rebecca Conger, and Selby U. Gration. "Reducing Noise in a College Library," *College & Research Libraries*, 42 (September 1981): 470–481.

Lynch, Beverly P. and Jo Ann Verdin. "Job Satisfaction in Libraries: Relationships of the Work Itself, Age, Sex, Occupational Group, Tenure, Supervisory Level, Career Commitment, and Library Department," *Library Quarterly*, 53 (October 1983): 434–447.

McClure, Charles R. "Academic Librarians, Information Sources, and Shared Decision Making," *Journal of Academic Librarianship*, 6 (March 1980): 9–15.

Saunders, Carol Stoak and Russell Saunders. "Effects of Flexitime on Sick Leave, Vacation Leave, Anxiety, Performance, and Satisfaction in a Library Setting," *Library Quarterly*, 55 (January 1985): 71–88.

Sharma, Prabha. "A Survey of Academic Librarians and Their Opinions Related to Nine-Month Contracts and Academic Status Configurations in Alabama, Georgia, and Mississippi," *College & Research Libraries*, 42 (November 1981): 561–570.

Van House, Nancy A. "Public Library Effectiveness: Theory, Measures, and Determinants," *Library and Information Science Research*, 8 (1986): 261–283.

Phi Coefficient

Adalian, Paul T., Jr., Ilene F. Rockman, and Ernest Rodie. "Student Success in Using Microfiche to Find Periodicals," *College & Research Libraries*, 46 (January 1985): 48–54.

Hernon, Peter and Maureen Pastine. "Student Perceptions of Academic Librarians," *College & Research Libraries*, 38 (March 1977): 129–139.

Cramer's V

Powell, Ronald R. and Sheila D. Creth. "Knowledge Bases and Library Education," *College & Research Libraries*, 47 (January 1986): 16–27.

Van House, Nancy A. "Public Library Effectiveness: Theory, Measures, and Determinants," *Library and Information Science Research*, 8 (1986): 261–283.

other for independent groups. The former is used when both groups of data are contained in each data record, while the latter applies in instances in which each case in the data file is to be assigned to one group or the other based on another variable ("StatPac Gold—Statistical Analysis Package for the IBM: Manual," 1988). The "samples are referred to as independent because they are drawn independently from a population without any pairing or other relationship between the two groups" (Ary et al., 1985, p. 158).

Table 7-1 illustrates the application of the *t*-test for samples of less than 30. When there are at least 30 cases in each sample, the sampling distribution of the difference between means is normal and we can assume a normal curve. (Nonetheless, we should plot the values on a scattergram and confirm the existence of a normal distribution.) We can then establish the area under the curve and calculate a standard deviation and a Z-score.[1,2]

For an example of a study using the *t*-test, see Hernon and McClure (1987b, Chapter 4). Staff members from two library departments were randomly assigned to one of two contrasting learning interventions (a workshop or slide-script presentation). The chair of each department certified that both groups were indeed similar in terms of experience and knowledge of the topic under investigation. Next, participants were pretested unobtrusively; they were unaware that they were being evaluated on the accuracy of their response to a set of reference questions. After completion of both intervention strategies, participants in both groups were posttested unobtrusively. Study participants did not attend any professional meetings, workshops, etc., during the time of data collection that might have affected their performance during unobtrusive testing. Further, participants were unaware of when unobtrusive testing would be conducted during the academic year.

The following two hypotheses were tested:

- The rate of accuracy (to the test questions) for both groups will improve as a result of the intervention (the group mean score from the posttest will be compared to the group mean from the pretest)
- There is no statistically significant difference ($p < .05$) in learning outcomes between the interventions. (The group mean scores from the two posttests will be compared.)

The first hypothesis was not supported . A *t*-test for matched pairs (comparing an individual's pretest to posttest performance) was computed for the correct an-

---

[1] Statistics textbooks discuss the computation of t-tests and show the variation in formulae for small samples that cannot be presumed to come from populations with a common variance.

[2] The means of an infinite number of randomly drawn samples from a population produce a normal curve when plotted in a frequency distribution. The differences between means of randomly drawn samples would do likewise. This distribution of differences between means is a sampling distribution of differences. This sampling distribution of differences has a standard deviation (see Chapter 5) that serves as a basis for finding the number of differences between means of randomly drawn samples that fall beyond given points.

Table 7-1.   Application of the *t*-test

Example:	The library is investigating two methods of teaching library skills to undergraduates. Fourteen freshmen were randomly assigned to method ONE and another 14 to method TWO. After two weeks of instruction, the librarians computed the following statistics from a library skills examination.

Method	$\bar{X}$	s
ONE	72	7
TWO	63	9

To test the hypothesis that the means of the two samples do not differ at the .05 level, we compute the standard error of the difference (sed)

$$sed = \sqrt{\frac{s_1^2}{N_1} + \frac{s_2^2}{N_2}}$$

S_1^2 and s_2^2 are the variances of each sample, while N_1 and N_2 refer to the number of cases in a sample.

$$sed = \sqrt{\frac{7^2}{14} + \frac{9^2}{14}} = 3.05$$

Computation of the *t*-test:

$$t = \frac{\bar{X}_1 + \bar{X}_2}{sed} = \frac{72 - 63}{3.05} = 2.95$$

Is the *t*-value of 2.95 significant?

If the sample size were large and we knew the *sed*, the *t* distribution approximates a normal curve. In our case, the sample size is less than 30 and the variance is pooled (pooling the data from both samples of the same population). We therefore consult a table of *t* distributions in a statistics textbook, using the following formula:

$$N_1 + N_2 - 2, \text{ or } 14 + 14 - 2 = 26$$

> Conclusion: A *t*-value of 2.056 is needed for significance at the .05 probability level. Because our *t*-value was larger (2.95), it is unlikely that the difference between the pairs of randomly selected samples is due to chance.

Table 7-2.   Printout from StatPac on the *t*-test

Pretest Correct Answer
Mean	=	1.37 ←
Variance	=	0.23
Standard Deviation	=	0.48
Standard Error of the Mean	=	0.36

Posttest Correct Answer
Mean	=	1.48 ←
Variance	=	0.35
Standard Deviation	=	0.50
Standard Error of the Mean	=	0.06

t-test Statistics
Difference (Mean X − Mean Y)	=	−0.111 ←
Standard Error of the Difference	=	0.088
t-statistic	=	1.261 ←
Degrees of Freedom	=	62
Probability of *t* (One-tailed test)	=	0.105
Probability of *t* (Two-tailed test)	=	0.205
Correlation Coefficient	=	− .063
Valid Cases	=	63
Missing Cases	=	0
Response Percent	=	100%

swers of all participants on both the pretest and posttest, regardless of the intervention to which they were assigned. As illustrated in Table 7-2, the mean score for the pretest was 1.37 and 1.48 for the posttest. The difference between the mean scores of the two sets was 0.111. There is no statistically significant difference between the two (*t*-statistic of 1.261). The mean scores for both the pretest and posttest are indeed similar. Group learning and application of the contents of an intervention cannot be attributed to either the workshop or slide-script presentation.

MANN-WHITNEY U TEST

The Mann-Whitney U Test, the nonparametric counterpart to the *t*-test for independent groups,[3] evaluates the difference between two population distributions for data reflecting ordinal, interval, or ratio measurement. In other words, we draw a sample of cases from two populations assumed to be identical and compare the extent to which these samples are similar. To do this, we compare each

---

[3] The Wilcoxon test for correlated samples is the nonparametric equivalent of the *t*-test for matched pairs. Data are assigned rank values and the differences between the ranks are calculated. The Wilcoxon test statistic is the minimum of positive and negative differences in ranks.

Table 7-3.   Application of the Mann-Whitney U Test

Example: We conduct a survey of college students, ones who are undergraduates in Education and those enrolled in master's programs in library and information science.

Scores for sample of undergraduates:
38, 45, 59, 64, 83
Scores for sample of graduate students:
20, 52, 57, 67, 85

Null Hypothesis: There is no statistically significant difference in the mean scores of both groups at the .05 level.

Pair Number	Score Undergraduate	Graduate Student	Undergrads Score Larger Than Grads	Grads Scores Larger Than Undergrads
1	38	20	X	
2	38	52		X
3	38	57		X
4	38	67		X
5	38	85		X
6	45	20	X	
7	45	52		X
8	45	57		X
9	45	67		X
10	45	85		X
11	59	20	X	
12	59	52	X	
13	59	57	X	
14	59	67		X
15	59	85		X
16	64	20	X	
17	64	52	X	
18	64	57	X	
19	64	67		X
20	64	85		X
21	83	20	X	
22	83	52	X	
23	83	57	X	
24	83	67	X	
25	83	85		X

Total number of pairs in which undergraduates score larger than graduate students: $12 = U$
Total number of pairs in which graduate students score larger than undergraduates: $13 = U'$

value in one sample with every value in the other. For every comparison, we see which value is larger.

Table 7-3, which illustrates the calculation of the Mann-Whitney U Test, indicates that we pair the number of cases in the first sample (five scores) with the number of cases in the second sample (the other five scores). Therefore, we have a total of 25 scores to pair. Assuming that none of the scores for a pair tied,[4] we count the number of instances in which each set of scores was larger. The scores of the undergraduates were larger in 12 instances (U) and those of the graduate students were larger in 13 instances (U'). The sum of U and U' equals the total number of pairs, or 25 in this case.

If both populations from which the samples are drawn are in fact identical, U and U' equal approximately $(n_1 n_2)/2$. To utilize U and U' in testing the null hypothesis that the populations are identical, we must determine the sampling distribution for each value. Statistics textbooks often reprint tables that report such computation. The *smaller* of the two statistics (either U or U') serves as the test statistic and is compared to the critical value in the table for the appropriate sample sizes and level of significance. If the observed value is the same as, or smaller than, the critical value shown in the table, the null hypothesis is rejected at the level of significance tested.

Statistical analysis software, such as StatPac, can easily perform the calculations and report the corresponding level of probability. Hand calculation of the data provided in Table 7-2 would be tedious. Therefore, we can simplify the calculation by ranking the 10 values from both samples in a single series:

Ranking	Scores
1	20 (Grad)
2	38 (Undergrad)
3	45 (Undergrad)
4	52 (Grad)
5	57 (Grad)
6	59 (Undergrad)
7	64 (Undergrad)
8	67 (Grad)
9	83 (Undergrad)
10	85 (Grad)

Undergraduates ranked as 2, 3, 6, 7, and 9; graduates were 1, 4, 5, 8, and 10. Next we sum each rank:

$$2 + 3 + 6 + 7 + 9 = 27 \ (R_1)$$
$$1 + 4 + 5 + 8 + 10 = 28 \ (R_2).$$

---

[4] The Kolmogorov–Smirnov (K-S) Test is used when both samples are larger and there are many tied ranks.

Together the R-values total 55. For verification on the accuracy of our computation, we could use the formula:

$$R_1 + R_2 = \frac{n(n+1)}{2}$$

$$27 + 28 = \frac{10(11)}{2} = 55.$$

The formula for computing U is:

$$U = n_1 n_2 + \frac{n_2(n_2+1)}{2} - R_2$$

$$U = (5)(5) + \frac{5(6)}{2} - 28 = 40 - 28 = 12$$

And $U' = n_1, n_2 - U$, or $(5)(5) - 12 = 13$.

Because 12 (U) is the smaller of the two values (U and U'), we compare that number with the critical values contained in a table in a statistics textbook.[5] However, in our case, the sample size is so small that most statistics books might not report a value; instead they indicate the probability. When $n_2 = 5$, $n_1 = 5$, and $U = 12$, the probability is .5 (see Siegel, 1956, p. 271), which is larger than than the value needed for significance in this case. Therefore, the null hypothesis cannot be rejected.

CHI-SQUARE TEST OF INDEPENDENCE

Librarians often collect data that represent either nominal or ordinal measurement. They then cast the data in the form of a contingency table, where the columns represent categories of one variable, rows portray categories of a second variable, and entries in the cells indicate the frequencies of cases for a particular row-column combination.

Crosstabs in statistical analysis software for mainframe computers, minicomputers, and microcomputers will produce contingency tables that compare independent questions or variables. Crosstabs utilizes the chi-square test for independence. The chi-square test, a nonparametric test, counts the number of subjects, objects, or events in various categories and examines the assumption that a

---

[5] Statistics textbooks may show a variation in the formula used in this example. They would do this when the sample size exceeds the values portrayed in their table. Under such circumstances, they will introduce a formula for which critical values are determined from a table on normal probabilities.

sample or given dataset of observed frequencies is representative of the population.

The formula for computation of chi-square (x^2) is:

$$x^2 = \Sigma \ \frac{(f_o - f_e)^2}{f_e}$$

where f_o is the actual or observed frequency for a cell and f_e is the expected frequency for the cell.

Table 7-4 illustrates the steps involved in computation of the formula. Knowing the chi-square value and the degrees of freedom, librarians can turn to a statistics textbook for a standard table of chi-square distributions. Here they can look up the critical value for either a one- or two-tailed test for a given level of significance (see Chapter 6) and quickly determine whether or not the computed statistic has significance: Should the hypothesis be supported or rejected? As an alternative, librarians might compute the chi-square value using statistical analysis software for a computer. Such software automatically signifies the level of

Table 7-4.　Calculation of the Chi-square Test

Example:	Library staff polled 160 students about their preference for library instruction. They had the choice of a lecture, tour, or workbook. Responses were compared to class level.

Class Level	Mode of Instruction		
	Lecture	Tour	Workbook
Freshmen	17	11	12
Sophomores	20	10	10
Juniors	16	12	12
Seniors	19	11	10

	The hypothesis is that there is no statistically significant difference between the type of instruction and class level (at the .05 level).
STEP 1:	Figure row and column totals.

Class Level	Mode of Instruction			Totals
	Lecture	Tour	Workbook	
Freshmen	17	11	12	40
Sophomores	20	10	10	40
Juniors	16	12	12	40
Seniors	19	11	10	40
Totals:	72	44	44	160

Table 7-4.   (*Continued*)

STEP 2:	Determine f_e values for each of the cells (or sets of numbers).

$$\frac{72 \times 40}{160} = 18 \qquad \frac{44 \times 40}{160} = 11 \qquad \frac{44 \times 40}{160} = 11 \qquad \frac{72 \times 40}{160} = 18$$

$$\frac{44 \times 40}{160} = 11 \qquad \frac{44 \times 40}{160} = 11 \qquad \frac{72 \times 40}{160} = 18 \qquad \frac{44 \times 40}{160} = 11$$

$$\frac{44 \times 40}{160} = 11 \qquad \frac{72 \times 40}{160} = 18 \qquad \frac{44 \times 40}{160} = 11 \qquad \frac{44 \times 40}{160} = 11$$

STEP 3:   For each cell, subtract f_e from f_o, square the difference $(f_o - f_e)^2$, and divide the result by f_e.

$$x^2 = \frac{(17 - 18)^2}{18} + \frac{(11 - 11)^2}{11} + \frac{(12 - 11)^2}{11} + \frac{(20 - 18)^2}{18} + \frac{(10 - 11)^2}{11} +$$

$$\frac{(10 - 11)^2}{11} + \frac{(16 - 18)^2}{18} + \frac{(12 - 11)^2}{11} + \frac{(12 - 11)^2}{11} + \frac{(19 - 18)^2}{18} +$$

$$\frac{(11 - 11)^2}{11} + \frac{(10 - 11)^2}{11}$$

STEP 4:   Sum the results of STEP 3 for all cells, thusly:

$$= .05 + 0 + .09 + .22 + .09 + .09 + .22 + .09 + .09 + .05 + .09 + .09 = 1.17$$

STEP 5:   Calculate degrees of freedom: $df = (c - 1)(r - 1) = (4 - 1)(3 - 1) = 6$. The meaning attached to any chi-square value depends on the degrees of freedom associated with the contingency table. The degrees of freedom (labeled *df*) is the number of observations free to vary with a constant parameter.

STEP 6:   Check a chi-square table in a statistics book for $df = 6$ and $p = .05$. The corresponding number in a statistics book is 12.592.

> Because the 1.17 value is less than 12.592, there is no statistically significant difference.

probability at which there is statistical significance. Nonetheless, either a hypothesis or research question should guide the interpretation of the chi-square value and table.

For the eight questions depicted in Figure 7-3, library staff members would first produce a frequency distribution. Next, they would want to compare two questions and study the following examples of null hypotheses:

- There is no statistically significant difference ($p < .05$) between gender of respondents and the number of hours spent in the library per week (questions 1 and 3)
- There is no statistically significant difference ($p < .05$) between gender of respondents and the willingness to seek help immediately (questions 1 and 5)
- There is no statistically significant difference ($p < .05$) between gender of respondents and hesitancy to ask for assistance (questions 1 and 6)
- There is no statistically significant difference ($p < .05$) between gender of respondents and the extent to which students are intimidated by staff sitting behind a reference desk (questions 1 and 7)

Figure 7-3.   Questionnaire on Student Perceptions of Academic Librarians*

1. Gender: a. Male____   b. Female____
2. Check appropriate class rank:
   a. Freshman____   d. Senior____
   b. Sophomore____   e. Unclassified____
   c. Junior____
3. How many hours each week do you spend in the library?
   a. None____   d. 6–10____
   b. 1–2____   e. 11–____
   c. 3–5____
4. If you checked "a" or "b" in the preceding question, was this because you find the library: (Check as many answers as applicable)
   a. Too quiet____   f. Too large____
   b. Too noisy____   g. Too small____
   c. Too drab____   h. Have no real need to go to the
   d. Too confusing____   library____
   e. Too old____   i. Other (please specify)____
5. When searching for library materials or information for research in a library unfamiliar to you, do you usually seek help immediately rather than trying to locate materials alone?
   a. Never____   c. Frequently____
   b. Sometimes____   d. Always____
6. Are you hesitant to approach a reference librarian to ask for assistance?
   a. Never____   c. Frequently____
   b. Sometimes____   d. Always____
7. Do you feel intimidated if the librarian helping you sits behind a desk?
   a. Never____   c. Frequently____
   b. Sometimes____   d. Always____
8. If you did not understand the librarian the first time you asked the question or could not find the material, does it bother you to ask the same librarian for further assistance?
   a. Yes____   b. No____. Explain.

*A few questions from Hernon and Pastine (1977).

- There is no statistically significant difference ($p < .05$) between gender of respondents and student willingness to ask the same librarian again for assistance (questions 1 and 8).

Staff members could also construct null hypotheses comparing class rank to questions 3 and 5 through 8. They could also build contingency tables comparing question 3 to the various parts of question 4. They might even want to compare gender of respondents to class rank (questions 1 and 2).

Table 7-5 offers an example of crosstabs and the chi-square test. Each cell has four lines of numbers. The first (e.g., 20 in the first cell) is the raw number or the

Table 7-5.   StatPac and the Chi-square Test

A comparison of gender of respondent to willingness to ask the same librarian again for assistance, using hypothetical data (questions 1 and 8 of Figure 7-3)

—BY— Gender—(Y Axis)		Request Assistance Again?—(X Axis)		
Number Row % Column % Total %		yes 1	no 2	Row Totals
Male	1	20 40.0 33.3 20.0	30 60.0 75.0 30.0	50 50.0
Female	2	40 80.0 66.7 40.0	10 20.0 25.0 10.0	50 50.0
Column Total		60 60.0	40 40.0	100 100.0

Chi-square	= 15.04	Valid cases	= 100
Degrees of freedom	= 1	Missing cases	= 0
Probability of chance	= 0.000	Response cases	= 100.0%
Phi	= 0.388		
Contingency coeff.	= 0.362		

There is a statistically significant difference between gender of respondent and willingness to request assistance again. Women are more likely than men to request assistance again.

number of males for stated "yes." The second line of numbers is the row percentage (e.g., 40% of the males responded with "yes"), and the third line is the column percentage (e.g., males accounted for 33.3% of the "yes" responses). The final line indicates the percentage of the total associated with that cell—in other words, of the 100 respondents to the survey, cell 1 accounts for 20%. Together, the four cells total 100%.

Yates' Correction

When the crosstabs produces a 2 × 2 table and the degrees of freedom equals one, the regular computation of chi-square results in an overestimation of the true value. A Type I error (rejection of a true hypothesis) may result (see Chapter 6). The Yates' correction compensates for the overestimation. It consists of subtracting .5 from the absolute difference between f_o and f_e (labeled $|f_o - f_e|$) for each category and then squaring the difference. The formula for the Yates' correction is:

$$x^2 = \Sigma \; \frac{(|f_o - f_e| - .5)^2}{f_e} \; .$$

Table 7-6 is an example of the application of the Yates' correction.[6]

To correct for many cells with counts of less than five, librarians might use a *recode* function and combine similar response categories; in other words, they might combine, for example, "never" and "sometimes" into one response category and "frequently" and "always" into another category. When 2 × 2 tables (the degrees of freedom equals one) have an expected frequency of less than five in one or more cells, they might apply either the Yates' correction or Fisher's exact test. For a discussion of the latter test, see Weiss (1968, pp. 265–269) and Hays (1963, pp. 155–156, 598–601).

PHI COEFFICIENT

Whereas the chi-square test reports whether variables are related, the Phi coefficient measures the strength of the relationship between two variables. The coefficient is applied in instances where there is a 2 × 2 contingency table; Cramer's V is applicable for larger tables. Phi also compares two crosstabs with unequal Ns (see, for example, Hernon and Pastine, 1977). Phi assumes a value of 0 when

---

[6] StatPac recognizes the instances in which Yates' correction should be applied and supplies a corrected chi-square value.

Table 7-6. The Chi-square Test with Application of Yates' Correction

Example: A survey reports the reaction of students in the College of Education and College of Behavioral Sciences to the use of *InfoTrac* as either favorable or unfavorable.

Observed Reaction	College of Education #	College of Behavioral Sciences #	Total #
Favorable Responses	10	20	30
Unfavorable Responses	22	8	30
Total #:	32	28	60

$$f_{e1} = \frac{(32 \times 30)}{60} = 16 \qquad f_{e2} = \frac{(28 \times 30)}{60} = 14$$

$$f_{e3} = \frac{(32 \times 30)}{60} = 16 \qquad f_{e4} = \frac{(28 \times 30)}{60} = 14$$

$$x^2 = \frac{(|10 - 16| - .5)^2}{16} + \frac{(|20 - 14| - .5)^2}{14} + \frac{(|22 - 16| - .5)^2}{16} + \frac{(|8 - 14| - .5)^2}{14}$$

$$x^2 = 1.89 + 2.16 + 1.89 + 2.16 = 8.1$$

Note: For $df = 1$ at $p = .05$, the critical chi-square value is 3.841.

> There is a statistically significant difference. College of Behavioral Science students were more likely to have a favorable response.

there is no relationship and a value of $+1$ when there is a perfect association; a value of -1 signifies a perfect negative association.

The formula for calculating Phi is:

$$\text{phi} = \sqrt{\frac{x^2}{n}}$$

x^2 is the chi-square statistic and n is the total number of cases. Software such as StatPac automatically reports the Phi coefficient as part of printout for crosstabs (see Table 7-5).

CRAMER'S V

Cramer's V is a slightly modified version of Phi that is suitable for contingency tables larger than 2×2. Because Phi can yield a value larger than 1 when it is used for a table with more than four cells (2×2), Cramer's V adjusts the Phi coefficient for either the number of rows or columns in the table depending on which of the two is smaller.

Cramer's V ranges from 0 to +1; the larger the value of V the greater is the association in the variables. Both Phi and Cramer's V values become equivalent in a 2 × 2 tables. The formula is:

$$V = \sqrt{\frac{Phi^2}{min\ (R - 1),\ (C - 1)}}$$

where V is Cramer's V, R is the number of rows in the crosstabs, C is the number of columns, and min is the minimum of $(R - 1)$ and $(C - 1)$.

REMINDER: HYPOTHESIS TESTING OR RESEARCH QUESTIONS GUIDE DATA ANALYSIS AND INTERPRETATION

At times, librarians have collected data and, without engaging in hypothesis testing or formulating research questions, have subjected the dataset to statistical analysis. They have assumed "that large quantities of data must have some meaning." However, "they demonstrate only that analyzing the daylights out of shaky data produces obscurity" (Zweizig, 1988, p. 403). They have drawn inferences to the population in their discussion of findings or employed statistical tests that place a sample in the context of its population. Unless theory and the body of existing practice provide a framework for collecting and interpreting data, "conclusions may be drawn that are based on the idiosyncratic characteristics of a sample" (Ibid., p. 404). When librarians engage in hypothesis testing, they either support or reject the hypothesis. They do not prove/disprove it. Moreover, there are not degrees of acceptance or rejection. For instance, they should not conclude that a relationship is highly, moderately, or mildly significant.

Kim and Little (1987) make such mistakes in their study. They also ask similar, but differently worded, questions on "walk-in questionnaires administered at a variety of public libraries (the exact number of data sources is hard to pin down)" (Zweizig, 1988, p. 404). Nonetheless, they treat responses to items on different questionnaires (even though the wording may differ) as "comparable data" (Ibid.). Zweizig's analysis of the Kim and Little handbook serves as a reminder: a dataset and inferential statistics must be placed in the context of the entire research process, including hypothesis testing. Hypothesis testing enables librarians to view a sample as part of a population. Remember large numbers in a cell may produce statistical significance.

SUMMARY QUESTIONS (FOR THE CHAPTER)

1.   Does question 1 in Figure 7-3 represent nominal, ordinal, interval, or ratio type data?

2. Does question 3 in Figure 7-3 represent nominal, ordinal, interval, or ratio type data?
3. Does question 6 in Figure 7-3 represent nominal, ordinal, interval, or ratio type data?
4. What are the comparative advantages and disadvantages of using the *t*-test or the Mann-Whitney U test?
5. When would researchers apply the Phi coefficient and when would they use Cramer's *V*? Can they have the same value?
6. Library managers are investigating two methods for teaching their staff to understand and apply statistics. Ten staff are assigned randomly to method A and 10 to method B. After a month of instruction, the following statistics were computed from a written examination.

Method	$\bar{X}$	s
A	82	8
B	74	10

Test the null hypothesis that there is no difference between the sample means (at the .05 level). NOTE: For 18 *df* (at the .05 level), a statistics textbook lists the probability at 2.101.

7. The reference staff have monitored the reference questions asked during the previous week and discovered the following:

Gender	Mode of Asking Question	
	Telephone	In-Person
Female	200	400
Male	300	500

Does the Yates' correction apply?
8. For question 7, make up a null hypothesis for testing at the .05 level?
9. Calculate the chi-square value for that hypothesis.
10. Interpret the results of the hypothesis testing for question 7. Note that the critical value for significance at .05 (1 *df*) is 3.841.

Appendix A provides the answers to the questions

Chapter Eight
Correlation

Correlation examines co-variation or the tendency of measures (variables) to vary or go together. If one variable increases, the other either increases or decreases. Often when librarians question the effect of one variable on another, they are expressing a correlation. A scattergram (such as the ones depicted in Figures 5-11 and 8-3) is a two-dimensional graph consisting of points whose coordinates are determined by the two variables under study. A scattergram illustrates the direction and extent to which two variables co-vary. It also indicates whether a relationship is linear.

A correlation coefficient measures the nature and extent of the relationship between two or more random variables. The relationship may range from a perfect negative correlation (−1.00) to a perfect positive correlation (+1.00). A positive correlation reflects a direct relationship between two variables; high scores on one variable are paired with high scores on the other variable. A negative correlation does not signify a lack of a relationship between the variables, but rather an opposite relationship. With a negative correlation, low values on one variable are paired with high values on the other variable.

The closer the coefficient is to a perfect positive or perfect negative correlation, the stronger or higher is the correlation. A correlation of zero indicates a lack of linearity but not necessarily the lack of a relationship between two variables. "Usually, inspection of the scattergram will indicate whether there is in fact no relationship or whether the relationship is sufficiently nonlinear to produce a zero correlation" (Blalock, 1972, p. 378). The power of a relationship is not affected by the negative or positive sign. A correlation, even a high one, does not necessarily indicate causation between two variables.[1,2]

---

[1] A correlation problem differs from a regression problem (see Chapter 9) in that a correlation measures a relationship between/among variables rather than predicting one variable from a knowledge of the independent variable.

[2] There are eight *basic* types of correlations:

1. *Curvilinear correlation*: a curved line best depicts the relationship between the variables. All linear relationships, which are depicted by a straight line, are monotonic. Curvilinear relationships may be monotonic or nonmonotonic.
2. *Linear correlation*: a straight line best depicts the relationship between the variables
3. *Multiple correlation*: the relationship between a single dependent variable and at least two independent variables

There are ready-made tables of the values of different correlation coefficients for various levels of significance and sample sizes. Statistics textbooks, such as Carpenter and Vasu (1978), reproduce such tables.

This chapter provides an overview of different types of correlation coefficients and their applications. Figure 8-1 identifies the different tests discussed in this chapter, while Figure 8-2 suggests examples of articles that have employed correlation coefficient tests either as the sole means of data analysis or one of many statistical applications. Chapter 9 builds upon the foundation presented here and introduces regression analysis for the development of models and the making of predictions about the value of one variable knowing the value of another variable.

Figure 8-1. Brief Descriptions of Some Correlation Coefficient Tests

Test	Description
Correlation matrix	This specialized form of a correlation table presents possible combinations of correlation values for a set of variables.
Gamma	This nonparametric test describes the correlation between two or more sets of ranked data. It is especially useful in instances in which there are numerous tied or grouped data. It is also useful for cross-tabulated data measured according to an ordinal scale.
Kendall's tau	This nonparametric test describes the correlation between two or more sets of ranked data. It is especially useful in instances in which there is an uneven number of cells and numerous occasions of tied data.
Pearson's r	This parametric correlation coefficient describes the degree of linear relationship (points on a scattergram fall along a straight line) between two variables measured at an interval or ratio level.
Somer's d	It is a measure of association for ordered contingency tables when there is both a dependent and independent variable, as well as tied scores.
Spearman's rho	This nonparametric test describes the degree of association between two sets of ranked data to determine their degree of equivalence. The ranks must represent the ordinal level.

4. *Negative correlation*: the dependent and independent variable(s) go in opposite directions
5. *Nonlinear correlation*: the relationship between the variables approximates a line that has one or two changes in direction
6. *Partial correlation*: the relationship between a variable in a multiple correlation and the dependent variables
7. *Positive correlation*: the value of the dependent and independent variables co-vary over time
8. *Simple correlations*: the association between one dependent and one independent variable.

These types of correlations do not comprise mutually exclusive categories. Either a simple correlation or a multiple correlation might be positive or negative, linear or nonlinear.

Figure 8-2. Examples of Writings Using Correlation Coefficients
_____

Pearson's *r*

Brooks, Terrence A. "The Systematic Nature of Library-Output Statistics," *Library Research*, 4 (Winter 1982): 341–353.

Clack, Mary E. and Sally F. Williams. "Using Locally and Nationally Produced Periodical Price Indexes in Budget Preparation," *Library Resources and Technical Services*, 27 (October/December 1983): 345–356.

D'Elia, George P. "The Determinants of Job Satisfaction among Beginning Librarians," *Library Quarterly*, 49 (1979): 283–302.

Edinger, Joyce A. and Steven Falk. "Statistical Sampling of Reference Desk Inquiries," *RQ*, 20 (Spring 1981): 265–268.

Gothberg, Helen M. and Donald E. Riggs. "Time Management in Academic Libraries," *College & Research Libraries*, 49 (March 1988): 131–140.

Hardesty, Larry and John Wright. "Student Library Skills and Attitudes and Their Change: Relationships to Other Selected Variables," *Journal of Academic Librarianship*, 8 (September 1982): 216–220.

Hardesty, Larry, Jamie Hastreiter, and David Henderson. "Development of College Library Mission Statements," *Journal of Library Administration*, 9 (1988): 11–34.

Hardesty, Larry, Nicholas P. Lovrich, Jr., and James Mannon. "Library-Use Instruction: Assessment of the Long-Term Effects," *College & Research Libraries*, 43 (January 1982): 38–46.

King, David N. and John C. Ory. "Effects of Library Instruction on Student Research: A Case Study," *College & Research Libraries*, 42 (January 1981): 31–41.

Kohl, David F. "High Efficiency Inventorying through Predictive Data," *Journal of Academic Librarianship*, 8 (May 1982): 82–84.

Lane, Larraine M. "The Relationship between Loans and In-House Use of Books in Determining a Use-Factor for Budget Allocation," *Library Acquisitions*, 11 (1987): 95–102.

McClure, Charles R. and Alan R. Samuels. "Factors Affecting the Use of Information for Academic Library Decision Making," *College & Research Libraries*, 46 (November 1985): 483–498.

Powell, Ronald R. "An Investigation of the Relationships between Quantifiable Reference Service Variables and Reference Performance in Public Libraries," *Library Quarterly*, 48 (January 1978): 1–19.

Scamell, Richard W. and Bette Ann Stead. "A Study of Age and Tenure As It Pertains to Job Satisfaction," *Journal of Library Administration*, 1 (Spring 1980): 3–18.

Van House, Nancy A. "Public Library Effectiveness: Theory, Measures, and Determinants," *Library and Information Science Research*, 8 (July/September 1986): 261–283.

Spearman's rho

Chudamani, K. S. and R. Shalini. "Journal Acquisition—Cost Effectiveness of Models," *Information Processing & Management*, 19 (1983): 307–311.

Danilowicz, C. and H. Szarski. "Selection of Scientific Journals Based on the Data Obtained from an Information Service System," *Information Processing & Management*, 17 (1981): 13–19.

Figure 8-2. *(Continued)*

He, Chunpei and Miranda Lee Pao. "A Discipline-Specific Journal Selection Algorithm," *Information Processing & Management*, 22 (1986): 405–416.

Hernon, Peter. *Use of Government Publications by Social Scientists*. Norwood, NJ: Ablex Publishing Corp., 1979.

———. "Use of Microformatted Government Publications," *Microform Review*, 11 (Fall 1982): 237–252.

———. and Gary R. Purcell. *Developing Collections of U.S. Government Publications*. Greenwood, CT: JAI Press, 1982.

McGrath, William E. "A Pragmatic Book Allocation Formula for Academic and Public Libraries with a Test for Its Effectiveness," *Library Resources and Technical Services*, 19 (Fall 1975): 356–369.

Powell, Ronald R. and Sheila D. Creth. "Knowledge Bases and Library Education," *College & Research Libraries*, 47 (January 1986): 16–27.

Correlation Matrix

Ahiakwo, O.N. and N.P. Obokoh. "Attitudinal Dimension in Library Overdues among Faculty Members—A Case Study," *Library and Information Science Research*, 9 (October/December 1987): 293–304.

D'Elia, George P. "The Determinants of Job Satisfaction among Beginning Librarians," *Library Quarterly*, 49 (1979): 283–302.

Marchant, Maurice P. *Participative Management in Academic Libraries*. Westport, CT: Greenwood Press, 1976.

McClure, Charles R. and Alan R. Samuels. "Factors Affecting the Use of Information for Academic Library Decision Making," *College & Research Libraries*, 46 (November 1985): 483–498.

McClure, Charles R. and Peter Hernon. *Improving the Quality of Reference Service for Government Publications*. Chicago, IL: ALA, 1983, pp. 70–71.

Murfin, Marjorie E. and Gary M. Gugelchuk. "Development and Testing of a Reference Transaction Assessment Instrument," *College & Research Libraries*, 48 (July 1987): 314–338.

Renner, Charlene and Barton M. Clark. "Professional and Nonprofessional Staffing Patterns in Departmental Libraries," *Library Research*, 1 (Summer 1979): 153–170.

Samuels, Alan R. "Assessing Organizational Climate in Public Libraries," *Library Research*, 1 (Fall 1979): 237–254.

Kendall's tau

Danilowicz, C. and H. Szarski. "Selection of Scientific Journals Based on the Data Obtained from an Information Service System," *Information Processing & Management*, 17 (1981): 13– 19.

McClure, Charles R. and Peter Hernon. *Improving the Quality of Reference Service for Government Publications*. Chicago, IL: ALA, 1983, pp. 70–71.

Pungitore, Verna L. "Perceptions of Change and Public Library Directors in Indiana: An Exploratory Study," *Library and Information Science Research*, 9 (October/December 1987): 247–264.

Figure 8-2.   *(Continued)*

Gamma

Hardesty, Larry, Nicholas P. Lovrich, Jr., and James Mannon. "Library-Use Instruction: Assessment of the Long-Term Effects," *College & Research Libraries*, 43 (January 1982): 38–46.

Hurt, C. D. "A Comparison of a Bibliometric Approach and an Historical Approach to the Identification of Important Literature," *Information Processing & Management*, 19 (1983): 151–157.

Jewell, Timothy D. "Student Reactions to a Self-Paced Library Skills Workbook Program: Survey Evidence," *College & Research Libraries*, 43 (September 1982): 371–378.

Somer's *d*

Gerry, Ellen and Susan Klingberg. "A Survey of Participative Management in California State University Libraries," *College & Research Libraries*, 49 (January 1988): 47–56.

PEARSON PRODUCT–MOMENT CORRELATION COEFFICIENT

Pearson's product–moment correlation coefficient, frequently known as Pearson's *r*, "estimates a population parameter" and is "our best guess about the value of the true correlation coefficient in the population" (Swisher and McClure, 1984, p. 170). The coefficient describes the degree of linear relationship between two variables and indicates "the tendency of points in a . . . [scattergram] to fall right along a straight line" (see Jaeger, 1983, pp. 72–79; Swisher and McClure, 1984, pp. 165–171).

The two groups of scores should be normally distributed (see Chapter 5). The level of measurement is either interval or ratio. A few extreme values in either variable will affect the correlation coefficient. Further, the magnitude of the value depends on the degree of general variability in the independent variable (Blalock, 1979, p. 401).

The coefficient belongs to the same statistical family as the mean and considers the size of the score for each variable. Pearson's *r*, a powerful parametric correlation, may be computed by using *Z*-scores (see Chapter 5 and a statistics textbook) or raw-scores. The formula for the computation of the correlation coefficient from raw scores is:

$$r = \frac{N\Sigma XY - \Sigma X \Sigma Y}{\sqrt{N\Sigma X^2 - (\Sigma X)^2} \ \sqrt{N\Sigma Y^2 - (\Sigma Y)^2}}.$$

X is the value of variable X, Y is the value of variable Y, and N is the number of subjects. To compute the correlation, we first sum the X and Y scores, square each X and Y score and sum the values of X^2 and Y^2, multiple each X score by its corresponding Y score, and summate the products. Next square the values X and Y, insert the values into the equation, and complete the calculation (see Table 8-1).

Squaring the value of r indicates the portion of variance in one variable that is accounted for by knowledge of the second variable. A correlation coefficient of .5 can be interpreted as $(.5)^2$, or 25% of the variation of one random variable is accounted for by differences in the other variable.[3]

Meddis (1975, p. 149), among others, provides a table that indicates the significance of r values for different Ns and confidence levels. Because r may have either a positive or negative sign, a one-tailed test is usually appropriate. A prediction of the sign generally can be made before the results are calculated. The two-tailed test may be used when a properly reasoned prediction cannot be advanced.

In figuring a correlation coefficient, librarians should review existing theory and practice before assuming that samples are drawn from the same population; they might also test the assumption using reliability coefficients (see McClure and Hernon, 1983, for an example). When librarians have obtained two values of r from two samples and want to know if the values are significantly different, they should consider the application of Fisher's transformation (see Meddis, 1975, p. 152).

The sample size should be taken into account when making an interpretation of the correlation coefficient. The larger the sample size, the smaller the value of r that is needed to give confidence that the correlation coefficient is characteristic of the population from which the sample was drawn. Similarly, the larger the sample size, the more confidence librarians have that the value of r would be approximately the same if another sample were drawn from the same population.

---

[3] As a reminder of the relationship between r and r^2 values, it might be useful to remember the following:

r	$r^2 \times 100$ (for %)
1.00	100%
.90	81%
.80	64%
.70	49%
.60	36%
.50	25%
.40	16%
.30	9%
.20	4%
.10	1%

Table 8-1. Computation of A Correlation Coefficient from Raw Scores

Example: Given the following scores on a library skills test and corresponding scores on a reading comprehension test, correlate the two sets of scores.

Null Hypothesis: There is no significant correlation between library skills test scores and the reading comprehension test scores.

Person	Skills (X)	Reading (Y)	X^2	Y^2	XY^2
A	4	7	16	49	28
B	1	5	1	25	5
C	6	8	36	64	48
D	4	2	16	4	8
E	5	5	25	25	25
F	4	6	16	36	24
G	1	3	1	9	3
H	3	4	9	16	12
	$\Sigma X = 28$	$\Sigma Y = 40$	$\Sigma X^2 = 120$	$\Sigma Y^2 = 228$	$\Sigma XY = 153$

$$r = \frac{N\Sigma XY - \Sigma X\Sigma Y}{\sqrt{N\Sigma X^2 - (\Sigma X)^2} \ \sqrt{N\Sigma Y^2 - (\Sigma Y)^2}}$$

$$r = \frac{8\,(153) - (28)(40)}{\sqrt{8(120) - (28)^2} \ \sqrt{8(228) - (40)^2}}$$

$$r = \frac{104}{(13.266)\,(14.967)}$$

$$\boxed{r = 0.524}$$

When n is 8, the critical value is .62 (Champion, 1981, p. 409). Because this value is greater than .524, the null hypothesis cannot be rejected.

It might be useful to insert an example from the literature to illustrate the use of Pearson's r. Kohl and Wilson (1986, p. 206) investigated the "effectiveness of course-integrated bibliographic instruction in improving coursework." From a pool of student term papers, they randomly selected 30. Both the instructor and a librarian independently evaluated the bibliographies of the papers. Using Pearson's r, the researchers compared the ratings of the bibliographies between the instructor and the librarian and discovered a statistically significant, positive correlation between the two ratings. However, there was no correlation between the ratings of the bibliographies and the grades that the students received on their papers—again the researchers used Pearson's r.

SPEARMAN'S RHO

Spearman's rank order correlation coefficient, a modified form of Pearson's r, is a nonparametric test commonly referred to as rho. Rho, which is used with data that measure variables at the ordinal level, is computed on sets of ranks instead of actual frequency scores (or Z-scores derived from them). Librarians rank the scores according to size, but they do not know how much larger or smaller a particular score is relative to another score. The relationship presented between variables should be linear or monotonic (no change in direction).

When ties in the ranks occur but only infrequently, the effect is negligible. However, with more ties in the ranks, consult Siegel (1956, pp. 207–210) or consider the use of Kendall's tau or gamma, which will be discussed later in the chapter.

To determine the significance of rho, librarians should refer to a table of critical values in a nonparametric statistics textbook, such as Siegel (1956). In many instances, Pearson's r and Spearman's rho will be fairly close in absolute value. For this reason, rho is sometimes used as an approximation of Pearson's r. In general, rho will be greater than r when the latter is computed on raw scores. This is because Pearson's r is sensitive to scores that are not linear, while Spearman's rho is only sensitive to those that are not monotonic or homogeneous. Rho is more convenient to use than the correlation ratio as an index of strength of a curvilinear but monotonic relationship.

A comparison of Pearson's r and Spearman's rho shows that:

- Both are reported as a two-digit number preceded by a decimal point
- Both have the range of possible values from −1.00 to +1.00
- Both can be tested for significance
- Both can be used in a correlation matrix
- For interval level data, Pearson's r is preferred
- For ordinal level data, or data obtained as ranks, Spearman's rho is more appropriate.

Spearman's rho can be used: (1) with interval level data if there is reason to doubt the precision of measurements that are reported; or (2) when the numbers are large and would require much manipulation to calculate the Pearson correlation coefficient. A good example is the size of the collection in large libraries. The numbers might be overwhelming and the reporting of collection size can be imprecise. A reasonable estimate can be made with the application of rho.

One-tailed tests are appropriate to use with rho. The probability of a directional value can often be stated, regardless of whether the direction is positive or negative.

The formula for computing rho is:

$$\text{rho} = 1 - \frac{6\Sigma D^2}{N^3 - N}$$

where N is the number of category options and D^2 is the square of the ranking difference.

Suppose that library staff rank nine subject areas of the Dewey collection according to the number of titles owned in each area. Next they rank the nine areas according to the frequency of circulation for each subject area. Believing that there is no statistically significant correlation (at the .05 level) between collection rank and the circulation rank, they calculate rho (see Table 8-2).[4] The critical value of rho (at the .05 level) when $N = 9$ is 0.60 (Siegel, 1956, p. 284). There is a highly positive correlation between the two ranks, or no statistically significant difference between the ranking for collection size and the ranking for circulation exists. Based on this finding, however, we should not necessarily assume that the library's collection generally meets the information needs of the clientele. Such an assumption merits further exploration.

Table 8-3 offers another example of the use of Spearman's rho. This time, a group of engineers ranked the types of library resources that they used for both work and personal interest. Again, the null hypothesis, we presume, suggests no statistically significant correlation between the two rankings. The critical value (at .05) for $N = 7$ is .714. There is a highly positive correlation between the two ranks, or no statistically significant difference between the ranking for work related and the ranking for personal interest exists. In both instances, the engi-

Table 8-2.   Calculation of Spearman's rho

Subject Area	Collection Rank	Circulation Rank	D	D²
General	1	4	−3	9
Philosophy	6	5	1	1
History	4	3	1	1
Social Sciences	5	7	−2	4
Fiction and Language	2	1	1	1
Sciences	8	9	−1	1
Technology	7	6	1	1
Art	3	2	1	1
Religions	9	8	1	1
		$N = 9$		$\Sigma D^2 = 20$

$$\text{rho} = 1 - \frac{6\Sigma D^2}{N^3 - N}$$

$$\text{rho} = 1 - \frac{6 \times 20}{9^3 - 9}$$

$$\text{rho} = 1 - \frac{120}{720} = 1 - 0.17 = 0.83$$

$$\boxed{\text{rho} = 0.83}$$

---

[4] Hernon and Richardson (1988, pp. 94–95) offer a different example of the use of Spearman's rho.

Table 8-3. Another Calculation of Spearman's rho

Types of Resources	Work	Personal Interests	D	D²
Conference proceedings	3	4	−1	1
Monographs	4	2	2	4
Periodicals	2	1	1	1
Newspapers	7	6	1	1
Technical reports	1	3	−2	4
Dissertations and theses	5	5	0	0
Other	6	7	−1	1
		N = 7	ΣD² =	12

$$rho = 1 - \frac{6\Sigma D^2}{N^3 - N}$$

$$rho = 1 - \frac{6 \times 12}{7^3 - 7}$$

$$rho = 1 - \frac{72}{336} = 1 - 0.214 = 0.786$$

$$\boxed{rho = 0.786}$$

neers tend to draw upon the same types of resources. Figure 8-3 is a graphic depiction of the two rankings showing the distribution around the regression line (see Chapter 9). The figure was produced through the use of StatPac. It might be noted that both StatPac and Minitab calculated the rho coefficient. However, StatPac provided the better visual display.

OTHER MEASURES OF CORRELATION

Kendall's tau, Goodman and Kruskal's gamma, and Somer's *d* are three different forms of relationship between ordered variables or rankings. All three handle ties. The different operating characteristics of each reflect their sensitivity to different types of relationships. Because they are sensitive to different features of a relationship, their respective interpretations differ. Therefore, the values are not comparable.

Basically, gamma has the least stringent criteria and tau the most. Somer's *d* falls in between. With ordinal data, librarians must decide which of the three is most appropriate. The decision should be made on the basis of the type of relationship expressed in the research hypothesis. Gamma is the best choice if the theory concerns merely a "weak monotonic relationship." If the theory concerns a "strictly monotonic asymmetric relationship" the Somer's *d* is best. Tau would be appropriate for theories concerning "category-rank linear relationships" (Kohout, 1974, p. 231).

Figure 8-3.   Graphic Depiction of the Correlation Described in Table 8-3

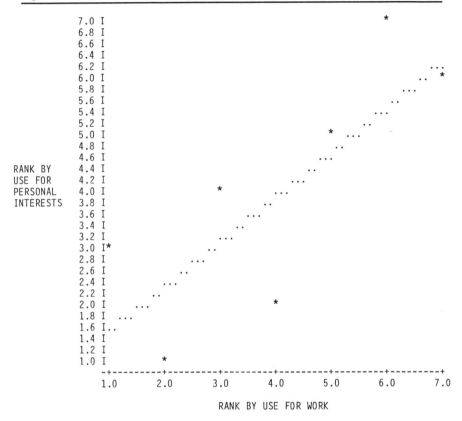

```
              7.0 I                                            *
              6.8 I
              6.6 I
              6.4 I
              6.2 I                                                    ...
              6.0 I                                                 .. *
              5.8 I                                              ...
              5.6 I                                            ..
              5.4 I                                          ...
              5.2 I                                        ..
              5.0 I                                  *  ...
              4.8 I                                      ..
              4.6 I                                   ...
RANK BY       4.4 I                                ..
USE FOR       4.2 I                             ...
PERSONAL      4.0 I              *           ...
INTERESTS     3.8 I                        ..
              3.6 I                      ...
              3.4 I                    ..
              3.2 I                  ...
              3.0 I*              ..
              2.8 I            ...
              2.6 I          ..
              2.4 I        ...
              2.2 I      ..
              2.0 I  ...              *
              1.8 I ...
              1.6 I..
              1.4 I
              1.2 I
              1.0 I        *
                  -+---------+---------+---------+---------+---------+---------+
                  1.0       2.0       3.0       4.0       5.0       6.0       7.0
```

                         RANK BY USE FOR WORK

Mean of X = 4.000	Correlation coefficient = 0.786	Valid cases = 7
S.D. of X = 2.160	Degrees of freedom = 5	Missing cases = 0
Mean of Y = 4.000	Slope of regression line = 0.786	Response % = 100
S.D. of Y = 2.160	Y intercept = 0.857	

Regression equation :   Y' = 0.786 X + 0.857
Standard error of estimate for regression   = 1.464
t statistic for correlation coefficient   = 2.840
Significance of correlation coefficient   = 0.036

Spearman's rank-order correlation coefficient = 0.786

Kendall's tau

Kendall's tau, or Kendall rank correlation coefficient, is a family of non-parametric tests that measure the correlation between two sets of rankings and that do not make assumptions concerning the distribution of cases on the variables. This section only provides a general overview of this family of tests.

The coefficient examines "all possible pairs of cases . . . noting whether or not the ranks are in the same order" (Blalock, 1972, p. 418). Tau can be generalized to a partial correlation coefficient (the possibility that the correlation between two variables is due to their association with a third variable) or data that have an unequal number of cells (Siegel, 1956, pp. 223–229). Further, tau applies to linear relationships, not nonlinear or curvilinear ones. Tau also requires ordinal level measurement.

The one-tailed test is appropriate because we expect the relationship only to go in one direction, whether that be positive or negative. Nonetheless, the two-tailed test can be used. As with other correlation techniques, statistics textbooks may contain a table for judging if the results are statistically significant.

Tau often indicates a lower strength of association than does rho. Rho tends to give relatively more weight to extreme differences, while tau offers equal weight to all differences. Kendall coefficients are more meaningful when numerous cases are classified into a few categories and the ranking of data produces a large number of tied ranks. Spearman's rho is preferred when the ratio of cases to categories is smaller and there are few ties at each ranking. The numerical value of tau and rho would be dissimilar, if both were computed on the same pair of rankings. Tau and rho have different underlying scales and are not comparable. Prior to selection of either tau or rho, librarians should consult Siegel (1956, pp. 217–219), Blalock (1979, pp. 437–441), or another statistics textbook.

To determine tau, we must order the ranks of one set from lowest to highest. We then assign a plus one ($+1$) value to each pair in the same order and a minus one (-1) to each pair in the opposite order. The degree of relationship between the two sets of ranks is indicated by the ratio of the actual total of $+1$s and -1s to the possible maximum total (if all were $+1$). Thus, it is a measure of agreement between the ranks assigned, or a sort of coefficient of disarray.

The formula for calculating tau is:

$$\text{tau} = \frac{S}{1/2\, N\, (N - 1)}$$

where S is the score of the sum of the difference in rank order, N is the number of subjects or objects, and $1/2\, N\, (N - 1)$ is the maximum possible score of the difference in rank order. The formula can be adjusted in order to deal with ties.

Table 8-4 uses the same example depicted in Table 8-3, but this time illustrates the calculation of Kendall's tau. Starting from the first number of the second row (personal use), we count the number of ranks to the right that are larger. From this number, we subtract the number of ranks to the right that are smaller. Because the probability of tau is .035 when $N = 7$ and $S = 13$ (Siegel, 1956, p. 285), there is a significant correlation between use of the resources for work and personal use. Engineers tend to use similar resources in both instances.

Pungitore (1987, p. 254) surveyed 125 directors of public libraries in the state of Indiana about their perceptions of organizational change. She questioned: Is

Table 8-4.   Calculation of Kendall's tau

	Types of Library Resources						
Type of Need	Tech Repts	Periodicals	Conf. Proc	Monographs	Diss. & Theses	Other	Newspapers
Work	1	2	3	4	5	6	7
Personal Use	3	1	4	2	5	7	6

$$S = (4 - 2) + (5 - 0) + (3 - 1) + (3 - 0) + (2 - 0) + (0 - 1) = 13$$

$$\text{tau} \quad \frac{S}{1/2\ N\ (N - 1)} = \frac{13}{1/2 \times 7\ (7 - 1)} = \frac{13}{21} = 0.62$$

$$\boxed{\text{tau} = 0.62}$$

there a possible relationship between the size of a library and the degree to which its director perceives change occurring? Her questionnaire solicited background information on the directors and included a twenty-item scale "designed to measure perceptions of change." She reduced data on population size served by the library and perceptions of change to ordinal level. She used Kendall's tau as the measure of association because it handles unequal cells. There was a positive moderate relationship with the perceptions of administrative and technological change. The correlation with service change perception was weak. As a consequence (Ibid., p. 255), the

> size of the community by itself may not be a very good indicator of the library director's perceptions of change. It might be hypothesized that other factors relating to the library's community . . . combine with population size to influence the director's perceptions of change.

Gamma

Gamma identifies the degree of correlation for ranked data at the ordinal, interval, or ratio level. The coefficient is especially useful when there are many ties in the ranking or grouped data (see Hurt, 1983, p. 153; and Mueller, Schuesslet, and Costner, 1977, pp. 207–222).

The formula for calculating gamma is:

$$\text{gamma} = \frac{P - Q}{P + Q}$$

where P is the sum of the number of agreements in the ranking or grouped data, and Q is the number of disagreements.

Taking the example presented in Table 8-2, we arrange the subjects in a descending rank order of collection size (X) and indicate the ranks of the circulation size (Y) on the right side, as shown in Table 8-5. Starting from the bottom of Y, we calculate P values by examining the number of agreements in the upper portion, i.e., how many numbers are larger than the first number in the bottom. Next, we count the larger numbers beginning with the second category "science" and proceed throughout the table. After determining the P values, we sum the P column. We calculate the Q values in the same way as we did the P values; however, this time, we count the smaller numbers in the upper part. We then determine the total for the Q value.

The critical value of gamma at .05 and $N = 9$ is 0.50 (Champion, 1981, p. 419); there is a significant positive relationship in the two ranks, collection and circulation size.

Table 8-6, which presents hypothetical data, discusses the calculation of gamma for grouped data. Assume that we are interested in determining if there is a correlation between patron age and the frequency of public library use. To calculate the P value (the agreement frequency), multiply the values that came from non-zero frequency in each cell (ignoring its row and column in the table) and summing the number of entries to the right and below that cell. For Q, multiply the values that came from non-zero frequency in each cell (ignoring its row and column in the table), by summing the number of entries to the left and

Table 8-5. Calculation of Gamma (Non-Grouped Data)

Subject Area	Collection Rank	Circulation Rank	P	Q
Religion	9	8	0	0
Sciences	8	9	0	1
Technology	7	6	2	0
Philosophy	6	5	3	0
Social Sciences	5	7	2	2
History	4	3	5	0
Art	3	2	6	0
Fiction and Language	2	1	7	0
General	1	4	5	3
		$N = 9$	$P = 30$	$Q = 6$

$$\text{gamma} = \frac{P - Q}{P + Q} = \frac{30 - 6}{30 + 6} = \frac{24}{36} = 0.67$$

gamma $= 0.67$

Table 8-6.   Calculation of Gamma (Grouped Data)

Age	Rank	Use Frequently	Use Rarely	Total
41 or more	3	18	7	25
21–40	2	28	32	60
1–20	1	4	11	15
Total		50	50	100

$$P = [18 \times (32 + 11)] + (28 \times 11) = 1{,}082$$

$$Q = [7 \times (28 + 4)] + (32 \times 4) = 352$$

$$\text{gamma} = \frac{P - Q}{P + Q} = \frac{1{,}082 - 352}{1{,}082 + 352} = \frac{730}{1{,}434} = 0.51$$

$$\boxed{\text{gamma} = 0.51}$$

below the cell. When n (sample size) is greater than 40, an approximation of a Z-value may be obtained (Champion, 1981, p. 331). Therefore,

$$Z = \text{gamma} \sqrt{\frac{P - Q}{n\,(1 - \text{gamma}^2)}} = \sqrt{\frac{1082 - 352}{100\,(1 - 0.51^2)}}$$

$$Z = 1.60$$

because Z equals $\pm$ 1.645 (at $p = .05$) in the table reprinted in statistics textbooks such as Champion (1981, p. 331), there is no relationship between age and the frequency of library use.

Somer's d

Somer's d, which measures ordinal association, takes ties into consideration when computing the denominator. However, the adjustment is made in a different way from other tests. There are three formulae for calculating Somer's d: two are asymmetric depending on whether the row or the column is considered to be the dependent variable. The symmetric version is used when researchers do not take into consideration which variable is dependent or independent. These formulae are:

$$d_{yx} = \frac{C - D}{C + D + T_y}$$

and

$$d_{xy} = \frac{C - D}{C + D + T_x}$$

as well as this symmetric version,

$$e = \frac{C - D}{C + D + T_x + T_y}$$

In these formulae, C and D are the sets of ranked scores and T represents the tied scores, with the x and y representing dependent and independent variables.

CORRELATION MATRIX

A correlation matrix is a specialized form of a correlation table. It is a visual display of the intercorrelations of a list of variables. The matrix therefore presents all possible combinations of correlation among a certain number of variables. The coefficients fill the lower-left or the upper-right of a correlation matrix. Usually they do not fill the entire matrix, unless a mirror image is shown. The values may range from +1.00 to −1.00.

Table 8-7 offers a hypothetical correlation matrix for variables compared through the application of Spearman's rho. The table illustrates a significant relationship among the different variables depicted.

Table 8-7.   Correlation Matrix (Displaying Spearman's rho)

	Library Volumes	Library Budget	No. of Library Professionals	No. of Paraprofessionals
Library volumes	—	.001	.001	.025
	Library budget	—	.001	.035
		No. of Library Professionals	—	.029
			No. of Library Paraprofessionals	—

SUMMARY QUESTIONS (BASED ON THE CHAPTER)

1. What level of measurement do we need to apply Pearson's *r* and Spearman's rho, Kendall's tau, and Gamma?
2. To use Pearson's *r*, what assumptions must we make?
3. Assume that we have ranked data, ties in the ranks, and unequal cells in the dataset, do you want to use a parametric or nonparametric test? Which test?
4. What is an advantage of constructing a correlation matrix?
5. Compute and interpret a correlation coefficient for the following grades of nine students, selected at random, from among those completing a library skills exercise and an English test.

Library Skills Grade	83	70	94	87	84	80	78	91	85
English Grade	90	74	80	65	63	87	84	93	73

6. Suppose that we sent a questionnaire to the faculty listing the journals that were being considered for cancellation and asking them to rank the journals on the list as to their priority for retention (with 1 being the journal they would most like to keep/not be canceled) and that we want to compare responses by academic department (the economics to political science department, and so forth). What type of correlation coefficient would we use to compare the rankings?
7. Returning to question 6, the librarians have compiled a list of 50 journals for cancellation and they want to compare their list to the 50 titles chosen by the faculty. Which correlation coefficient should we select to make the comparison? Should we use a one- or two-tailed test? In which direction might we expect the correlation coefficient to go?
8. If we generate ranked data with numerous tied scores, which correlation coefficients might we use?
9. If we want to determine if there is a relationship between the size of the student body and the size of the library's periodical collection, which correlation coefficient would we use?
10. Compute each type of correlation using software such as StatPac and Minitab. Which package do you prefer? Why?

Appendix A provides the answers to the questions

Chapter Nine
Analysis of Variance, Regression, and Factor Analysis

This chapter provides an introduction to regression, analysis of variance, and factor analysis. The discussion of factor analysis is the most cursory because we found the fewest examples of its application in the literature and because many datasets that librarians collect and maintain may not support such analysis. Factor analysis is most applicable where researchers have taken extreme care in the collection of data demonstrating reliability and internal validity. The data must also group logically into units or factors. Much action research in librarianship does not meet these criteria.

The published literature contains many examples where researchers have applied regression and analysis of variance. In fact, each test represents a family of tests and applications. StatPac Gold, for instance, offers 11 analysis of variance designs or models. Clearly, librarians must carefully research the variations and discover the one most appropriate to their *reflective inquiry* (statement of the problem, logical structure, objectives, and hypotheses/research questions), and research design. Analysis of variance has application to bibliographic instruction programs and other instances in which librarians compare the means of three or more samples. Regression is used in modeling (planning, budgeting, and so forth) and in collection development. It merits repeating that this chapter is a general introduction, one that encourages readers to find out more about the tests discussed here.

Figure 9-1 explains the major statistical tests discussed in this chapter, while Figure 9-2 offers examples of statistics books that explain the tests in more detail. Figure 9-3 provides examples of the application of regression, analysis of variance, and factor analysis in the literature of library and information science.

ANALYSIS OF VARIANCE

Analysis of variance (ANOVA) is a systematic way of studying variability. Similar to the *t*-test, ANOVA compares the mean scores of groups. Unlike the

Figure 9-1.   Description of the Key Statistical Tests Discussed in This Chapter

Test	Description
Analysis of Variance	This test compares the means of two or more group samples. One-way analysis of variance has one independent variable, two-way ANOVA considers two independent variables, and three-way ANOVA has three independent variables.
Factor Analysis	It reduces many variables to a few representative ones. The test examines interrelationships among a set of observed variables. Each variable is a dependent variable that is a function of a set of factors.
Regression	It examines the relationship between two or more variables. Simple regression predicts one variable when the other is known.

Figure 9-2.   Examples of Writings on Analysis of Variance, Factor Analysis, and Regression

Analysis of Variance[a]

Dunn, Olive J. and Virginia A. Clark. *Applied Statistics*. New York: Wiley, 1987.

Fidell, Linda S. and Barbara G. Tabachnick. *Using Multivariate Statistics*. New York: Harper and Row, 1982.

Harris, Richard J. *A Primer of Multivariate Statistics*. New York: Harcourt Brace, 1985.

Factor Analysis

Armstrong, J. S. and P. Soelberg. "On the Interpretation of Factor Analysis," *Psychological Bulletin*, 70 (1968): 361–364.

Harman, H. *Modern Factor Analysis*. Chicago, IL: The University of Chicago Press, 1967.

Horst, P. *Factor Analysis of Data Matrices*. New York: Holt, Rinehart and Winston, 1965.

Kerlinger, Fred N. *Foundations of Behavioral Research*. New York: Holt, Rinehart and Winston, 1973, pp. 659–692.

Kim, Jae-On. "Factor Analysis," in *SPSS: Statistical Package for the Social Sciences*, edited by Norman H. Nie et al. New York: McGraw-Hill, 1975, pp. 468–514.

Wells, William D. and Jagdish N. Sheth. "Factor Analysis," in *Handbook of Marketing Research*, edited by Robert Ferber. New York: McGraw-Hill, 1974, pp. 458–471.

Regression Analysis

Berry, William D. and Stanley Feldman. *Multiple Regression in Practice*. Sage University Paper 50. Beverly Hills, CA: Sage, 1985.

Claycamp, Henry J. "Correlation and Regression Methods," in *Handbook of Marketing Research*, edited by Robert Ferber. New York: McGraw-Hill, 1974, pp. 394–408.

Newbold, Paul and Theodore Bos. *Stochastic Parameter Regression Models*. Sage University Paper 51. Beverly Hills, CA: Sage, 1985.

[a]See also Sage University Paper Series (Beverly Hills, CA: Sage Publications). This series has contained several volumes on analysis of variance.

Figure 9-3.   Examples of Writings Using the Statistical Analyses Presented in This Chapter

Analysis of Variance

Brooks, Terrence A. "Using Time-Series Regression to Predict Academic Library Circulations," *College & Research Libraries*, 45 (November 1984): 501–505.

D'Elia, George P. "The Determinants of Job Satisfaction among Beginning Librarians," *Library Quarterly*, 49 (1979): 283–302.

Funk, Mark E. and Carolyn Anne Reid. "The Usefulness of Monographic Proceedings," *Bulletin of the Medical Library Association*, 76 (January 1988): 14–21.

Hardesty, Larry L. "The Influence of Selected Variables on Attitudes of Classroom Instructors toward the Undergraduate Educational Role of the Academic Library," *ACRL Third National Conference (Seattle, April 4–7, 1984) Proceedings*, 3rd (1984), pp. 365–377.

King, David N. and John C. Ory. "Effects of Library Instruction on Student Research: A Case Study," *College & Research Libraries*, 42 (January 1981): 31–41.

Koohang, Alex A. "Effects of Age, Gender, College Status, and Computer Experience on Attitudes toward Library Computer Systems (LCS)," *Library and Information Science Research*, 8 (October/December 1986): 349–355.

Luyben, Paul D., Leonard Cohen, Rebecca Conger, and Selby U. Gration. "Reducing Noise in a College Library," *College & Research Libraries*, 42 (September 1981): 470–481.

Lynch, Beverly P. and Jo Ann Verdin. "Job Satisfation in Libraries: Relationships of the Work Itself, Age, Sex, Occupational Group, Tenure, Supervisory Level, Career Commitment, and Library Department," *Library Quarterly*, 53 (October 1983): 434–447.

————. "Job Satisfaction in Libraries: A Replication," *Library Quarterly*, 57 (April 1987): 190–202.

Markham, Marilyn J., Keith H. Stirling, and Nathan M. Smith. "Library Self-Disclosure and Patron Satisfaction in the Reference Interview," *RQ*, 22 (Summer 1983): 369–374.

Nielsen, Brian and Betsy Baker. "Educating the Online Catalog User: A Model Evaluation Study," *Library Trends*, 35 (Spring 1987): 571–585.

Powell, Ronald R. "An Investigation of the Relationships between Quantifiable Reference Service Variables and Reference Performance in Public Libraries," *Library Quarterly*, 48 (January 1978): 1–19.

Pungitore, Verna L. "Perceptions of Change and Public Library Directors in Indiana: An Exploratory Study," *Library and Information Science Research*, 9 (October/December 1987): 247–264.

Scamell, Richard W. and Bette Ann Stead. "A Study of Age and Tenure As It Pertains to Job Satisfaction," *Journal of Library Administration*, 1 (Spring 1980): 3–18.

Regression Analysis

Bengston, Dale S. and Dorothy Shields. "A Test of Marchant's Predictive Formulas Involving Job Satisfaction," *Journal of Academic Librarianship*, 11 (May 1985): 88–92.

(continued)

Figure 9-3.   (*Continued*)

Casper, Cheryl A. "Estimating the Demand for Library Service: Theory and Practice," *Journal of the American Society for Information Science*, 29 (September 1978): 232–237.

Collins, Susan M. "Determining Effective Staff Levels in Special Libraries," *Special Libraries*, 74 (October 1984): 284–291.

Cooper, Alan. *Trend Forecasting Using Regression Analysis: A Guide for Library Managers*. Loughborough, England: Loughborough University, 1982.

D'Elia, George P. "The Determinants of Job Satisfaction among Beginning Librarians," *Library Quarterly*, 49 (1979): 283–302.

Hodowanec, George V. "An Acquisition Rate Model for Academic Libraries," *College & Research Libraries*, 39 (November 1978): 439–447.

——. "Analysis of Variables Which Help to Predict Book and Periodical Use," *Library Acquisitions: Practice and Theory*, 4 (1980): 75–85.

Metz, Paul. "The Role of the Academic Library Director," *Journal of Academic Librarianship*, 5 (July 1979): 148–152.

Pierce, Thomas J. "An Empirical Approach to the Allocation of the University Library Book Budget," *Collection Management*, 2 (Spring 1978): 39–58.

Powell, Ronald R. "An Investigation of the Relationships between Quantifiable Reference Service Variables and Reference Performance in Public Libraries," *Library Quarterly*, 48 (January 1978): 1–19.

Pungitore, Verna L. "Perceptions of Change and Public Library Directors in Indiana: An Exploratory Study," *Library and Information Science Research*, 9 (October/ December 1987): 247–264.

Renner, Charlene and Barton M. Clark. "Professional and Nonprofessional Staffing Patterns in Departmental Libraries," *Library Research*, 1 (Summer 1979): 153–170.

Tolle, John E. *Public Access Terminals: Determining Quantity Requirements*. OCLC, 1984.

Williams, Robert V. "Sources of the Variability in Level of Public Library Development in the United States: A Comparative Analysis," *Library Research*, 2 (Summer 1980/81): 157–176.

Factor Analysis

D'Elia, George P. "The Determinants of Job Satisfaction among Beginning Librarians," *Library Quarterly*, 49 (1979): 283–302.

Hardesty, Larry. "Book Selection for Undergraduate Libraries: A Study of Faculty Attitudes," *Journal of Academic Librarianship*, 12 (March 1986): 19–25.

McClure, Charles R. *Information for Academic Library Decision Making*. Westport, CT: Greenwood Press, 1980.

—— and Alan R. Samuels. "Factors Affecting the Use of Information for Academic Library Decision Making," *College & Research Libraries*, 46 (November 1985): 483–498.

Noble, Grant and Steve O'Connor. "Attitudes toward Technology as Predictors of Online Catalog Usage," *College & Research Libraries*, 47 (1986): 605–612.

Suprenant, Thomas T. "Learning Theory, Lecture, and Programmed Instruction Text: An

Figure 9-3.   (*Continued*)

Experiment in Bibliographic Instruction," *College & Research Libraries*, 43 (January 1982): 31–37.

Williams, Robert V. "Sources of the Variability in Level of Public Library Development in the United States: A Comparative Analysis," *Library Research*, 2 (Summer 1980/81): 157–176.

---

t-test, it can compare two or *more* groups.[1] As Huck, Cormier, and Bounds (1974, p. 58) indicate,

> Both procedures yield identical results in a two-group comparison, but the one-way ANOVA is more versatile because it can also be used to compare three or more groups. The one-way ANOVA is, in effect, an extension of the t test to a greater number of groups compared.

Another benefit of analysis of variance is that it is designed to protect against a possible Type I error, which can occur when using the *t*-test and the number of groups or categories increases. Although the *t*-test can compare each pairing, using the single test of analysis of variance for all groups simultaneously is preferable.

There are different types of ANOVA models. The two basic designs are one-way and two-way models. In a one-way model, the dependent variable represents a level within a single factor. In a two-way design, the dependent variable depicts the interaction of two factors.

In analysis of variance, the dependent variable must be measured at the interval or ratio level. However, the independent variables, called factors, could be at the nominal level. One-way analysis of variance is an investigation of the possible effects of a single factor. Studying the simultaneous effects of two or more factors involves two-way analysis of variance or multivariate analysis.

As with the *t*-test, analysis of variance tests a null hypothesis stating that there is no difference in the dependent variable resulting from any of the factors or independent variables. When computing the analysis of variance, "the variation in the averages of these samples, from one sample to the next, will be compared to the variation among individual observations within each of the samples" (Jaeger, 1983, p. 234). The statistic that is computed is called an *F-ratio*, a ratio of variances. This statistic (the *F*-statistic) summarizes the variation among the

---

[1] The Kruskal–Wallis test is the nonparametric equivalent to an analysis of variance. The test ranks scores and determines if the sums of ranks are so disparate that they are not likely to be from samples drawn from the same population.

sample averages, which is compared to the variation among individual observations within the samples.

Because ANOVA is a parametric test, we assume a normal distribution, with randomly drawn samples, and a linear relationship. This test involves interval or ratio data and homogeneity of variance or equal variance. ANOVA does not reveal where significant differences among groups exist. It simply indicates that a difference exists somewhere among the groups. We may assume that there is a difference between the largest and smallest mean. However, it is difficult to say whether there is a significant difference between the largest and second or third smallest mean. To examine the significance of difference between specific means, some researchers use the Scheffé procedure, once the F-statistic is determined, while others apply the t-test.

An ANOVA or summary table is the central part of the analysis and interpretation. Table 9-1 provides an example of a summary ANOVA table. The *source* refers to the variable being studied. The term *between groups* is used even though it is grammatically correct to say "among" for three or more groups. The next column is *df*. Degrees of freedom is calculated for the first row by subtracting one from the number of groups in the study. To find the *df* for the total row, subtract one from the total number of scores in the study. The *df* for the second row, within groups, is the difference of the other two rows. In the example, the total number of scores in the study was 10.

The third column is the *sum of squares* or *SS*. The calculation for the sums of squares is similar to that of calculating variance (as in Chapter 5), except that the result is not divided by $N - 1$. The total row will always be the sum of the other two rows.

To obtain the *mean square* or *MS*, simply divide the *SS* by the *df* in the same row. No value is ever given for the total *MS*. To obtain the *F-value* of the fifth column, divide the *MS* for between groups by the *MS* for within groups; that is, divide 8 by 2 to get 4. (Table 9-2 reprints the formula used to calculate the F-value. This formula is then applied in the case of Table 9-3.) The numbers in this example were chosen to make the calculations easy to see. (The example is taken from Huck, Cormier, and Bounds, 1974, p. 59.)

All of the calculations lead to finding the F-value, which is used to determine if the differences are statistically significant. To interpret the F-value, one must

Table 9-1. ANOVA Summary Table

Source	df	SS	MS	F
Between groups	2	16	8	4
Within groups	15	30	2	
Total	17	46		

Table 9-2.   Calculation of the F-value

$$F = \frac{\text{Between category variance}}{\text{Within category variance}} = \frac{\dfrac{\text{Sum of Squares } (SS)_{between}}{k-1}}{\dfrac{\text{Sum of Squares } (SS)_{within}}{N-k}}$$

$$= \frac{\text{Mean Squares } (MS)_{between}}{\text{Mean Squares } (MS)_{within}}$$

$$SS_{within} = \Sigma\Sigma(X_{ik} - \bar{X}_k)^2 = \Sigma X_{ik}^2 - \Sigma\frac{(\Sigma X_k)^2}{N_k}$$

$$SS_{between} = \Sigma\frac{(\Sigma X_{ik})^2}{N_k} - \frac{(\Sigma\Sigma X_{ik})^2}{N}$$

$$SS_{total} = \Sigma\Sigma(X_{ik} - \bar{X}_T)^2 = \Sigma\Sigma X_{ik}^2 - \frac{\Sigma\Sigma(X_{ik})^2}{N}$$

$$SS_{total} = SS_{within} + SS_{between}$$

$$df_{between} = k - 1 \ (n_1 \text{ in the } F \text{ table})$$

$$df_{within} = N - k \ (n_2 \text{ in the } F \text{ table})$$

where

$\Sigma\Sigma$ = double summation, summing over both rows and columns
N = number of total samples
k = number of categories
N_k = sample size for the kth sample
X_{ik} = ith (individual) raw score in the kth sample
$\bar{X}_k$ = kth sample mean
$\bar{X}_T$ = grand mean

Note: SS_{within} is sometimes referred to as $SS_{unexplained}$ or SS_{error} (in a summary table), because it is a measure of random sampling error from the population. To derive SS_{within}, we can subtract the $SS_{between}$ from the SS_{total}.

use the F table found in many statistics textbooks. The degrees of freedom from the summary table are used to locate the critical value of F, based on the chosen level of significance. If the value that was calculated is larger than the value found in the table, then there is a significant difference and the null hypothesis will be rejected. If the value calculated is smaller than that expressed in the table, the difference is not significant and the null hypothesis can be accepted. If there is a significant difference between the sample means, a researcher often reports an asterisk next to the calculated F-value. At the bottom of the table, the researcher states the level of significance used in hypothesis testing.

Several one-way ANOVA's can be combined into one summary table. In such instances, the total row may be omitted, although it is still used in the calculations.

Example

One popular use of one-way analysis of variance is to compare how three (or more) groups react to a certain factor. One problem that librarians face is the noise level in a library. If study areas are placed near public service desks, the activities at the desk, as well as conversation among staff members, can be an annoyance. Assume that researchers undertake a study to determine how the noise level affects students studying in the library and that a pool of students were randomly assigned to three groups. Further, assume that the researchers conducted the study in a library classroom freed from outside distractions and that a librarian sat at a desk in the classroom.

Each group of students received a simple set of problems (basic arithmetic) to solve. With the first group, the librarian sat quietly at the desk and did not speak; the room was quiet. With the second group, the librarian was visited by students from outside the room. The conversations were kept at a low level, and only one or two people were present at a time. With the third group, the activity was greatly increased. In addition, other librarians at the desk engaged in conversations but in normal speaking tones.

Each group had the same amount of time to solve the set of problems. The number of problems was greater than any member of a group could finish in the allotted time. The number of questions solved was used as the scores for each group. Table 9-3 summarizes the numerical calculations. The calculated value of F must be compared to the critical value of F for the same degrees of freedom, using a standard table found in many statistics books.

Statistical analysis software will provide the key data on the printout. Table 9-4 reproduces the ANOVA summary table using StatPac, while Table 9-5 illustrates the table provided by Minitab.

Two-way Analysis of Variance

Two-way analysis of variance considers two independent variables. Two groups that differ from each one in two dimensions are compared. In the hypothetical example previously mentioned in which three groups of students solved problems under different noise settings, if another factor or independent variable were added (i.e., the difficulty of the problems), then two-way analysis of variance could be used. For example, if there were two sets of problems—an easy and a difficult set—and each were given under the three noise conditions, then six combinations could be analyzed.

The interaction that may be found is the main advantage of using two-way analysis of variance. This interaction would be the effect of two of the variables on another variable. If the data for a two-variable study were graphed, the lines would show a difference in slope if there were interaction. Parallel lines would indicate that there was no interaction.

Table 9-3. Problem Solving under Different Noise Levels

	Group 1	Group 2	Group 3
	18	16	10
	17	14	9
	15	13	7
	15	12	6
	13	10	5
$T =$	78	65	37
$N =$	5	5	5

For a summary table, we need to make the following calculations:

df for Row 1	3 groups $-$ 1 = 2
df for Row 2	15 $-$ 3 = 12
df for Row 3	15 scores $-$ 1 = 14
SS for Row 1	$(78)^2/5 + (65)^2/5 + (37)^2/5 - (78 + 65 + 37)^2/15$
	$6084/5 + 4225/5 + 1369/5 - 32400/15$
	$1216.8 + 845 \quad + 273.8 \quad - 2160 = 175.6$
SS for Row 2	SS of Row 3 $-$ SS of Row 1 = 228 $-$ 175.6 = 52.4
SS for Row 3	$(18)^2 + (17)^2 + (15)^2 + (15)^2 + (13)^2 +$
	$(16)^2 + (14)^2 + (13)^2 + (12)^2 + (10)^2 +$
	$(10)^2 + (9)^2 + (7)^2 + (6)^2 + (5)^2$
	$- (78 + 65 + 37)^2/15$
	$= 324 + 289 + 225 + 225 + 169 + 256 +$
	$196 + 169 + 144 + 100 + 100 + 81 + 49$
	$+ 36 + 25 - 2160$
	$= 2388 - 2160 = 228$
MS for Row 1	SS/df
	$= 175.6/2 = 87.8$
MS for Row 2	SS/df
	$= 52.4/12 = 4.37$
F-value	$87.8/4.37 = 20.09$

ANOVA Summary Table

Source	df	SS	MS	F
Between groups	2	175.6	87.8	20.09
Within groups	12	52.4	4.37	
Total	14	228.0		

The preceding example tested the null hypothesis: There is no statistically significant difference in the mean scores of the three student groups at the .05 level. From a standard F distribution table, the critical value of F in this example is 3.88 at the .05 level

(continued)

Table 9-3.   (Continued)

> when df between groups is 2 and df within groups is
> 12. Because the F-value of 20.09 is greater than
> 3.88, the null hypothesis can be rejected. It appears
> that the noise level may have an effect on the stu-
> dents' performance.

Analysis of Covariance

Analysis of covariance (ANCOVA) is a form of analysis of variance in which the differences between the groups on a variable are analyzed after taking into account any initial differences in the measurement of the variable. A common example found in library literature is the pretest measure. The pretest is a covariate in each analysis. Variation in the dependent variable due to the influence of the covariate is then explained.

Multivariate Analysis of Variance

Multivariate analysis of variance (MANOVA) is used to compare multiple independent factors. MANOVA is useful in controlling the error rate. If individual analyses of variance were conducted for each factor, the result could be a high

Table 9-4.   ANOVA Summary Table (StatPac)

Source of Variation	DF	Sum of Squares	Mean Squares	F	Significance Level
Between groups	2	175.600	87.800	20.107	0.000
Within groups	12	52.400	4.367		
Total	14	228.000			

		Group Statistics		
GROUP	N	Missing	Mean	SD
Group 1	5	0	15.600	1.949
Group 2	5	0	13.000	2.236
Group 3	5	0	7.400	2.074

t-test between group means—values of p are for a two-tailed test. Note: Statistics are printed only if p is less than or equal to .050

t = 6.205	Group 1 − Group 1	
p = .008	Group 3 − Group 3	
t = 4.237	Group 2 − Group 2	
p = .024	Group 3 − Group 3	

Table 9-5.   ANOVA Summary Table (Minitab)

```
MTB >    SET SCORES FOR GROUP A INTO C1
DATA>    18 17 15 15 13
DATA>    END
MTB >    SET SCORES FOR GROUP B INTO C2
DATA>    16 14 13 12 10
DATA>    END
MTB >    SET SCORES FOR GROUP C INTO C3
DATA>    10 9 7 6 5
DATA>    END
MTB >    AOVONEWAY ON C1-C3
```

ANALYSIS OF VARIANCE

SOURCE	DF	SS	MS	F
FACTOR	2	175.60	87.80	20.11
ERROR	12	52.40	4.37	
TOTAL	14	228.00		

INDIVIDUAL 95 PCT CI'S FOR MEAN BASED ON
POOLED STDEV

LEVEL	N	MEAN	STDEV				
				_____+_____+_____+_____+__			
C1	5	15.600	1.949				(____*____)
C2	5	13.000	2.236			(____*____)	
C3	5	7.400	2.074	(____*____)			
				_____+_____+_____+_____+__			
				7.0	10.5	14.0	17.5

```
POOLED STDEV = 2.090
MTB>
```

error rate. If the MANOVA found significant results, then individual analyses of variances for each variable could be conducted.

REGRESSION

While correlation and regression both indicate association between variables, correlation studies assess the strength of that association. Regression analysis examines the association from a different perspective; it is used to *predict* the value of one variable by knowing the value of another variable. Regression, a parametric test that uses either interval or ratio data, provides information to evaluate the "goodness-of-fit" or the extent to which the regression line explains the actual data. In calculating the regression line, the assumption is made that the data are normally distributed and that any point on a scattergram is representative of any value for X and Y in the population. This may not be the case. To predict what one department or one library may do on the basis of what another department or library does may be misleading. To predict outside the limits of observed values may produce error since the regression model assumes normal distribution over the range of predicted values and datasets actually observed. In reality, predicted values may not be normally distributed.

Scattergrams display the distribution and may indicate if there are sampling, data entry, or coding errors. Such errors stand out because they differ from other plotted points and because they deviate markedly from the regression line.

If a null hypothesis is not rejected, the inference is that Y does not depend on X. This may not be true because the absence of a linear relationship has been established only over the range of values in the sample; the values may not be representative of the population. Clearly, the appropriateness of regression analysis depends on the research design, hypotheses, and reliability and validity assessments. The usefulness of a regression model is further constrained by the underlying assumptions that there is independence in the error estimates of X and Y. For example, an error made in estimating a circulation count based on one set of budget figures is independent of the error associated with estimating a circulation count based on another set of figures. Another assumption relates to constant variance, that is, the data points cannot be close to the regression line on one end and not the other. Further, the variance of each of the two variables should be the same or nearly so. If any of these assumptions cannot be applied to predicted values, the utility of the regression model is undermined.

A problem in regression analysis can occur in *ex post facto* research when inferences are drawn from unmatched pairs. For example, in comparing the scores on a bibliographic instruction test in one university with those at another university, there is the possibility that the mean scores of these two groups differ. Conclusions based on a regression model therefore could be deceiving. The main problem with comparing matching groups of different populations is that pre-existing conditions are not always addressed.

While correlation coefficients indicate whether variables are related, if the correlation between X and Y is coincidental, a regression or a prediction based on the regression is not valid. Even though calculations may indicate a large correlation between or among variables and a linear relationship,[2] it is possible that a Type I error has been committed. As is evident, it is important to scrutinize the logic behind an association and to review carefully the published literature (both theoretical and application studies) for guidance in the formulation of hypotheses and in presuming an association between or among variables.

Calculation of the Regression Equation

The first step in the calculation of a regression equation is to draw a scattergram. The resulting pattern depicted on the graph can indicate a type of relationship between variables as well as the direction of that relationship. If Y increases as X does, the relationship is positive; if Y decreases as X increases, the relationship is

---

[2] A test for a linear association, or linearity, is performed using Pearson's r.

negative. With only a small number of data points, the type of relationship may be apparent. Even with a small dataset, assumptions about the nature and direction of the relationship can be made.

It is common practice to allow the variable X to serve as the independent or predictor variable. The variable Y, known as the effect or response variable, is the dependent variable. The independent variable (X) is plotted on the x-axis with the dependent variable (Y) plotted on the y-axis.

Regression analysis finds the line or curve that best represents the data points in the scattergram. In order to draw the straight line through the data points on the scattergram, the line of "best fit" between the X and Y variables must first be calculated. The mathematical expression for linear regression involving two variables is:

$$Y = mX + b$$

where b equals the intercept of the straight line with the y-axis, m equals the slope of the line, X is the independent variable, and Y is the dependent variable. The formula for the slope of the regression line (m) is:

$$m = n \sum XY - (\sum X)(\sum Y)/n \sum X^2 - (\sum X)^2$$

where $\sum X$ and $\sum Y$ = sums of X and Y respectively, $\sum XY$ = sum of the products of X and Y, and $\sum X^2$ = sum of the squares of X. The formula for b, the intercept of the line with the y-axis, is:

$$b = \bar{Y} - m\bar{X}$$

where $\bar{X}$ and $\bar{Y}$ are the means of X and Y.

It should be noted that m and b represent unknown population parameters. The formula $Y = mX + b$ is based on a population and not a sample. Although regression analysis will be computed on the basis of a sample from a population, it is done so in the context of the population and all unobserved values of the variable. Suffice it to say here, other tests (see Chapter 7) will assist in determining how well the sample represents the unknown population whose parameters are given by m and b.

Returning to the formula for calculating the slope of the regression line, the sum of the squares of the variables X and Y are involved in this formula. The line of "best fit" is, by definition, the line that minimizes the sum of the squares of the vertical distances of the data points from the line. This method locates the regression line on the scattergram. Known as the *least squares method*, it predicts values of Y' from values of X.

As an example, X represents the average number of reference questions asked per hour and Y is the average number of reference materials used (left on tables) per hour. Let us assume that staff have monitored use of reference materials and determined that patrons only reshelve an insignificant number of titles once they have obtained the information needed.

Table 9-6 illustrates the computation of the regression coefficient (b), which is the indicator of rate of change in Y for a unit change in X. The regression line is used to predict a value of Y (known as Y') from a value of X. To draw the line of "best fit," substitute any two values of X into the equation for Y, plot the points, and draw a line between those two points. This is the graph of the least squares line. To predict Y', draw a vertical line from any point on the x-axis to the regression line and a horizontal line from the regression line at that point to the y-axis (see Figure 9-4).

Figure 9-5 is an example of the graph and summary data printed in StatPac. The summary data include the correlation coefficient. A value close to $+1.00$ for the correlation coefficient, Pearson's r, indicates that the line will be almost perfect; most points will fall exactly on the line or close to it.

Table 9-6.   Computation of the Regression Coefficient

X = average number of reference questions asked per hour
Y = average number of reference materials used per hour

X	Y	XY	X²
5.0	3.5	17.50	25.00
4.5	3.0	13.50	20.25
5.5	3.5	19.25	30.25
6.0	4.0	24.00	36.00
4.0	3.0	12.00	16.00
4.5	2.5	11.25	20.25
3.5	2.0	7.00	12.25
4.0	2.5	10.00	16.00
5.0	3.0	15.00	25.00
$\Sigma X = 42$	$\Sigma Y = 27$	$\Sigma XY = 129.5$	$\Sigma X^2 = 201$

$$\bar{X} = 4.67 \quad \bar{Y} = 3$$

$$m = \frac{N\Sigma XY - (\Sigma X)(\Sigma Y)}{N\Sigma X^2 - (\Sigma X)^2}$$

$$m = \frac{9\,(129.50) - 42(27)}{9\,(201) - (42)^2} = .7$$

$b = Y - mX$

$b = 3 - .7(4.67) = -.27 =$ intercept on y-axis

$Y = b + mX = -.27 + .7\,(X) =$ regression line

Figure 9-4.   Depiction of Regression Line

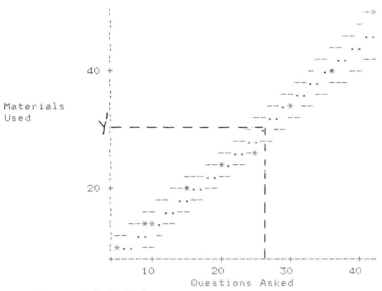

Regression Analysis

 Scattergram of Data & Regression Line & Confidence Intervals

* = Observed Data Value
. = Predicted Data Value
\- = 99.0% Confidence Limit

Standard Error of the Estimate

The value of a variable that is predicted from knowledge of another variable is only an estimate. The predicted value has an error associated with it. This error might be a sampling error or an error due to factors impacting on the individual variable beyond the control of the researcher. The error associated with a sample is known as the *standard error of the estimate* (S_e). We need an index to determine the magnitude of this error, which is the difference between the actual value of Y and the predicted value of Y' when Y' is predicted from a value of X. This error is designated in terms of the variance. The variance is a measure of the accuracy of prediction as shown in Chapter 5. The standard error of the estimate is given as:

$$S_e = sd_y \sqrt{1 - r^2}$$

where r^2 is the amount of variation explained by the association of two variables. Sd_y is the standard deviation of y.

Figure 9-5.   Regression Graph Drawn on StatPac

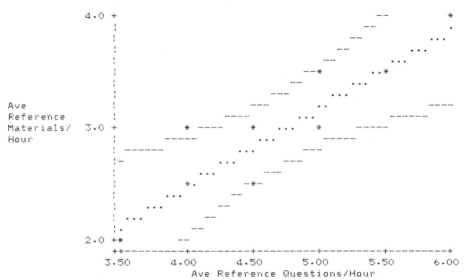

```
Regression Analysis

        Scattergram of Data & Regression Line & Confidence Intervals

        4.0 +                                             --              *
            :                                          --                 .
            :                                       --            ...
            :                                    --          ...
            :                                 --*        ..*
            :                              --        ...
            :                           ---        ...
Ave         :                     ---     ..                    ----
Reference   :                  ----    ...               ------
Materials/  3.0 +         *  ----      *    ...    *    ------
Hour        :              -----      ...            ------
            :           -------      ...        ----
            : -             ...          ----
            :            ...       ---
            :        *.            -*-
            :      ...       --
            :   ...      --
            :  ...    --
            :.
        2.0 +*        --
            ++----------+----------+----------+----------+----------+
           3.50      4.00      4.50      5.00      5.50      6.00
                       Ave Reference Questions/Hour
* = Observed Data Value
. = Predicted Data Value
- = 99.0% Confidence Limit
```

```
                    Summary Statistics  (N=9)

IV = Ave Reference Questions/Hour  Mean of residuals =-0.0000
Mean of IV = 4.6667                S.D. of residuals = 0.2622
S.D. of IV = 0.7906

DV = Ave Reference Materials/Hour  Mean Abs. % Error = 7.1914
Mean of DV = 3.0000                Mean % Error      =-0.8069
S.D. of DV = 0.6124                Mean Square Error = 0.0611

Correlation coefficient = 0.9037  Degrees of freedom = 7
R-Squared               = 0.8167  S.E. of estimate   = 0.2803
```

	Coefficient	Estd Std Error	T-Value	Significance
Intercept	-0.2667	0.5924	-0.4501	0.6662
Slope	0.7000	0.1254	5.5841	0.0008

Figure 9-5. (*Continued*)

Regression Analysis

Table of Observed Data, Predicted Data, and Error

Rec.	IV	Observed DV	Predicted DV	Error	Percent Error	99.0% Conf. Limits	
1	5.0	3.5	3.2	0.3	7.6	2.9	3.6
2	4.5	3.0	2.9	0.1	3.9	2.5	3.2
3	5.5	3.5	3.6	-0.1	-2.4	3.1	4.1
4	6.0	4.0	3.9	0.1	1.7	3.3	4.6
5	4.0	3.0	2.5	0.5	15.6	2.1	3.0
6	4.5	2.5	2.9	-0.4	-15.3	2.5	3.2
7	3.5	2.0	2.2	-0.2	-9.2	1.6	2.8
8	4.0	2.5	2.5	-0.0	-1.3	2.1	3.0
9	5.0	3.0	3.2	-0.2	-7.8	2.9	3.6

For the purposes here, it is sufficient to understand that this value is a measure of the confidence we can assign to the selected sample with respect to the population. From the formula, as r^2 increases the variance decreases; the more variance (r^2) explained, the smaller the standard error of the estimate. We can see this by substituting a value of 1 for r:

$$S_e = sd_y \sqrt{1 - r^2} = sd_y \sqrt{1 - 1} = 0 = \text{no error.}$$

In the case of $r = 1$, all points on the scattergram fall on the regression line, with there being no variation. This brief example indicates the accuracy of the prediction of Y' where r is ± 1 and there is no error. The closer the absolute value of r to 1, the more accurate the prediction.

Multiple Regression

Multiple regression, an extension of simple regression, examines the relationship between a dependent variable and two or more independent variables. The computation of multiple regression is complex and beyond the scope of this discussion. Statistical analysis software, such as StatPac and Minitab, can perform the computation. However, prior to the use of such software, it is important to review the user's manual and the discussion of the procedure. While regression analysis is usually performed on interval- or ratio-level data in a normal distribution, with randomly selected variables, these programs can linearize data and perform tests for other levels of measurement.

Example from Literature

Taylor and Viegas (1988) used eight years of patronage and circulation data "at the School of Education at the University of Mississippi to portray the performance of their branch library" (p. 322). They translated performance into four questions (p. 323):

- "What were the strengths and weaknesses of the library in terms of collection?"
- "Was the library providing adequate student services?"
- "Did the library support research requirements?"
- "Was the branch library a financial burden to the main library system?"

They used multiple regression to analyze the patronage and circulation data and thereby answer the four questions.

Unfortunately they do not explain the variables comprising the "patronage data" and how these data elements were collected. For example, was in-house use monitored and treated as part of patronage data? In addition, the application of regression analysis to the four questions should not provide sufficient answers upon which to base library decision making and planning. First, collection strengths and weaknesses must be considered in the context of a library's mission, goals, and objectives. Second, how is "adequate" operationally defined and why the subdivision of patronage data—students and student services? In effect, are patronage data merely student data? Third, how do the data elements distinguish between library support for research requirements and other types of requirements? And, finally, how can patronage and circulation data sufficiently address whether or not the branch library was "a financial burden to the main library system?" Clearly, the authors read too much into their findings. Regression analysis of patronage and circulation data, by itself, cannot provide adequate answers to the four study questions.

FACTOR ANALYSIS

Factor analysis ascertains whether the interrelationships among a set of observed variables are explicable in terms of a small number of unobserved variables or factors. The two basic purposes of factor analysis are "to explore variable areas in order to identify the factors presumably underlying the variables; and . . . to test hypotheses about the relations among variables" (Kerlinger, 1973, p. 245). Factor analysis explains a set of data in a smaller number of dimensions than one starts with. In other words, this type of analysis does two things: it (1) views each of the variables as a dependent variable that is a function of an underlying set of factors; and (2) considers all the variables at the same time.

In essence, factor analysis comprises a method of examining a correlation matrix (see Chapter 8). A *factor loading* therefore becomes the correlation of a variable with the factor. Factor loadings range from -1.00 to $+1.00$, similar to correlation coefficients. A set of factors should contain highly positive or negative loadings for the concepts under investigation. Further, if we investigated a concept such as *organizational climate*, variables such as *democratic governance* and *esprit de corps* might account for a sizable percentage of the total variance among the scales employed. As is evident, the operational definition of concepts, and their translation into something measurable and demonstrating construct validity, guide the use and interpretation of factor analysis. Both theory and the literature influence the development of definitions and the formation of a smaller number of dimensions.

Computer technology has opened up new approaches and developments in the use of factor analysis. It is now easier to manipulate data in machine-readable form than to perform long and complex calculations by hand or with the aid of a pocket calculator. The danger, however, is that researchers might let the dataset dictate the use of statistical tests and the interpretation of the findings. More than ever, librarians must have greater insights into the datasets that they use and be certain of the data's reliability and validity before applying statistical tests, such as factor analysis. In addition, they should engage in hypothesis testing that takes into account existing theory and knowledge as reflected in the published literature.

SUMMARY QUESTIONS (BASED ON THE CHAPTER)

1. Analysis of variance is a statistical test that compares which measure of central tendency for two or more groups?
2. What is the difference between one-way and two-way analysis of variance?
3. How does analysis of variance compare to the *t*-test?
4. What does the F ratio mean?
5. In an ANOVA table, what do SS and MS represent?
6. Construct a straight line that approximates the data for the number of CD-ROM stations, the independent variable, with the number of people waiting to use the stations, the dependent variable. Find the equation for the line and predict the number of people waiting for a CD-ROM terminal, when $X = 6$. Use the data below to construct the scattergram.

X	1	2	3	4	5	6
Y	7	6	5	4	3	

7. As a manager of collection development operations, you are interested in looking at the association between the number of library books circulated and the number of students in each of six departments in the university. From the data provided below, calculate the regression equation and predict the number of books that will circulate when a department, with an initial student enrollment of 110, is created.

X: Number of students in department
Y: Number of books circulated by department

X	50	60	70	80	90	100
Y	75	80	85	90	95	100

8. If the correlation coefficient is $r = .5$ and the standard deviation $= .1$, calculate the standard error of the estimate for the preceding question.

9. A library manager wants to predict the number of reference questions asked based on the amount of expenditure for library promotional activities. From the data provided below, calculate the regression equation.

X: Cost in thousands of dollars
Y: Number of reference questions asked

X	2000	3000	1500	3500	1000
Y	180	220	160	240	140

10. Predict the number of reference questions asked if the library's promotional budget is $4,000.

Chapter Ten

Examples of Statistical Applications

Previous chapters have discussed specific statistical tests and offered summary questions to reinforce statistical concepts and computations. This chapter offers hypothetical situations and highlights the tests that apply in these instances. The purpose here is to provide readers with an opportunity to sort through the various tests discussed in this book and identify those most applicable to a given situation.

USE OF AN ONLINE SEARCH SERVICE

The library of a research institute serves a user community of about 300 people, most of whom are researchers in material science and nuclear engineering. For the past five years, the library has offered online search services, including access to DIALOG, BRS, and so forth. For all this time, library staff have kept records on the users of the services, including who they were, what they requested, and if the search located pertinent and important source material.

Analysis of the library's records reveals that 200 different people have used a search service at least once. Sixty-five of these users consulted a service more than 10 times, while 45 requested a search 5–9 times and 90 made 1–4 uses. The staff did not know if the researchers decided to use the service due to a particular method by which the library has promoted the search service. If they have, the library can emphasize that method (or those methods) of publicity. At the same time, the staff will gain insights into how to reach out to the 100 nonusers of a service.

The staff decided to conduct a study guided, in part, by the following objectives, research question, and hypothesis:

- To identify the method that has attracted the greatest number of people to a search service. *Question*: How have the users of the service become aware of that service?
- To compare the rankings of methods used by the frequency by which users have consulted a service (more than 10 times, 5–9 times, and 1–4 times).

Hypothesis: There is no significant correlation in the rankings among the three groups.

The library staff sent a brief questionnaire to the users of a service asking them to rank eight methods by which they might have become aware of the search services. The eight are: the annual library seminar about the services offered, informal discussion with staff (such as through reference desk service), a recommendation made by a colleague, a recommendation made by a librarian, consulting the library brochure, reading the bulletin board or posters, scanning the library newsletter, or other.

Among the respondents to the survey were 36 of the 65 heavy users (more than 10 times), 27 of the 45 moderate users (5–9 times), and 48 of the 90 infrequent users (1–4 times). Figure 10-1 summarizes the number of respondents by method of publicity.

To address the first objective and its research question, we can use descriptive statistics and determine percentages. Of the 111 respondents, 36 were heavy users, 27 were moderate users, and the remaining 48 were infrequent users. Figure 10-1 indicates the breakdown of the eight methods by respondent type. Note that we are basing the answer to the research question on the percentage of heavy (55.4%), moderate (60%), and infrequent (53.3%) users who responded to the survey. At least 40% of each group did not complete and return the questionnaire. The question becomes: "Are we satisfied with the return rate as the basis for making a policy decision?"

Turning to the second objective, the staff investigated the hypothesis that there is no significant correlation in the rankings among the three groups. Clearly, there are options that the staff can pursue in the selection of a statistical test. Because they are comparing the rankings of the groups and given the type of survey, they have selected a nonparametric test. Examining the rankings, they saw that there are few ties in the rankings and that cells are equal. Therefore, they decided to apply Spearman's rho. They compute three such values: comparison of heavy to moderate users, heavy to infrequent users, and moderate to infrequent users. Table 10-1 offers an example of the computation and interpretation of findings. When $N = 8$ and $p = .05$, the critical value is 0.643. Therefore there is a positive correlation between the two ranks; the null hypothesis is rejected. Both groups tend to get information from similar types of publicity methods.

STAFFING THE CIRCULATION DESK

College A is a small, independent school with an enrollment of 1,000 full-time equivalent students. The college library has had a difficult time retaining the work-study students who staff the circulation desk. Work-study staffing is

Figure 10-1.   Source of Awareness for Online Services

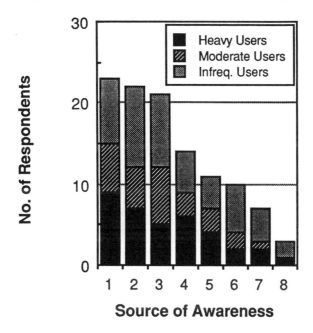

1: Annual Seminar
2: Informal Discussion with Staff
3: Recommendation by Colleague
4: Recommendation by Librarian
5: Library Brochure
6: Bulletin Board or Posters
7: Newsletter
8: Other

the only method that the library has to maintain current hours of operation. The library is open almost 100 hours per week during the academic term, until midnight from Sunday through Friday.

With the opening on campus of a new Student Center that included a swimming pool, many new and desirable work-study positions became available for the first time. Departments that traditionally had a wide choice of students were finding it more difficult to attract student employees and to maintain appropriate coverage of work-related activities. Good student workers were leaving library employment to seek positions elsewhere on campus.

Table 10-1. Computation of Spearman's Rho for Heavy and Infrequent Users

Method	Heavy User Rank	Infrequent User Rank	D	D²
Annual Seminar	1	3	−2	4
Informal Discussion	2	1	1	1
Recommendation by Colleague	4	2	2	4
Recommendation by Librarian	3	5	2	4
Brochure	5	6.5	−1.5	2.25
Bulletin Board or Posters	6.5	4	2.5	6.25
Newsletter	6.5	6.5	0	0
Other	8	8	0	0
$N = 8$				$\Sigma D^2 = 21.5$

$$\text{rho} = 1 - \frac{6\Sigma D^2}{N^3 - N} = \frac{6 \times 21.5}{8^3 - 8} = 1 - \frac{129}{404} = 0.74$$

The director of the library surmised that one way to influence students to remain on the library staff would be to increase their degree of involvement in setting and meeting library goals and objectives. With the head of circulation, she devised a new program that involved a series of three goal-setting workshops for students and staff in the circulation department. From the pool of 50 work-study students starting to work in the library that September, they randomly selected 27 participants for the new program. Those not selected to participate received the regular circulation desk training and were simply assigned tasks. The director asked the head of circulation to report back to her at the end of the academic year on the program and whether it reduced the number of work-study students leaving library employment.

The hypothesis being tested is that the goal-setting workshops reduced student loss; there was an appreciably smaller number of students lost from the workshop group (.05 level of significance).

Such a simple hypothesis is actually difficult to support or reject because valid conclusions would have to be based on detailed insights into the 50 work-study students in order to determine that the two groups were indeed similar. Random assignment indeed is important. However, before students are informed of which group they are assigned, the librarians would probably check personnel forms and document that both groups are similar. A major problem that would acquire attention would be that the work-study students, at some point, would know about the existence of two groups. Some students who did not participate in the workshops might resign because they did not believe that the organization appreciated them. After all, are not the participants in the workshop favored? Conversely, workshop participants might feel special and so inform other student workers. Clearly, the study that the librarians want to conduct is not as easy as it first seems.

At any rate, the librarians proceed with the study. The following May, they discover that 18 of the 27 workshop participants have remained on the library staff, while 10 of the 23 nonparticipants were still on the staff. The director wanted to know if these results were significant, that is, do these data tell anything about the efficacy of the goal-setting workshop program? Should the library continue to fund this particular retention program and involve all student workers in it?

The study could be structured in such a way that parametric tests, including the t-test apply. However, given the control and validity issues identified, they decide that the chi-square test is most appropriate. The data collected involve nominal measurement. The chi-square test will determine if there is a relationship between variables (a 2×2 contingency table). However, results should be interpreted with great caution.

The librarians use statistical analysis software and generate a table, such as that depicted in Table 10-2. Because the contingency table is 2×2, the software automatically applies Yates' correction. There is no statistically significant difference between the number of student losses and whether or not the person participated in the workshops.

Without the use of the chi-square test, the librarians might be tempted to simply look at the raw numbers or percentages and conclude that 18 of 26 workshop participants (66%) remained on the staff, while only 10 of 23 nonparticipants (43%) remained. The temptation may be to apply significance to the surface appearance of one number being greater than another, rather than actual significance of the relationship between the variables being compared. Either way, the librarians are letting the statistics speak for themselves. Statistics must be placed in context of the entire research process. As already noted, conclusions must be tempered by the research design used as well as the attempts to control for internal validity. Random selection to either group does not provide a sufficient validity check. This example serves as a reminder of a theme stressed throughout the book—study findings must be viewed in context. Perhaps for managerial decision making this study might offer some useful impressions. The study, however, may not withstand scrutiny as a tightly controlled research investigation. The example illustrates the difficulty of conducting an experiment.

USAGE AND AVAILABILITY OF CD-ROM STATIONS

Alpha University is a medium-sized institution with a student body of 14,000, fifteen master's-level and nine doctoral programs. The university is becoming a regional research and teaching base for an expanding industrial economy. Omega Library, located on the campus, has made a significant commitment to the

Table 10-2. Application of the Chi-square Test

Remained on Library Staff—Y-axis)
_____ BY _____ Whether or Not a Workshop Participant—(X-axis)

Number Row % Column % Total %	yes 1	no 2	Row Totals
yes	18 64.3 66.7 36.0	10 35.7 43.5 20.0	28 56.0
no	9 40.9 33.3 18.0	13 59.1 56.5 26.0	22 44.0
Column Totals	27 54.0	23 46.0	50

Corrected Chi-square	= 1.851
Degrees of freedom	= 1
Probability of chance	= 0.174
Phi	= .192
Valid cases	= 50
Missing cases	= 0
Response rate	= 100%

NOTE: Other statistics, e.g., Somer's d, could be reported.

development of its resources and services that support the University's mission. One of the factors that has had considerable impact on the university as a whole is technology. An ever increasing number of departments and university services related to technology have made it apparent that the use of technology can benefit members of the university community.

In addition to automating technical services and circulation functions in the main library and the four branches, the main library recently implemented technology to assist its public service functions in the reference department. One of the goals of the reference department in the main library is to provide efficient and effective service to patrons. To accomplish this goal, the library recently made available an online public access catalog of in-house resources and online search capabilities for access to external databases. One search service, BRS After Dark, was offered at no charge. However, shortly after the service was initiated, costs associated with this service nearly doubled due to a change in pricing structure. This proved to be very costly for the library. After re-evaluation of this service by reference staff management, free searches were discontinued and an effort to obtain internal grant funds for searching was made.

The purpose of the grant request was to provide five CD-ROM (compact disc read-only-memory) databases and to install these databases in the reference section of the main library.

In the summer of 1987, the university provided the funding necessary to purchase one-year subscriptions to five CD-ROM databases along with the corresponding hardware necessary for their operation. The library provided the furniture and supplies. The CD-ROM databases were selected on the basis of availability, observed use of print and electronic indexes by the reference staff, and the number of students and faculty in the university. The curriculum that the Technical Branch Libraries support was not included in the project due to offsite facilities for these disciplines.

The CD-ROM databases selected and their descriptions are as follows:

- *ABI/INFORM*—coverage includes all phases of business management and administration. Type of coverage is directed toward business and industry. Includes specific product and industry information. Presently indexes approximately 700 publications
- *ERIC*—complete database of educational material from Educational Resources Information Center (ERIC). This index corresponds to two print indexes, *Resources in Education* and *Current Index to Journals in Education*. ERIC indexes research reports, journals, and dissertations in addition to periodical literature
- *MEDLINE*—produced by the U.S. National Library of Medicine, MEDLINE is one of the major sources for biomedical information. This index corresponds to the printed indexes of *Index Medicus*, *Index to Dental Literature*, and *International Nursing Index*. In addition to indexing over 3,000 journals, MEDLINE covers monographs and symposia. The coverage is international
- *PsycLIT*—produced by the American Psychological Association, this index covers over 1,300 journals, technical reports, monographs, dissertations, studies reporting original research, reviews, conference reports, panel discussions, and case studies in the field of psychology
- *Sociofile*—this index corresponds to the print source, *Sociological Abstracts*. International in scope, the database covers sociology and related disciplines in the social and behavioral sciences. Sociofile indexes over 1,200 journals and other publications.

By October 1987, it became apparent that there were problems concerning the use of the CD-ROM stations. The reference staff observed that lines were forming at one or more of the stations throughout the day and evening. Patron's queries to the staff about the availability of additional stations were commonplace. Patrons also were observed leaving a line or going elsewhere when the station they needed was in use. It became apparent that five CD-ROM stations, each having a different index, were not sufficient to meet the level of service the library wanted to provide.

The reference staff conducted a literature review to determine if other libraries had had a similar problem and, if so, what steps they had taken. Although the literature indicated that many use studies have been performed in academic libraries, no literature study had quantitatively examined the number of CD-ROM stations needed to satisfy user needs within a fixed amount of time without there being a problem of lines or queuing. Neither had any study measured the number of students who leave the area where the stations are located due to the unavailability of the CD-ROM station in which they indicated an interest.

If such studies were available, they could provide guidelines to assist reference staff members in solving this type of problem. They could also provide a model that could be replicated in other libraries of similar size. (Figure 10-2 offers examples of writings pertinent to the discussion and resolution of the problem depicted in this example.)

Reference staff members questioned if a significant number of patrons:

- Were leaving the area without using the stations because of the unavailability of the stations
- Had to wait to use the stations because other patrons were searching.

They also wondered if it were possible to determine the number of stations needed to satisfy demand with a 90% probability of success. All staff members

Figure 10-2. Examples of Pertinent Writings

Borgman, Christine L. and Neal K. Kaske. "Online Catalogs in the Public Library: A Study to Determine the Number of Terminals Required for Public Access," in *Proceedings of the 43d ASIS Annual Meeting*, vol. 19. White Plains, New York: Knowledge Industry Publications, 1980, pp. 273–275.

Burr, Robert L. "Evaluating Library Collections: A Case Study," *Journal of Academic Librarianship*, 5 (November 1979): 256–260.

Hodowanec, George V. "Analysis of Variables Which Help to Predict Book and Periodical Use," *Library Acquisitions: Practice and Theory*, 4 (1980): 75–85.

Knox, A. Whitney and Bruce A. Miller. "Predicting the Number of Public Computer Terminals Needed for an On-Line Catalog: A Queuing Theory Approach," *Library Research*, 2 (Spring 1980–1981): 95–100.

McGrath, William E. "Predicting Book Circulation by Subject in a University Library," *Collection Management*, 1 (Fall/Winter 1976): 7–26.

_____. "Relationship between Hard/Soft, Pure/Applied and Life/Nonlife Disciplines and Subject Book Use in a University Library," *Information Processing & Management*, 14 (1978): 17–28.

Tolle, John E. *Public Access Terminals: Determining Quality Requirements*. Dublin, Ohio: OCLC, 1984.

were agreed that a study to investigate the following objectives would assist them in making a decision about what system requirements could better satisfy patron demand. The objectives of the study were:

- To determine the number of patrons who leave the area in which the CD-ROM stations are placed without referencing them because others are using these stations
- To determine the cumulative number of patrons waiting to use the stations over a fixed amount of time
- To establish the number of CD-ROM terminals needed in order to assure patrons of a .10 probability of them being able to use a station without waiting, that is, a patron wanting to do a search would be successful, without waiting, 90% of the time.

Methodology

The reference staff assigned trained student workers to observe activity at the CD-ROM stations. The librarians assigned two students to this activity in blocks of two hours from 9 a.m. to 9 p.m. each day, except Saturday and Sunday. On Saturday, they assigned students from 9 a.m. to 5 p.m. and on Sunday from 2 p.m. to 10 p.m. These hours correspond to the library weekend schedule.

For each day, the students completed a reporting sheet listing the time that a patron began a search, the time that person concluded a search, the number of people waiting to use a station, and the number leaving the line for each CD-ROM station. Figure 10-3 reprints the reporting sheet. Because the library has 135 student staff helpers and because no other major projects were underway, the director decided to have data collection extend from October 1, 1987 to November 30, 1987 and from March 1, 1988 to April 30, 1988, with the exception of holidays. These time periods for the study were selected because they had been established as the periods of greatest demand, as reflected by the number of circulation records, interlibrary loan requests, and reference desk transactions in previous years.

Student helpers worked a minimum of 30 minutes with a reference librarian initially. If that librarian was satisfied that the student knew how to record the observations accurately, that student was permitted to collect data. Still, at periodical intervals, reference personnel monitored data collection and the accuracy of the information supplied on the sheets. If a student was unsure that a patron wanted to use a station or if that person was there simply to visit friends, the student was instructed to ask that person if s/he was waiting to use a station.

The survey was conducted every other day for two weeks in September 1987, to determine if any problems in the methodology were apparent. The staff also compiled weekly summaries from the completed reporting sheets.

Figure 10-3.   Reporting Sheet

CD-ROM Station (name) _____			Date _____	
Start Time	Finish Time	Amount of Time	Number Waiting	Number Leaving
	Total Time: Average Time:		Total:	Total:

In May, 1988, the library completed the study and analyzed the data. Tables 10-3 and 10-4 indicate the type of data that they collected.

Statistical Applications

In order to determine what statistical method could best serve as a model for determining CD-ROM station need, it was necessary to inventory the existing conditions. In this case, the demand for CD-ROM stations appeared greater than the system's ability to support the service. Given this condition, a queue develops. An approach to determining how to balance the demand on a system (in this case, the number of patrons wanting to use the system) with the capacity of the system (in this case, the number of CD-ROM stations) involves a statistical procedure that quantifies delay. The statistical application model for the sample involved here is probability theory.

Probability sampling is defined as a kind of sampling in which every member or object in the population has a chance of being selected. The sampling takes place by chance, that is, it is random. The likelihood, or probability, that an event will occur is taken into account when calculating estimates from the observed sample. It is often of interest to determine how many times an event is

Table 10-3.   Example of A Completed Form

CD-ROM Station (name) ABI/INFORM

Start Time	Finish Time	Amount of Time	Number Waiting	Number Leaving
9:05	9:20	15	0	0
9:20	9:35	15	1	0
9:35	9:47	12	1	1
9:47	10:05	17	4	2
10:05	10:20	15	2	0
10:20	10:43	23	1	0
10:43	10:53	10	3	2
10:53	11:03	10	1	0
11:03	11:30	27	3	3
11:30	11:52	22	2	1
11:52	12:07	15	1	0
12:07	12:40	33	3	1
12:40	12:58	18	2	0
12:58	1:09	11	1	1
1:09	1:35	26	0	0
1:35	2:00	25	1	0
2:00	2:35	35	1	1
2:35	2:47	12	2	1
2:47	3:23	36	3	3
3:23	4:05	47	3	1
4:05	4:22	17	2	0
4:22	4:45	empty		
4:45	5:11	26	0	0
5:15	6:03	48	1	0
6:03	6:20	17	2	0
6:20	6:48	28	3	2
6:48	7:11	23	2	1
7:11	7:40	29	1	0
7:40	8:01	21	0	0
8:01	8:23	22	1	0
8:23	8:50	27	2	1
		628	49	21

Total Number of Users: 30
Average Time/Use: 22.73 minutes

WEEKLY SUMMARY—ABI/INFORM

Number of Users: 217
Average Time/Search: 21.73
Number Waiting: 81
Number Leaving: 62

Table 10-4. Station Use Summary Statistics

Date	Number of Users	Average Time/ Use	Number Waiting	Number Leaving
		ABI/INFORM		
10/87	653	24.31	1287	629
11/87	670	18.80	1404	691
3/88	660	19.20	1374	734
4/88	647	17.40	1421	796
	2630	79.71	5486	2850
		ERIC		
10/87	953	31.02	624	324
11/87	1140	28.90	671	399
3/88	1187	30.12	546	379
4/88	920	28.01	639	501
	4200	118.05	2480	1603
		MEDLINE		
10/87	742	33.06	301	124
11/87	803	27.97	259	98
3/88	721	28.34	211	117
4/88	674	27.81	187	151
	2940	117.18	958	490
		PsycLIT		
10/87	1044	23.12	179	154
11/87	1015	24.57	214	201
3/88	998	21.02	196	231
4/88	1083	22.91	222	189
	4140	91.62	811	775
		Sociofile		
10/87	875	26.70	201	318
11/87	930	28.12	282	401
3/88	845	25.73	309	373
4/88	890	26.84	400	399
	3540	107.39	1192	1491

likely to occur. In the case of the CD-ROM stations, there is a probability (p) that some patrons will be unsuccessful at finding the station they need available. This study attempted to find out how many successful and unsuccessful events were occurring and how to reduce the number of unsuccessful events.

To find the probability that a CD-ROM station is either available or unavailable when needed, three assumptions have to be made. First, a random number (n) of individuals will participate. Second, n is normally distributed and, third, the probability for the success of each event is the same. These conditions characterize a binomial distribution, one that describes the chance behavior of the number of times an event occurs in a given number of trials. When n is very large and the probability of occurrence of an event (p) is very small, there is a Poisson distribution. The corresponding formula is:

$$P(x) = \lambda^x \, e^{-\lambda}/x!$$

$P(x)$ equals the probability that x number of users will arrive in a given period of time, lambda (λ)[1] is the expected number of arrivals during that period of time, e is the natural logarithm or 2.71828, and $x!$ is 0,1,2,3, ... Note that in the formula x is a superscript over lambda and then lambda is a negative superscript over e.

The Poisson distribution is a useful probability model for events occurring randomly over time, as in the selection of one book from a large number of books. In the problem of CD-ROM station availability, there are a large number of patrons who could try to use a station during any one period of time, but normally only a few instances of this situation would occur in a given time. The statistical models used in queuing analysis can provide information on how many stations will be required to meet a desired level of service. The reference staff decided that less than a 90% chance of success at finding the terminal needed without having to wait was unacceptable. If a patron at any given point in time could have a 90% chance of finding the CD-ROM station they needed available, the service level requirement would be acceptable.

Table 10-4 provides summary data for Sociofile. Some 3,540 patrons used that CD-ROM station for a total of 86,400 minutes. The average search time was 26.847 minutes. When calculating the Poisson distribution to determine probability, it is necessary first to calculate lambda. To calculate this value, we use the following data:

λ = 3540 (total users)/(86400 (minutes))/26.847 (average time) = 1.20 users/time available.

The average time is divided into the minutes first and then that result is divided into 3540.

Determination of the probability that four patrons would arrive at any given hour ($x!$ or x factorial) to use the terminals is a two-step process. First, $4 \times 3 \times 2 \times 1 = 24$. Second,

$$(1.1)^4 \, (e^{-1.1})/4 \times 3 \times 2 \times 1 = 1.4641 \times .3328/24 = .021.$$

---

[1] Lambda, a measure of association for crosstabs, applies to nominal data. Lambda involves a prediction of the value of the dependent variable, knowing the value of the independent variable. Known as a *proportional reduction in error* statistic, lambda selects the category with the most cases—modal category. For the example illustrated here, lambda is the expected number of arrivals in any given period of time.

Therefore, there would be a 2.1% chance that four users would arrive during the period of an hour. Over a period of 12 hours with 48 users arriving, it could be expected that there would be about 15 minutes in which four users would arrive. This can be seen if we multiply .021 (2.1%) by 12 hours/day: .021 × 12 hours = .252 hours/day. This amount can be multiplied by 60 (the number of minutes in an hour). Therefore, .252 hours × 60 min/hour = 15.12, or approximately 15 minutes.

Application of the Poisson distribution method to the results of the survey indicates the probabilities of x users entering the system (see Table 10-5). According to the Poisson distribution, the library can usually expect between one and three users to arrive at the terminals in the course of an hour.

These results can be verified by comparing them to the observed results and testing them with the chi-square test. This test can compare an observed sample distribution with a theoretical frequency distribution. The chi-square test, the appropriate nonparametric test for nominal or ordinal level measurement, examines the sample or Poisson distribution of the number of occurrences of patron use within a normal distribution; the assumption is, indeed, that the variables were normally distributed.

The chi-square test could examine the observed service time distribution (O) and the corresponding theoretical frequencies (E). The low chi-square value indicates that there is a "goodness-of-fit." A level of significance of .05 or 5% with four degrees of freedom ($n - 1$ of the sample equals $5 - 1$, or 4) must exceed 9.49 (see the chi-square table in a statistics textbook). However, our value is less. Therefore, there is no reason to assume that the model cannot be described by the Poisson distribution. Since, by definition, one of the conditions of the Poisson distribution is random events, no association between variables was expected and correlation tests were inappropriate. Nonetheless, using statistical analysis software, the librarians could construct a correlation matrix for Spearman's rho values. In doing so, no correlation between any two stations was found. Therefore, the librarians assume that these variables are random and independent of each other.

The observed values of chi-square were well described by the theoretical model. Table 10-6 offers summary chi-square values that were determined

Table 10-5.   Application of the Poisson Distribution

Number of Arrivals	Poisson Distribution	Expected Number of Hours during Survey That Will Equal X
0	.333	3.996
1	.366	4.392
2	.201	2.412
3	.074	.888
4	.021	.252
5	.004	.048

through the use of StatPac Gold. Table 10-7 provides a sample calculation of a chi-square value.

To apply the Poisson distribution according to the formula previously given, it is necessary to determine the number of users/time available (λ). For Sociofile, we find that

$$\lambda = 3540 \text{ users}/(86400)/26.847 = 1.10 \text{ users/time available.}$$

Table 10-6.   Chi-square Values for Three CD-ROM Terminals

No. of Users/hr.	P(x)	Cum P(x)	Theoretical Arrival Rate E	Observed Arrival O
		ABI/INFORM		
0	.407	.047	17.5	16
1	.365	.772	15.69	17
2	.165	.937	7.09	6
3	.050	.987	2.15	3
4	.011	.998	0.473	1
				43

Total Number Users in 4 Months = 2630
Time Available for Use   = 86,400/29.5125 min/search
Chi-Square   = .5392
Degrees of Freedom   = 4

		ERIC		
0	.333	.333	23.3	21
1	.366	.699	25.62	28
2	.201	.900	14.07	15
3	.074	.974	5.18	6
4	.021	.995	0.021	0
				70

Total Number Users in 4 Months = 4200
Time Available for Use   = 86,400/21.73min/search
Chi-Square   = .3123
Degrees of Freedom   = 4

		MEDLINE		
0	.368	.368	13.61	16
1	.368	.736	13.61	12
2	.184	.920	6.8	7
3	.061	.981	2.25	2
4	.015	.996	0.555	1
				37

Total Number Users in 4 Months = 2940
Time Available for Use   = 86,400/29.295min/search
Chi-Square   = .4207
Degrees of Freedom   = 4

Table 10-7. Sample Chi-square Calculation

$$x^2 = \Sigma(O - E)^2/E$$

x^2 = chi-square
O = the number of cases observed
E = the number of cases expected (theoretically)

x	O	E(P(x)(49))	O − E	(O − E)²	(O − E)²/E
0	13	16.3	−3.3	10.89	.66
1	20	17.93	1.15	1.24	.069
2	10	9.84	.16	.0256	.0026
3	5	3.62	1.38	1.90	.526
4	1	1.029	− .029	.00084	.0008
5	0	.049	1.049	.0024	.0489

x = .7557
df = 5
level of significance = 98.98

To apply the Poisson distribution formula for Sociofile, we use 1.10 as λ and $P(x)$ as the probability that x number of users will arrive in a given time at that station. Table 10-8 indicates that to satisfy the criteria that a user should arrive and have only a 10% chance of waiting, the cumulative probability, cum $P(x)$, must be least .90. From the table, it is evident that two terminals ought to satisfy the requirements for this station.

Clearly, the Poisson distribution describes the data and estimates the number of terminals needed. (Many statistics textbooks devote a section to a discussion of the Poisson distribution.) To meet the stated objectives for service requirements, the library will have to add one terminal to each existing station; therefore, the number of terminals will double (from the five at present to ten).

Probability theory can characterize what happens in a library when random events occur over a given period of time. While hand calculations are tedious and prone to error, statistical analysis software can produce reliable results, assuming that the data were correctly entered and carefully gathered.

Table 10-8. Application of the Poisson Distribution Formula for *Sociofile*

x	P(x)	cum P(x)
0	.333	.333
1	.366	.699
→ 2	.201	→ .900
3	.074	.974
4	.021	.995
5	.004	.999

Chapter Eleven
Communication of Research Findings

PREPARATION OF THE REPORT/MANUSCRIPT

What to Include

Logical organization and presentation of a report are essential. Figure 11-1 offers a typical scheme for organizing a report. Each section should logically lead to the next and provide supporting information that will encourage reader understanding and acceptance of the completed research. Terms therefore should be clearly defined, assumptions identified, and indicators of reliability and validity provided.

A question-by-question presentation of data does not lend itself to easy readability and comprehension. Rather, the findings section typically addresses hypotheses and/or research questions. Ideally, a paper should include descriptive statistics presented in the form of tables and figures, and perhaps other graphic presentations that assist in the understanding, comparison, and application of the findings (see Tate, 1989).

A paper submitted for publication "speaks" to the editor and editorial board of a journal, and their perceptions about reader interests. A published article communicates with fellow researchers and, it is hoped, a larger community. Attracting that larger community requires the selection of a significant topic, making the article appealing and eye-catching, and perhaps provocative. Of course, an internal report delivered to library managers "speaks" to the information needs of these individuals. Decision makers do not want to labor through a detailed and lengthy report that is not well written.

Research has shown that the format in which information is presented has an independent effect on decision-making facilitation (Bybee, 1981, p. 364). An unattractive, hard-to-read, disorganized, and incoherent paper is not likely to assist in decision making. Researchers must adapt "information presentation formats to decision making" and the intended audience (Ibid., p. 343).

Ease of readability, combined with the significance of a topic to a reader, influence the extent to which a research article is scanned or read in its entirety by a large audience. Readability "involves the communication of ideas" and

Figure 11-1.   Typical Organization of a Report/Manuscript

1. Title Page
2. Table of Contents (applies to a report, not a manuscript)
3. Abstract or Executive Summary
4. Introduction
   A. Background
   B. Key Terms and Concepts
5. Statement of the Problem
6. Literature Review
   A. Places the problem in context
   B. Draws upon findings and experiences of previous research
7. Logical Structure (conceptual framework)
   This is similar to a menu in a restaurant. The logical structure identifies all the items (including variables) from which the researcher selects. The researcher then justifies the selections.
8. Objectives, Hypotheses and/or Research Questions
   A. Define key terms
   B. Identify assumptions
9. Procedures
   A. Research design—sampling?
   B. Methodology(ies) used
   C. Reliability and validity indicators
10. Limitations of Study
11. Findings
    A. Introduction to how the presentation is organized
    B. Appropriate tables, graphs, figures, and description
    C. Relation of findings to other similar studies
    D. Interpretation of the findings (what do they mean?)
12. Summary, Conclusions, and Recommendations
    Recommendations are extremely important for reports submitted to library managers. What should be done as a result of these findings?
13. Notes
14. Appendices
    A. Copy of the data collection instrument(s) used in the study
    B. Other items as appropriate
15. Bibliography
    A. Sources/references referred to in the body of the paper
    B. Sources/references for additional information
16. Index (applies to a report, not a manuscript)

reader success in understanding the ideas, reading the article "at optimum speed and . . . [finding that article] interesting" (Richardson, 1977, p. 20). More basically, readability attempts to ensure "that a given piece of writing reaches and affects its audience in the way that the author intends" (Tekfi, 1987, p. 262).

The Use of Software Writing Aids

One author who had a research study accepted for publication in a major journal in the discipline of library and information science told one of the authors of this book that the editor of that journal shared a comment by one of the reviewers of the manuscript. That comment was "this paper is so much better written than most other papers I have reviewed. I am tempted to recommend publication solely on the basis of the excellent writing." Reinforcing this comment is the experience of the same author of this book. He has served for more than a decade as either the managing editor or editor of a journal. Figure 11-2 summarizes writing style weaknesses that he has actually observed in manuscripts submitted for publication.

Figure 11-2.   Common Writing Deficiences in Manuscripts Submitted for Publication

Awkward sentences	Not following submission requirements of the journal—providing an abstract, etc.
Extensive quoting from sources	Not footnoting where necessary
Handling of he or she/he	Not paraphrasing where useful
Heavy repetition of same word in paragraph—lack of variety in noun and verb choices	Passive voice
It's for its	Sentence fragments
Lack of illustrations and tables—inferior quality of art work	Thoughts open to different interpretations, or thoughts not well organized
Lack of transition between sentences and paragraphs	Trite expressions
Lack of clearly stated thesis at beginning of paper	Typos and misspellings
Need a conclusion that returns to thesis	Verb and noun disagreement
Need to capture reader interest	Wordiness
No use of subheadings in paper	Wrong verb tense

Some papers lack a statement of the problem or properly worded hypotheses (see Chapter 6). They may also omit components of the report identified in Figure 11-1. Potential authors might obtain a copy of a journals's "guide to contributors," in part to ensure that they have supplied the specified number of copies and adhered to the stylistic requirements specified for footnotes and references. In a number of instances, the writing style of manuscripts submitted for publication is weak. The authors might make excessive use of passive voice. Further, their manuscripts might contain syntax errors, wordy sentences, sentence fragments, awkward and unclear sentences, and split infinitives.

Chapter 3 discussed the use of microcomputer software that serve as writing aids. This section illustrates that the use of such aids can identify potential weaknesses in one's writing and, it is hoped, lead to a better quality of writings among the manuscripts submitted for publication. This type of software enables authors to review their sentence structure and word choices. Using either WordPerfect or WordStar, Version 5, authors can also program the format of the bibliography as they wordprocess the text of the manuscript, thereby ensuring that they are meeting the journal's specifications.

At times, authors are under strict requirements about the number of words to use in a review essay or book review. Writing aid software counts the number of words and may contain a spelling checker. Authors should also consult a thesaurus (perhaps one attached to wordprocessing software) to guarantee that a paragraph, for example, does not make repeated use of the same verb.

Figure 11-3 takes portions of an article and, for the purposes of this demonstration, has introduced some common mistakes related to writing. (These mistakes were not contained in the published article.) Figures 11-4 and 11-5 represent a summary of the diagnostic performed by RightWriter, versions 2 and 3. The latter version *flags* more items and contains a refined readability formula. Authors should evaluate the recommendations offered by writing aid software. Instead of automatically accepting all of the recommendations,[1] they should determine which suggestions are applicable and which are not.

Grammatik III[tm], a product of Reference Software (330 Townsend Street, Suite 123, San Francisco, CA 94107), costs approximately the same as RightWriter. It performs many functions similar to RightWriter; however, Grammatik III picks up more grammar, stylistic, phrase, and mechanical errors. It discovered, for instance, the incorrect use of "there" in the second line of text in Figure 11-3.

Figure 11-6 contains the rewritten sections of the paper. Note that ultimately we did not accept all the suggestions offered by the writing aid software. The version contained in the figure still requires a high reading level. Shorter and simpler sentences would have dramatically reduced the readability level.

---

[1] RightWriter displays a limited understanding of word usage. For example, it equates "implementing" with "a tool" and "institute" as "start." It also has a limited vocabulary; e.g., it fails to recognize "desirability" as a word. RightWriter, however, does distinguish between "affect" and "effect."

Figure 11-3.   Portions of an Article*

Librarians do not completely comprehend the nature and extent of of student perceptions about them and there role in the educational process. With the trend in academia toward independent study, bibliographic instruction, and the application of educational psychology to reference desk service, precise knowledge of student perceptions and receptivity to librarians is needed. The extent and types of misperceptions must be realized before the image of librarianship can be upgraded with regard to students.

In order to acquire more insights into student perceptions, the study was guided by the following research question: Do students believe that librarians do less than they actually do in terms of duties? The question was examined in the context of the following variables: age, class level, subject area in which students are majoring,, gender, student purpose for using the library and number of hours spent each week in using the library; and whether students received a library lecture conducted through the classroom or a library orientation.

As for duties of reference librarians, students emphasized their role in locating needed information. Five percent indicated collection building, but none suggested participation in bibliographic instruction programs. Suspected activities included, among others, managing the library, classifying and shelving books, and knowledge of their department. Mann-Whitney analysis indicates differences in the variables of sex ($p < .01$), age ($p < .05$), purpose for using the library ($p. < .001$), and having library classroom instruction ($p < .001$). Class level, however, was not significant.

Students have difficulty in differentiating among library staff as to their roles. As long as their needs are met, they appear to be indifferent as to whether or not the person is actually a "librarian."

Librarians need constantly to emphasize their subject expertise and the reasons why students should differentiate among library staff members. Service desks staffed by professionals should be clearly marked and apparent. Bibliographic instruction programs should promote and instruct not only about library collections and search strategies, but also the role and abilities of academic librarians as educators.

Hopefully, the researchers have taken the necessary precautions to ensure that their findings did not come from a self-selected group. However, future studies must further persuade nonusers that although they are not currently utilizing the library, librarians still benefit from their comments.

*Adapted from Hernon and Pastine (1977). Certain writing mistakes have been intentionally inserted into the text to illustrate the value of software that serves as writing aids.

Research may require a higher reading level than the "average" American posseses. Studies apparently have not probed the preferred reading levels of librarians. Presumably, many librarians will examine technical report literature and scholarly writings; such works may well average higher than grade level 15 in readability. However, instead of reading an article, they might browse it. Reading comprehension and maintaining reader interest become more difficult with hard-to-read studies.

The Use of Graphics

Graphic techniques, such as bar graphs, line graphs, and pie charts, provide a visual representation of the data. Some journals, however, may discourage the

Figure 11-4.   Application of RightWriter (Version 2) to the Article*

Librarians do not completely comprehend the nature and extent of of student perceptions about them and there role in the
<<REPEATED WORD>>
educational process. With the trend in academia toward independent study, bibliographic instruction, and the application of educational psychology to reference desk service, precise knowledge of student perceptions and receptivity to librarians is needed. The extent and types of misperceptions must be realized
<<PASSIVE VOICE: is needed.>>
<<LONG SENTENCE: 31 WORDS>>
<<COMPLEX SENTENCE>>
before the image of librarianship can be upgraded with regard to
<<PASSIVE VOICE: be realized>>
students.
In order to acquire more insights into student perceptions,
<<WORDY. REPLACE In order to BY to>>
the study was guided by the following research question: Do
<<PASSIVE VOICE: was guided>>
students believe that librarians do less than they actually do in terms of duties? The question was examined in the context of the
<<LONG SENTENCE: 33 WORDS>>
<<PASSIVE VOICE: was examined>>
following variables: age, class level, subject area in which students are majoring,, gender, student purpose for using the
<<UNNECESSARY COMMA>>
library and number of hours spent each week in using the library; and whether students received a library lecture conducted through the classroom or a library orientation.
<<LONG SENTENCE: 54 WORDS>>
<<COMPLEX SENTENCE>>
As for duties of reference librarians, students emphasized their role in locating needed information. Five percent indicated collection buildling, but none suggested participation in bibliographic instruction program. Suspected activities included, among others, managing the library, classifying and shelving books, and knowledge of their department. Mann-Whitney
<<COMPLEX SENTENCE>>
analysis indicates differences in the variables of sex (p < .01), age (p < .05), purpose for using the library (p. < .001), and having library classroom instruction (p < .001). Class level,
<<LONG SENTENCE: 29 WORDS>>
<<COMPLEX SENTENCE>>
however, was not significant.
Students have difficulty in differentiating among library staff as to their roles. As long as their needs are met, they
<<PASSIVE VOICE: are met,>>
appear to be indifferent as to whether or not the person is
<<WEAK: appear to be>>
<<REPLACE: as to whether BY whether>>
actually a "librarian."

Figure 11-4.   (*Continued*)

<<LONG SENTENCE: 23 WORDS>>
Librarians need constantly to emphasize their subject expertise and the reasons why students should differentiate among
<<IS THIS VAGUE? expertise>>
library staff members. Service desks staffed by professionals
should be clearly marked and apparent. Bibliographic instruction
<<PASSIVE VOICE: be clearly marked>>
programs should promote and instruct not only about library collections and search strategies, but also the role and abilities of
academic librarians as educators.
<<LONG SENTENCE: 26 WORDS>>
<<COMPLEX SENTENCE>>
Hopefully,   the   researchers   have   taken   the   necessary
<<CONSIDER OMITTING Hopefully>>
precautions to ensure that their findings did not come from a
<<REPLACE ensure BY SIMPLER: be sure>>
self-selected group. However, future studies must further persuade nonusers that although they are not currently utilizing
<<REPLACE utilizing BY SIMPLER: use>>
the library, librarians still benefit from their comments.

SUMMARY

READABILITY INDEX: 15.01
Readers need a 15th grade level of education to understand.
The writing is complex and may be difficult to read.

STRENGTH INDEX: 0.00
The writing can be made more direct by using:
- the active voice
- shorter sentences
- more common words
SENTENCE STRUCTURE RECOMMENDATIONS:
   1.   Most sentences contain multiple clauses.
   Try to use more simple sentences.

---

*RightWriter, RightSoft Inc., 4545 Samuel Street, Sarasota,
FL 34233-9912.

use of graphics even if the author supplies copies in camera-ready form. The
reason is that graphics consume more space in the article. With many journals
now under strict limitations on the length of an issue or volume, editors are often
careful about the number of pages allotted to a given manuscript. On the other
hand, graphics can play a larger role in monographs, internal reports, and oral
presentations before decision makers or a conference audience.

Review of the Final Paper

Prior to submission of a manuscript to a publisher, editor, funding group, or
decision maker, the researcher should review Figure 11-7, his/her answers to

Figure 11-5.   Application of RightWriter (Version 3) to the Article

Librarians do not completely comprehend the nature and extent of of student perceptions about them and there role in the
<<REPEATED WORD>>
educational process. With the trend in academia toward
<<IS THIS JUSTIFIED? trend>>
independent study, bibliographic instruction, and the application of educational psychology to reference desk service, precise knowledge of student perceptions and receptivity to librarians is needed. The extent and types of misperceptions must be
<<PASSIVE VOICE: is needed>>
<<SPLIT INTO 2 SENTENCES?>>
<<LONG SENTENCE: 31 WORDS>>
realized before the image of librarianship can be upgraded with
<<PASSIVE VOICE: be realized>>
<<PASSIVE VOICE: be upgraded>>
regard to students.
<<WORDY. REPLACE with regard to BY about>>
In order to acquire more insights into student perceptions,
<<WORDY. REPLACE In order to BY to>>
<<REPLACE acquire BY SIMPLER get or gain?>>
the study was guided by the following research question: Do
<<PASSIVE VOICE: was guided>>
students believe that librarians do less than they actually do in terms of duties? The question was examined in the context of the
<<WORDY. REPLACE in terms of BY in or for>>
<<SPLIT INTO 2 SENTENCES?>>
<<LONG SENTENCE: 33 WORDS>>
<<PASSIVE VOICE: was examined>>
following variables: age, class level, subject area in which students are majoring,, gender, student purpose for using the
<<IS THIS PUNCTUATION CORRECT? ,,>>
library and number of hours spent each week in using the library; and whether students received a library lecture conducted through the classroom or a library orientation.
<<SPLIT INTO 2 SENTENCES?>>
<<LONG SENTENCE: 54 WORDS>>
As for duties of reference librarians, students emphasized their role in locating needed information. Five percent indicated collection building, but none suggested participation
<<REPLACE indicated BY FORM
OF SIMPLER show or say?>>
in bibliographic instruction programs. Suspected activities included, among others, managing the library, classifying and shelving books, and knowledge of their department. Mann-Whitney
<<SPLIT INTO 2 SENTENCES?>>
analysis indicates differences in the variables of sex (p < .01),
<<REPLACE indicates BY FORM OF
SIMPLER show or say?>>
age (p < .05), purpose for using the library (p. < .001), and

Figure 11-5.   (*Continued*)

<<IS THIS A COMPLETE SENTENCE?>>
having library classroom instruction (p < .001). Class level,
<<IS THIS AMBIGUOUS?>>
<<IS THIS A COMPLETE SENTENCE?>>
however, was not significant.
Students have difficulty in differentiating among library staff
as to their roles. As long as their needs are met, they
<<PASSIVE VOICE: are met>>
appear to be indifferent as to whether or not the person is
<<WEAK: appear to be>>
<<WORDY. REPLACE as to whether BY about whether>>
actually a "librarian."
<<SINGLE WORD ENCLOSED BY QUOTES>>
Librarians need constantly to emphasize their subject expertise and the reasons why students should differentiate among
<<IS THIS JUSTIFIED: expertise>>
library staff members. Service desks staffed by professionals
should be clearly marked and apparent. Bibliographic instruction
<<PASSIVE VOICE: be clearly marked>>
<<REPLACE apparent BY SIMPLER clear or plain?>>
programs should promote and instruct not only about library collections and search strategies, but also the role and abilities of
academic librarians as educators.
<<SPLIT INTO 2 SENTENCES?>>
<<LONG SENTENCE: 26 WORDS>>
Hopefully, the researchers have taken the necessary
<<WEAK SENTENCE START: Hopefully>>
precautions to ensure that their findings did not come from a
<<REPLACE ensure BY SIMPLER be sure?>>
self-selected group. However, future studies must further persuade nonusers that although they are not currently utilizing
<<REPLACE currently BY SIMPLER now?>>
<<REPLACE utilizing BY FORM OF SIMPLER use?>>
the library, librarians still benefit from their comments.

SUMMARY

READABILITY INDEX: 13.90
    4th   6th   8th   10th   12th   14th
| **** | **** | **** | **** | **** | **** | **** | **** | **** | **** |
SIMPLE |------- GOOD -------| COMPLEX
    Readers need a 14th grade level of education.
    The writing is complex and may be difficult to read.

STRENGTH INDEX: 0.00
    0.0   0.5   1.0
| * | | | | | | | | | |
WEAK   STRONG
    The writing can be made more direct by using:
                - the active voice

(*continued*)

Figure 11-5.   (*Continued*)

- shorter sentences
- less wordy phrases
- fewer weak phrases
- more common words

SENTENCE STRUCTURE RECOMMENDATIONS:

1. Most sentences contain multiple clauses.
    Try to use more simple sentences.

Figure 11-6.   Rewritten Portions of the Article Depicted in Figure 11-3

Librarians do not completely comprehend the nature and extent of student perceptions about them and their role in the educational process. With the trend in academia toward independent study, bibliographic instruction, and the application of educational psychology to reference desk service, the library profession would benefit from precise knowledge of student perceptions and receptivity to librarians. Before upgrading the image of librarians, librarians must realize the extent and types of student misperceptions.

To acquire more insights into student perceptions, the researchers investigated by the following research question: Do students believe that librarians do less than they actually do? The question was examined in relation to following variables: age, class level, subject area in which the students major, gender, student purpose for using the library and number of hours spent each week in using the library, and whether students had received a bibliographic instruction presentation.

As for duties of reference librarians, students emphasized their role in locating needed information. Five percent indicated collection building, but none suggested participation in bibliographic instruction programs. Suspected activities included, among others, managing the library, classifying and shelving books, and knowledge of their department. Mann-Whitney analysis indicates differences in the variables of sex ($p < .01$), age ($p < .05$), purpose for using the library ($p. < .001$), and having library classroom instruction ($p < .001$). Class level, however, was not a statistically significant variable.

Students have difficulty in differentiating among library staff as to their roles. As long as they receive the information needed, they are indifferent whether the person is actually a librarian.

Librarians need constantly to emphasize their subject expertise and the reasons why students should differentiate among library staff members. Service desks staffed by professionals should be easily identifiable. Bibliographic instruction programs should promote and instruct not only about library collections and search strategies, but also the role and abilities of academic librarians as educators.

The researchers have taken the necessary precautions to ensure that their findings did not come from a self-selected group. However, future studies must further persuade nonusers that although they are not currently using the library, librarians still benefit from their comments.

Grade Level of Writing: 16
Number of Words: 344

Figure 11-7.   Suggested Criteria for Judging a Research Report*

1. Background
   a. Is the title descriptive, accurate, and of a reasonable length?
   b. Does the introduction give a clear indication of the general scope of the research?
   c. Is the problem clearly stated, analyzed into definite subordinate questions or issues?
   d. Is the logic of the analysis of the problem sound?
   e. What is the hypothesis or research question?
   f. Is the hypothesis of social or theoretical significance, and stated so that it can be resolved or tested?
   g. Are the independent and dependent variables clear? Any logical consequences or implications?
   h. Are the basic assumptions needed to support the hypothesis made clear?
   i. Are operational or working definitions provided?
   j. Is the coverage of previous, related research adequate? Is the . . . [report] related to the earlier studies?
2. Design of the Study
   a. Does the research design seem adequate and logical for the solution of the problem?
   b. Are the reasons for its choice adequately explained?
   c. Was the methodology explained in an understandable way so that it can be replicated?
   d. If important terms are used in an unusual sense, are they defined?
   e. Are the data to be collected adequate for the solution of the problem?
   f. Are the data sufficiently quantitative (when appropriate) for the solution of the problem?
   g. Are the instruments used by the investigator adequate reflections of the conceptual variables of the study?
   h. If sampling procedures were used, were they adequately explained?
   i. If the sample was supposedly random, was it in fact chosen so that each member of the population had an equal chance of being selected?
3. Treatment of the Data
   a. Are the data presented as an integral part of the logical solution of the problem?
   b. What techniques were used to analyze the quantitative or qualitative data? Do they seem to be appropriate and effective?
   c. Were graphical and/or tabular formats appropriately used to display pertinent data?

Figure 11-7. *(Continued)*

---

    d. Is there evidence of care and accuracy in the collection and treatment of the data?

    e. Is irrelevant material or information excluded?

    f. Do the inferences based on the data seem to be sound?

4. Summary and Conclusions

    a. Do the conclusions actually serve to answer questions or issues raised in the study?

    b. Are all conclusions based essentially on data made known to the reader?

    c. Are conclusions free from mere unsupported opinions?

    d. Are the limitations or qualifications of the conclusions clearly and concisely expressed?

    e. Are applications and recommendations, when included, judiciously made?

    f. Can the conclusions be generalized to a larger population?

    g. Did the researcher appear to be aware of the theoretical implications, if any, of the research?

    h. Did the researcher make recommendations for future research?

5. Appendices

    a. If there is an appendix, is it supplementary in nature, rather than essential to an understanding of the text?

    b. Does it include all original data?

6. Bibliography

    a. Does it appear that one style manual was followed, i.e., is the bibliographic style consistent?

---

  *Reprinted from Powell (1985), pp. 167–169.

such questions, and the "common deficiencies of papers" identified by Rayward (1980, p. 217). The better the quality of the paper—substance and presentation—the more likely that the paper will be acceptable to the funder, publisher, or editorial board. Also it is more likely that a well-written, internal report will have an impact—that is, lead to change and improved decision making.

PUBLICATION

Library researchers might decide to pursue formal publication of their study. As an alternative to placing the report in the ERIC clearinghouse system, or even the database of the National Technical Information Service, they might opt for either journal or monograph publication. For an article, they would probably seek

Figure 11-8.   Selected Readings and Directories on Publishing

Alley, Brian and Jennifer Cargill. *Librarian in Search of A Publisher: How to Get Published*. Phoenix, AZ: Oryx Press, 1986.

American Book Trade Directory. New York: Bowker, 1988.

Barzun, Jacques. "Behind the Blue Pencil," *Publisher's Weekly*, 226 (September 6, 1985): 28–30.

Budd, John. "Publication in Library & Information Science: The State of the Journal Literature," *Library Journal*, 113 (September 1, 1988): 125–131.

Directory of Publishing Opportunities in Journals and Periodicals. Chicago, IL: Marquis Academic Media, 1979–.

Dorn, F. J. "Do Scholarly Authors Need Literary Agents?," *Scholarly Publishing*, 14 (October 1982): 79–86.

Faas, Larry A. "Factors Involved in the Preparation and Submission of Manuscripts to Professional Journals," 1982 (ED 228 649).

Freeman, J. "Negotiating a College Textbook Contract," *PS*, 17 (Winter 1984): 41–48.

Hanna, S. S. "Looking for a Publisher: An Author's Odyssey in Academe," *Publisher's Weekly*, 224 (November 11, 1983): 17–19.

Hubbard, Linda S., ed. *1987 Publishers Directory*. 2 vols. Detroit, MI: Gale, 1986.

Johnson, Richard D. "Current Trends in Library Journal Editing," *Library Trends*, 36 (Spring 1988): 659–672.

————. "The Journal Literature of Librarianship," *Advances in Library and Information Science*, vol. 12. New York: Academic Press, 1982, pp. 127–150.

Literary Marketplace with Names and Numbers. New York: Bowker, 1972/73– (there is also an international literary marketplace).

Miles, Jack. "How to Lose Money Electronically: Word Processing and Social Structure of Scholarly Publishing," *Library Journal*, 109 (November 15, 1984): 2125–2128.

Mullins, Carolyn J. *A Guide to Writing and Publishing in the Social and Behavioral Sciences*. New York: Wiley, 1977.

Rinzler, C. E. "When Is a Manuscript Acceptable," *Publishers Weekly*, 224 (September 23, 1983): 26–28.

Sellen, Betty Carol. *Librarian/Author: A Practical Guide on How to Get Published*. New York: Neal-Schuman, 1985.

Shubik, M., et al. "On Contracting with Publishers: Author's Information Updated," *American Economic Review: Papers and Proceedings*, 73 (May 1983): 26–28.

Stevens, Norman D. and Nora B. Stevens. *Author's Guide to Journals in Library and Information Science*. New York: The Haworth Press, 1982.

Webb, T. "Authors as Compositor: Word Processor to Typesetter," *Scholarly Publishing*, 15 (January 1984): 177–190 (this periodical publishes other relevant articles).

Williams, M. "Writer and the Editor," *Scholarly Publishing*, 14 (February 1983): 149–154.

Writer's Market. Cincinnati, OH: Writer's Digest, 1930– .

publication in a *refereed* journal, one that submits papers to a formal, peer review process.

Figure 11-8, which identifies examples of readings and directories on publishing, may be of use to the first-time or occasional author. Nonetheless, this person is best advised to discuss his/her publishing interests with established authors and request suggestions on the best ways to proceed. As an alternative, the potential author might query a journal editor about his/her possible interest in receiving a paper on a particular topic. The author should still develop the paper so that it might appeal to different journals. In case one journal rejects the paper, other options for submission remain.

IMPROVING THE QUALITY OF THE LITERATURE

Publication ideally should lead to improvement in the quality of the literature of library and information science. Obviously, writings should reflect more (if not all) of the steps in the research process (see Chapter 1) and take every precaution to minimize threats to internal validity and reliability. In addition to relating study findings, more published research should discuss the quality of the data collected. If the data are not reliable, the degree to which they are valid is likely to decline; if the findings are not valid, the degree to which action research has utility is injured. The social science research process may require trade-offs among these criteria, especially in the case of management studies.

The literature of library and information science ought to include more examples of basic and applied research, including the development and testing of models. The evaluation of library programs, services, operations, and collections comprises a type of action research. When librarians conduct such research, that research should address managerial information needs, have direct application to decision making, and avoid the "so what" charge. Action research should contain fewer examples of "how we did it good in our library" and be consistent with established theory and principles.

The research literature should reflect a broader array of research topics and methodologies. When research involves the reporting and interpretation of data, the investigators, at least, should use descriptive statistics. It is hoped that more studies will involve the use of inferential statistics, even the more fundamental ones emphasized in Chapters 8 and 9.

With attention given to the types of concerns briefly identified here, the image, quality, and utility of the literature should increase. The danger, though, is that increasing the quality and sophistication of the literature may well outpace the ability of many librarians to understand and profit from the research. The skills of librarians as consumers and practitioners of research must keep pace with improvements in the quality of the literature. Clearly, "the skill of 'consuming' research is easily as important as conducting research" (Swisher and McClure, 1984, p. 16).

As a result, there is a need for continuing education programs on research and the role of statistics. Such programs could be offered through professional associations and library schools. More librarians might also take formal course offerings on research, evaluation, and statistics. Clearly, practitioners and library educators must work together to ensure that future challenges are met and librarianship remains an important profession and discipline in the communication and information fields. Meeting this challenge, however, necessitates that research becomes an integral part of library and information science and that more attention be given to the theoretical underpinnings of the discipline.

Perhaps the *purposes* and *goals* of the Library Research Round Table of the American Library Association might serve as an excellent foundation around which to build a dynamic and viable research literature. The purposes are to:

- Contribute toward the extension and improvement of library research
- Provide public program opportunities for describing and evaluating library research projects and for disseminating their findings
- Inform and educate ALA members concerning research techniques and their usefulness in obtaining information with which to reach administrative decisions and solve problems
- Expand the theoretical base of the field.
- Serve as a forum for discussion and action on issues related to the literature and information needs for the field of library and information science.

The five goals are as follows:

- Promote research which develops theory and paradigms for library and information science
- Explore the value of research in problem solving through the application of theoretical models
- Encourage investigation of research methods used in other disciplines
- Promote rigor in research methods
- Explore the practical applications of research findings to professional practice.

With the accomplishment of these aspirations, the research literature of library and information science would mature and perhaps become a model for those in other professions and disciplines.

PLANNING THE USE OF MANAGEMENT STATISTICS

As emphasized in a *SPEC FLYER* distributed by the Association of Research Libraries (1987, unpaged),

The collection and use of management statistics are of almost universal concern to academic library administrators as part of their effort to accurately describe their libraries' performance, evaluate and enhance effectiveness, and plan for the future. Although the need for management statistics and the potential for their use in decision making is acknowledged by research libraries, most are still searching for ways to reconcile internal needs with external requirements, and to develop systems for effective use of statistics.

Furthermore, "ARL libraries are devoting much time and effort to the preparation of statistical reports, both for themselves and external agencies" (Ibid.). The *SPEC FLYER* points out that these libraries were most likely to manipulate data through the use of LOTUS 1–2–3. The Statistical Package for the Social Sciences (SPSS), presumably the mainframe version, was cited second, and Super-Calc was listed third. Visicalc, Symphony, and dBASE III were infrequently mentioned. The type of software discussed in this book as well as in Hernon and Richardson (1988) apparently had minimal or no use.

This finding reinforces the conclusion of Wallace (1985) and this book that librarians predominately collect nominal level data and subject datasets to selected statistical analysis—primarily the calculation of percentages and perhaps a few other descriptive statistics. As this book has emphasized, librarians have other possibilities and should be aware of these.

In conclusion, quoting again from the *SPEC FLYER* (Ibid.),

The overriding purpose for data collection and analysis is to support good decision-making and planning. To do this requires an understanding of not only how to work with statistics, but also how to determine which combinations of data elements are valid for specific purposes—to reduce library tasks to their common denominators. With such a base, libraries could then address the issue of which statistics . . . can be used . . . to support management decisions and even the design of generic management information or decision support systems.

Research is a critically important management tool that assists librarians in planning and maintaining an environment of change and growth. Research and statistics support, but do not replace, decision making and planning.

Managers must ask "why" and "how can we improve?" Answers to these questions might necessitate data collection, the use of statistics, and the types of issues discussed in this book. More librarians and library school students ought to be aware of parametric and nonparametric tests, measurement scales, Type I and II errors, one- and two-tailed tests, statistical inference and hypothesis testing, independent and dependent variables, and so forth.

A diverse readership should understand the research literature of library and information science. That literature should encourage theory development, movement of library and information science from a field or profession to a discipline, and planning, action, and improvement. The purpose of consulting the literature, conducting research, and using statistical applications is to increase library effectiveness and efficiency; respond better and more forcefully to the information needs of present and potential clientele; and assume a leadership role among competing information providers in monitoring the information environment and providing access to knowledge records.

An underlying theme of this book is that the literature should be consulted, fully understood, and applied. Statistics are often an integral part of research that quantifies and measures units. Clearly, as more libraries develop decision support systems, question assumptions and ask "why" instead of "how," become involved in the collection of fill rates and other performance measures, and generate a host of other statistics, they must find ways to summarize datasets and separate significant from insignificant findings. Statistics cannot be avoided or left exclusively to researchers and statisticians. We must all embrace statistics but do so under a framework—the research process. Even the application of statistics to a dataset involves interpretation, while creation of the dataset may depend on numerous "judgement calls" (see McGrath, Martin, and Kulka, 1982). Rarely does library science operate as a natural science with the research conducted in a laboratory under tightly controlled conditions.

As Swisher and McClure (1984, p. 192) observe,

> Thus action research, without understanding the research process, statistical techniques, and decision making, is both dangerous and self-deluding. Given the complexities of our libraries, the myriad factors from the environment that affect library and information services, and the endless constraints under which librarians strive to provide a broad range of information services, action research that assists in improving effectiveness of information services which better meet the needs of clientele is a responsibility of *all* librarians. Research ignorance is not bliss.

Further, ". . . conducting action research as a basis for making decisions and taking action is one of the *most important* activities" in which libraries engage (Ibid., p. 193). "The essence of action research is constantly to question, study, and improve the effectiveness of library information services and operations" (Ibid.). Statistics therefore should not be feared but properly understood and appropriately applied.

Appendix A
Answers to Summary Questions

Chapter 5

1. CAS: 2, CHS: 6, and COM: 4.
2. CAS: 16.7%, CHS: 50.0%, and COM: 33.3%
3.

Score	Frequency	Percentage	Cumulative Frequency	Cumulative Percentage
56–60	1	3.6	1	3.6
61–65	1	3.6	2	7.2
66–70	3	10.7	5	17.9
71–75	2	7.1	7	25.0
76–80	4	14.3	11	39.3
81–85	5	17.9	16	57.2
86–90	8	28.6	24	85.8
91–95	3	10.7	27	96.5
96–100	1	3.6	28	100.1

4. See answer to question 3.
5. 50th percentile: 81–85
   Lower percentile: 71–75
   Upper quartile: 86–90

6.

Library	Range	Variance	Standard Deviation
X	1100–1350	7000	83.67
Y	150–1000	137750	371.15
Z	850–950	1416.67	37.64

Y has the most variance and the least consistency in the number of titles circulated in the six-month period. Z has the least variance and the most consistency in the number of titles circulated for the same period.

7. The standard deviation shows how much each score varies around the mean. Instructors reflect wider variation in their knowledge of library skills. They appear to have less knowledge about library use (mean of 55.5) than do professors (mean of 82.5). Note that further insights would require hypothesis testing and the use of inferential statistics.

8. Z-scores:
−0.06	−1.47	−1.00	0.52	1.23
1.23	0.76	−1.35	−0.30	−0.06
−1.58	1.11	−1.70	0.64	−0.65
0.52	0.41	0.41	1.11	−0.30
0.76	−1.35	0.88	1.23	−1.00

   T-scores:
49.4	35.3	40.0	55.2	62.3
62.3	57.6	36.5	47.0	49.4
34.2	61.1	33.0	56.4	43.5
55.2	54.1	54.1	61.1	47.0
57.6	36.5	58.8	62.3	40.0

9. 29%

10. Mean = 0.286; standard deviation = 0.026

    Z-scores:
−0.62	2.08
−1.58	0.92
−0.23	−0.23
0.54	−0.42
0.15	−0.62

    T-scores:
43.8	70.8
34.2	59.2
47.7	47.7
55.4	45.8
51.5	43.8

Chapter 7

1. Nominal.
2. Ordinal.
3. Ordinal.
4. The t-test, a parametric test, is more powerful than a nonparametric test. However, it can be difficult to meet all the assumptions, for example, normality of distributions and having interval or ratio data.

   The Mann-Whitney U Test requires fewer assumptions but is less powerful than the t-test. Nonetheless, the Mann-Whitney U Test is one of the most powerful nonparametric tests.
5. The Phi coefficient applies to 2 × 2 tables, where $df = 1$. Cramer's V applies to tables with more cells.

   Yes, both can have the same value when there is a 2 × 2 table.
6. $t = 1.98$. The t-value is less than 2.101. The null hypothesis cannot be rejected. There is no difference between the sample means of Methods A and B.

7. Yes, because this is a 2 × 2 table.
8. There is no significant difference between gender of the person asking questions and the mode of asking questions (telephone and in-person).
9. With Yates' correction applied, it is 2.42. The chi-square value without the correlation is 2.59.
10. Because 2.42 is less than 3.841, we support the null hypothesis as stated in question 8. There is no significant difference.

Chapter 8

1. Pearson's r requires interval or ratio data. The other tests use ordinal, interval, or ratio data.
2. The assumptions are that (1) the relationship between two variables should be essentially linear, (2) two groups of scores need to be distributed normally, (3) the mean and standard deviation reflect the data, and (4) the scores need to be represented in an interval or ratio scale.
3. Nonparametric. Kendall's tau.
4. A correlation matrix provides different combinations of correlation among many variables. As a result, researchers obtain an overview of the possible relationship between variables.
5. Pearson's r is 0.092. For n equals 9, the critical value at the .05 level is 0.6664. Therefore, there is no relationship between the test scores on the library skills exercise and those on the English test.
6. Spearman's rho, unless there is a large number of tied scores.
7. Spearman's rho, using a one-tailed test. One list focuses on titles for retention and the other examines titles for cancellation. Given the opposite emphasis, there should be a negative correlation.
8. We could use Kendall's tau, gamma, or Somer's d depending on the research hypothesis.
9. Pearson's r, if the assumptions of a parametric test are met.

Chapter 9

1. The mean.
2. One-way ANOVA has one independent variable and two-way ANOVA has two independent variables.
3. The t-test only compares two means, while ANOVA compares two or more.
4. It is a ratio of the variance among the means.
5. SS is the sum of squares and MS is the mean square, computed by dividing SS by df in the same row.
6. The accompanying figure illustrates the line.

CD-ROM Stations versus Number of Patrons Waiting

Regression Analysis

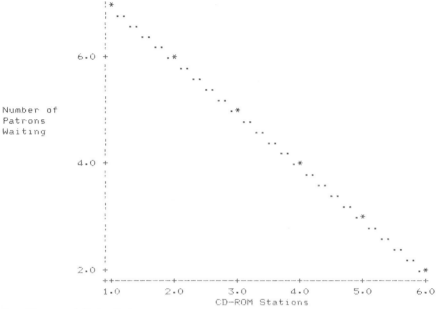

Scattergram of Data & Regression Line & Confidence Intervals

```
         !*
         !  . .
         !      . .
         !        . .
         !          . .
   6.0  +             .*
         !               . .
         !                 . .
         !                   . .
Number of!                     . .
Patrons  !                       .*
Waiting  !                         . .
         !                           . .
         !                             . .
         !                               . .
   4.0  +                                 .*
         !                                   . .
         !                                     . .
         !                                       . .
         !                                         .*
         !                                           . .
         !                                             . .
         !                                               . .
   2.0  +                                                  .*
        ++-----------+-----------+-----------+-----------+-----------+
         1.0         2.0         3.0         4.0         5.0         6.0
                                CD-ROM Stations
```

* = Observed Data Value
. = Predicted Data Value
– = 99.0% Confidence Limit

Summary Statistics (N=6)

IV = CD-ROM Stations	Mean of residuals = 0.0000
Mean of IV = 3.5000	S.D. of residuals = 0.0000D+00
S.D. of IV = 1.8708	
DV = Number of Patrons Waiting	Mean Abs. % Error = 0.0000D+00
Mean of DV = 4.5000	Mean % Error = 0.0000D+00
S.D. of DV = 1.8708	Mean Square Error = 0.0000D+00
Correlation coefficient =-1.0000	Degrees of freedom = 4
R-Squared = 1.0000	S.E. of estimate = 0.0000D+00

	Coefficient	Estd Std Error	T-Value	Significance
Intercept	8.0000	0.0000D+00	9999+	0.0000
Slope	-1.0000	0.0000D+00	9999+	0.0000

X	Y	XY	X²
1	7	7	1
2	6	12	4
3	5	15	9
4	4	16	16
5	3	15	25
X = 15	Y = 25	XY = 65	X² = 55

$$Y = mX + b$$

$$m = -1$$

The slope is negative 1. For every decrease in X, there is a corresponding decrease in Y (if $X = 6$, $Y = 2$). Two people.

7. The accompanying figure illustrates the line.

Students/Department vs # Circ./Department

```
Regression Analysis

    Scattergram of Data & Regression Line & Confidence Intervals

         ¦                                                                  . . *
         ¦                                                            . . . .
   100 + ¦                                                       * . . . .
         ¦                                                  . . . .
         ¦                                             . . . .
         ¦                                       . . * . .
 #       ¦                                  . . . .
 Circ./  ¦                             * . . .
 Department ¦                      . . . .
         ¦                    . . . .
         ¦               . . * .
         ¦          . . . .
    80 + ¦      * . . .
         ¦   . . . .
         ¦ . . . .
         ¦ * .
       ++-----------+-----------+-----------+-----------+-----------+-----------+
         50          60          70          80          90         100         110

                             # Students/Department
```

* = Observed Data Value
. = Predicted Data Value
— = 99.0% Confidence Limit

```
            Summary Statistics  (N=7)

IV = # Students/Department      Mean of residuals = 0.0000
Mean of IV = 80.0000            S.D. of residuals = 0.0000D+00
S.D. of IV = 21.6025

DV = # Circ./Department         Mean Abs. % Error = 0.0000D+00
Mean of DV = 90.0000            Mean % Error      = 0.0000D+00
S.D. of DV = 10.8012            Mean Square Error = 0.0000D+00

Correlation coefficient = 1.0000    Degrees of freedom = 5
R-Squared               = 1.0000    S.E. of estimate   = 0.0000D+00

            Coefficient   Estd Std Error   T-Value   Significance
            -----------   --------------   -------   ------------
Intercept     50.0000      0.0000D+00      9999+       0.0000
Slope          0.5000      0.0000D+00      9999+       0.0000
```

X	Y	XY	X^2
50	75	3750	2500
60	80	4800	3600
70	85	5950	4900
80	90	7200	6400
90	95	8550	8100
100	100	10000	10000
X = 450	Y = 525	XY = 40250	X^2 = 35500

$$m = .5$$

The regression line is a straight line with a slope of $+.5$. If a new department is added with 110 students, the graph indicates that 105 books can be expected to circulate.

8. $S_e = .087$
9. The accompanying figure illustrates the line.

Cost in Thousands versus # Reference Questions

```
Regression Analysis

        Scattergram of Data & Regression Line & Confidence Intervals

            ¦                                                              *
            ¦                                                          . .
      250 +                                                  . . .
            ¦                                                    . .
            ¦                                              * . .
            ¦                                          . .
            ¦                                      . . .
            ¦                                    . .
            ¦                              * . .
            ¦                            . .
  #         ¦                          . . .
            ¦
  Reference ¦                      . .
            ¦
  Questions 200 +                . . .
            ¦                  . .
            ¦              . . .
            ¦            . .
            ¦        * . .
            ¦      . .
            ¦    . . .
            ¦  . .
            ¦ * . .
            ¦ . .
      150 +    . . .
            ¦  . .
            ¦* . .
          ++----------+----------+----------+----------+----------+----------+
            1000      1500      2000      2500      3000      3500      400(

                              Cost in Thousands
  * = Observed Data Value
  . = Predicted Data Value
  - = 99.0% Confidence Limit
```

```
                Summary Statistics  (N=6)

IV = Cost in Thousands          Mean of residuals  = 0.0000
Mean of IV = 2500.0000          S.D. of residuals  = 0.0000D+00
S.D. of IV = 1183.2160

DV = # Reference Questions       Mean Abs. % Error  = 0.0000D+00
Mean of DV = 200.0000           Mean % Error       = 0.0000D+00
S.D. of DV = 47.3286            Mean Square Error  = 0.0000D+00

Correlation coefficient = 1.0000   Degrees of freedom = 4
R-Squared               = 1.0000   S.E. of estimate   = 0.0000D+00

          Coefficient   Estd Std Error   T-Value   Significance
          -----------   --------------   -------   ------------
Intercept   100.0000     0.0000D+00      9999+       0.0000
Slope         0.0400     0.0000D+00      9999+       0.0000
```

X	Y	XY	X^2
2000	180	36000	4000000
3000	220	660000	9000000
1500	160	240000	2250000
3500	240	840000	12250000
1000	140	140000	1000000
X = 11000	Y = 940	XY = 2240000	X^2 = 28500000

$$m = .4$$

10. If $X = \$4000$, Y' (predicted value of Y) $= 260$.

Appendix B
Statistical Analysis Software

This book highlights the use of two packages, StatPac and Minitab. The purpose is to illustrate the application of statistical analysis software that operate on the microcomputer. For large datasets, librarians could use a mainframe computer or download smaller sets onto floppy disks for use on a hard disk drive. Clearly, the technology is advancing and presenting librarians with options. They can use mainframe computers, minicomputers, and microcomputers. They may combine the use of statistical analysis software with other types of software, i.e., spreadsheets. StatPac, for example, has produced special packets that operate in conjunction with spreadsheets and perform one function—calculation of chi-square values, correlation coefficients, and so forth.

As has been discussed, Hernon and Richardson (1988) present over 70 different statistical analysis software packages that operate on microcomputers, both the Macintosh or IBM or IBM equivalent. The personal favorite of ours is StatPac. It is versatile, easy to use, and produces easy-to-read printout. Nonetheless, other packages, including Minitab, have positive features. It is important that librarians experiment with different packages and discover the one(s) that best meet their particular needs. The same is true for library school courses covering management, research methods, evaluation of library collections and services, and statistics.

Researchers who use statistics on a regular basis might prefer command-driven software or software that offers two modes (either command- or menu-driven). Occasional users of statistical analysis software might prefer menu-driven software, or perhaps packages that operate in conjunction with spread-sheets. Menu-driven software will be particularly useful in libraries where clerical and student staff are in charge of data input and the execution of specified analyses. Such software does not take as long to master.

Hernon and Richardson (1988) offer 23 evaluative criteria for the selection of general purpose statistical packages. These criteria merit review. In addition, that book contains a self-paced tutorial on the use of StatPac. We encourage the use of statistical analysis software. The combination of statistics with microcomputers underscores that statistical analysis software can be an important tool for library managers, especially those wanting decision support systems. Nonetheless, the use of statistics requires a solid foundation in research and knowledge of the various steps in the research process.

Bibliography

The ALA Survey of Librarian Salaries, 1988. Project directors Mary Jo Lynch and Margaret Myers. Chicago, IL: American Library Association, 1988.

Alder, Henry L. and Edward B. Roessler. *Introduction to Probability and Statistics.* San Francisco, CA: W.H. Freeman and Co., 1977.

Allen, Geoffrey G. "Management and the Conduct of In-House Library Research," *Library and Information Science Research*, 8 (1986): 155–162.

———. "The Management Use of Library Statistics," *IFLA Journal*, 11 (1985): 211–222.

Andrews, Frank M., Laura Klenn, Terrence N. Davidson, Patrick M. O'Malley, and Willard L. Rodgers. *A Guide for Selecting Statistical Techniques for Analyzing Social Science Data.* Ann Arbor, MI: University of Michigan, Institute for Social Research, Survey Research Center, 1974.

Argyris, Chris. "Some Limits of Rational Man Organizational Theory," *Public Administration Review*, 33 (1973): 257–269.

Ary, Donald, Lucy C. Jacobs, and Asghar Razavieh. *Introduction to Research in Education.* 3rd edition. New York: Holt, Rinehart and Winston, 1985.

Association of Research Libraries. Office of Management Studies. *Planning for Management Statistics.* Washington, D.C.: Association of Research Libraries, 1987.

Atkins, Stephen E. "Subject Trends in Library and Information Science Research, 1975–1984," *Library Trends*, 36 (Spring 1988): 633–658.

Benham, Frances and Ronald R. Powell. *Success in Answering Reference Questions: Two Studies.* Metuchen, NJ: Scarecrow, 1987.

Blalock, Hubert M., Jr. *Social Statistics.* New York: McGraw-Hill, 1972, 1979.

Bommer, Michael R.W. and Ronald W. Chorba. *Decision Making for Library Management.* White Plains, NY: Knowledge Industry Publications, Inc., 1982.

Borgman, Christine L. *End User Behavior on the Ohio State University Libraries' Online Catalog: A Computer Monitoring Study.* Dublin, OH: OCLC, 1983.

Bourne, C.P. "Some User Requirements Stated Quantitatively in Terms of the 90% Library," in *Electronic Information Handling*, edited by Allen Kent and Orrin E. Taulbee. Washington, D.C.: Spartan Books, 1965, pp. 93–110.

Bradburn, Norman M., Lance J. Rips, and Steven K. Shevell. "Answering Autobiographical Questions: The Impact of Memory and Inference on Surveys," *Science*, 236 (April 10, 1987): 157–161.

Broadus, Robert N. "The Applications of Citation Analyses to Library Collection Building," in *Advances in Librarianship.* New York: Academic Press, 1977, pp. 299–335.

Bruer, J. Michael. "Management Information Aspects of Automated Acquisitions Systems," *Library Resources & Technical Services*, 24 (Fall 1980): 339–342.

Buckland, Michael K. *Library Services in Theory and Context*. New York: Pergamon Press, 1983.

Bunge, Charles A. *Professional Education and Reference Efficiency*. Springfield, IL: Illinois State Library, 1967.

Burr, R.L. "Evaluating Library Collections: A Case Study," *Journal of Academic Librarianship*, 5 (1979): 256–260.

Busha, Charles H. and Stephen P. Harter. *Research Methods in Librarianship*. New York: Academic Press, 1980.

"Buyer's Guide: Presentation Graphics," *Personal Computing*, 13 (February 1989): 121–176.

Bybee, C.R. "Fitting Information Presentation Formats to Decision-Making: A Study in Strategies to Facilitate Decision-Making," *Communication Research*, 8 (1981): 343–370.

Carlson, G. *Search Strategy by Reference Librarians*. Part 3 of Final Report on the Organization of Large Files. Sherman Oaks, CA: Hughes Dynamics Inc., Advanced Information Systems Division, 1964 (available from NTIS, PB 166192).

Carmines, Edward G. and Richard A. Zeller. *Reliability and Validity Assessment*. Beverly Hills, CA: Sage Publications, 1979.

Carpenter, Ray L. and Ellen Storey Vasu. *Statistical Methods for Librarians*. Chicago, IL: American Library Association, 1978.

Champion, Dean J. *Basic Statistics for Social Research*. New York: MacMillan, 1981.

Chen, Ching-chih and Peter Hernon. *Information Seeking: Assessing and Anticipating User Needs*. New York: Neal-Schuman, 1982.

Clack, Mary E. and Sally F. Williams. "Using Locally and Nationally Produced Periodical Price Indexes in Budget Preparation," *Library Resources and Technical Services*, 27 (October/December 1983): 345–356.

Cleveland, William S. *The Elements of Graphing Data*. Monterey, CA: Wadsworth Advanced Books and Software, 1985.

Cochran, W.G. "Some Methods for Strengthening the Common Chi-Square Tests," *Biometrics*, 10 (1954): 417–451.

Cooper, W.S. "Expected Search Length: A Single Measure of Retrieval Effectiveness Based on the Weak Ordering Action of Retrieval Systems," *American Documentation*, 19 (1968): 30–41.

Crowley, Terence and Thomas Childers. *Information Service in Public Libraries: Two Studies*. Metuchen, NJ: Scarecrow Press, 1971.

Davis, Charles H. "Editorial," *Library and Information Science Research*, 10 (1988): 1.

D'Elia, George. "A Response to Van House," *Public Libraries*, 27 (Spring 1988): 28–31.

Dowlin, Kenneth E. "The Use of Standard Statistics in an On-Line Library Management System," *Public Library Quarterly*, 3 (Spring/Summer 1982): 37–46.

Drott, M. Carl. "Random Sampling: A Tool for Library Research," *College & Research Libraries*, 30 (March 1969): 119–125.

Evaluating Bibliographic Instruction: A Handbook. Chicago, IL: American Library Association, Association of College and Research Libraries, Bibliographic Instruction Section, 1983.

Ferguson, George. *Statistical Analysis in Psychology and Education*. New York: McGraw-Hill, 1981.

Freund, John E. *Statistics: A First Course*. Englewood Cliffs, NJ: Prentice Hall, 1976.

Futas, Elizabeth. *The Library Forms Illustrated Handbook*. New York: Neal-Schuman, 1984.

Gulick, L. and L. Urwick, eds. "Notes on the Theory of Organization," in *Papers on the Science of Administration*. New York: Columbia University Press, 1937, pp. 1–45.

Hallman, Clark N. "Designing Optical Mark Forms for Reference Statistics," *RQ*, 20 (Spring 1981): 257–264.

Halperin, Michael. "Waiting Lines," *RQ*, 16 (Summer 1977): 297–299.

Harwell, Michael R. "Choosing between Parametric and Nonparametric Tests," *Journal of Counseling and Development*, 67 (September 1988): 35–38.

Hawks, Carol P. "The GEAC Acquisitions System as a Source of Management Information," *Library Acquisitions: Practice and Theory*, 10 (1986): 245–253.

Hays, William L. *Statistics for Psychologists*. New York: Holt, Rinehart, and Winston, 1963.

Hecht, Myron, Herbert Hecht, and Laurence Press. *Microcomputers: Introduction to Features and Uses*. NBS Special Publication 500–110. Institute for Computer Science and Technology, National Bureau of Standards, U.S. Department of Commerce. Washington, D.C.: GPO, 1984.

Hernon, Peter. "Information Needs and Gathering Patterns of Academic Social Scientists, with Special Emphasis Given to Historians and Their Use of U.S. Government Publications," *Government Information Quarterly*, 1 (1984): 401–429.

———. "Utility Measures, Not Performance Measures, for Library Reference Service?," *RQ*, 26 (Summer 1987): 449–459.

Hernon, Peter and Charles R. McClure. "Quality of Data Issues in Unobtrusive Testing of Library Reference Service: Recommendations and Strategies," *Library and Information Science Research*, 9 (April/June 1987a): 77–93.

———. *Unobtrusive Testing and Library Reference Services*. Norwood, NJ: Ablex Publishing Corp., 1987b.

Hernon, Peter, Charles R. McClure, and Gary R. Purcell. *GPO's Depository Library Program*. Norwood, NJ: Ablex Publishing Corp., 1985.

Hernon, Peter and Maureen Pastine. "Student Perceptions of Academic Librarians," *College & Research Libraries*, 38 (March 1977): 129–139.

Hernon, Peter and John V. Richardson. *Microcomputer Software for Performing Statistical Analysis*. Norwood, NJ: Ablex Publishing Corp., 1988.

Huck, Schuyler W., William H. Cormier, and William G. Bounds, Jr. *Reading Statistics and Research*. New York: Harper & Row, 1974.

Hurt, C.D. "A Comparison of A Bibliometric Approach and An Historical Approach to the Identification of Important Literature," *Information Processing & Management*, 19 (1983): 151–157.

Iehl, Ronald E. and Edward J. Kazlauskas. "Use of SPSS to Enhance Management Decision Making," in *Information Interaction: Proceedings of the 45th ASIS Annual Meeting*, vol. 19, edited by Anthony E. Petrarca, Celianna I. Taylor, and Robert S. Kohn. White Plains, NY: Knowledge Industry Publications, Inc., 1982, pp. 141–143.

Jaeger, Richard M. *Statistics: A Spectator Sport*. Beverly Hills, CA: Sage, 1983.

Janis, Irving L. and L. Mann. *Decision Making*. New York: The Free Press, 1977.

Johnson, Edward R. and Stuart H. Mann. *Organizational Development for Academic Libraries*. Westport, CT: Greenwood Press, 1980.

Kast, Fremont E. and James E. Rosenzweig. *Organization and Management: A Systems and Contingency Approach*. 4th edition. New York; McGraw-Hill, 1985.

Kelly, Sarah A., Pamela Q.J. Andre, and James B. Morrison. "Agricultural Information: A Comparison of Information Delivery Alternatives," *Microcomputers for Information Management*, 5 (June 1988): 113–128.

Kenney, L. "The Implications of the Needs of Users for the Design of a Catalogue: A Survey at the International Labor Office," *Journal of Documentation*, 22 (1966): 195–202.

Kerlinger, Fred N. *Foundations of Behavioral Research*. New York: Holt, Rinehart, and Winston, 1973.

Kim, Choong Han and Robert David Little. *Public Library Users and Uses: A Market Research Handbook*. Metuchen, NJ: Scarecrow, 1987.

Kohl, David F. and Lizabeth A. Wilson. "Effectiveness of Course-Integrated Bibliographic Instruction in Improving Coursework," *RQ*, 26 (Winter 1986): 206–211.

Kohout, Frank J. *Statistics for Social Scientists: A Coordinated Learning System*. New York: Wiley, 1974.

Koontz, Harold and Cyril O'Donnell. *Management: A Systems and Contingency Analysis of Managerial Functions*. New York: McGraw-Hill, 1979.

Lancaster, F.W. *The Measurement and Evaluation of Library Services*. Washington, D.C.: Information Resources Press, 1977.

_____. *If You Want to Evaluate Your Library* . . .. Champaign, IL: University of Illinois, Graduate School of Library and Information Science, 1988.

Lazorick, Gerald. "Patterns of Book Use Using the Negative Binomial Distribution," *Library Research*, 1 (1979): 171–188.

Lee, Alec. *Applied Queuing Theory*. New York: St. Martin's Press, 1966.

Luthans, Fred. *Introduction to Management: A Contingency Approach*. New York: McGraw-Hill, 1976.

Lynch, Mary Jo. *Library Data Collection Handbook*. Chicago, IL: American Library Association, 1981.

_____. *Sources of Library Statistics, 1972–1982*. Chicago, IL: American Library Association, 1983.

Marchant, Maurice P. *Participative Management in Academic Libraries*. Westport, CT: Greenwood Press, 1976.

_____, Nathan M. Smith, and Keith H. Stirling. "SPSS As a Library Research Tool." Occasional Research Paper No. 1. Provo, UT: Brigham Young University, School of Library and Information Sciences, 1977.

McCartt, Ann. "The Application of Social Judgment Analysis to Library Faculty Tenure Decisions," *College & Research Libraries*, 44 (September 1983): 345–357.

McClure, Charles R. *Information for Academic Library Decision Making: The Case for Organizational Information Management*. Westport, CT: Greenwood Press, 1980.

_____. "Management Information for Library Decision Making," in *Advances in Librarianship*, vol. 13, edited by Wesley Simonton. New York: Academic Press, 1984, pp. 1–47.

_____. "A View from the Trenches: Costing and Performance Measures for Academic Library Public Services," *College & Research Libraries*, 47 (July 1986): 323–336.

_____, Amy Owen, Douglas L. Zweizig, Mary Jo Lynch, and Nancy A. Van House. *Planning and Role Setting for Public Libraries: A Manual of Options and Procedures*. Chicago, IL: American Library Association, 1987.

McClure, Charles R. and Peter Hernon. *Improving the Quality of Reference Service for Government Publications*. Chicago, IL: American Library Association, 1983.

McGrath, Joseph E., Joanne Martin, and Richard A. Kulka. *Judgment Calls in Research*. Beverly Hills, CA: Sage, 1982.

Meddis, Ray. *Statistical Handbook for Non-statisticians*. New York: McGraw-Hill, 1975.

Metz, Paul. "The Role of the Academic Library Director," *Journal of Academic Librarianship*, 5 (July 1979): 148–152.

Molina, E.C. *Poisson's Exponential Binomial Limit*. New York: Van Nostrand, 1942.

Morton, Bruce. "Statistical Data as a Management Tool for Reference Managers, or Roulette by the Numbers," *The Reference Librarian*, 19 (1987): 87–109.

Mueller, John S., Karl F. Schuesslet, and Herbert L. Costner. *Statistical Reasoning in Sociology*. Boston, MA: Houghton Mifflin, 1977.

Murfin, Marjorie E. and Gary M. Gugelchuck. "Development and Testing of a Reference Transaction Assessment Instrument," *College & Research Libraries*, 48 (July 1987): 314–338.

Nelson, Jerold. "Faculty Awareness and Attitudes toward Academic Library Reference Services: A Measure of Communication," *College & Research Libraries*, 34 (September 1973): 268–275.

O'Conner, Daniel O. "Evaluating Public Libraries Using Standard Scores: The Library Quotient," *Library Research*, 4 (1982): 51–70.

Orr, R.H. and E.E. Olson. "Quantitative Measures as Management Tools." Materials prepared for a continuing education course of the Medical Library Association. Chicago, IL: Medical Library Association, 1968.

Paisley, William J. "Behavioral Studies on Scientific Information Flow: An Appendix on Method." New London, NH: Gordon Research Conference on Scientific Method, 1969.

Permut, J.E., A.J. Michel, and M. Joseph. "The Researcher's Sample: A Review of the Choice of Respondents in Marketing Research," *Journal of Marketing Research*, 13 (1976): 278–283.

Popa, Opritsa D., Deborah A. Metzer, and James A. Singleton. "Teaching Search Techniques on the Computerized Catalog and on the Traditional Card Catalog: A Comparative Study," *College & Research Libraries*, 49 (May 1988): 263–274.

Powell, Ronald R. *Basic Research Methods for Librarians*. Norwood, NJ: Ablex Publishing Corp., 1985.

_____ and Sheila D. Creth. "Knowledge Bases and Library Education," *College & Research Libraries*, 47 (January 1986): 16–27.

_____. "Sources of Professional Knowledge for Academic Librarians," *College & Research Libraries*, 49 (July 1988): 332–340.

Pungitore, Verna L. "Perceptions of Change and Public Library Directors in Indiana: An Exploratory Study," *Library and Information Science Research*, 9 (October/December 1987): 247–264.

Rayward, W. Boyd. "Publishing Library Research," *College & Research Libraries*, 41 (May 1980): 210–219.

Richardson, John V., Jr. "Readability and Readership of Journals in Library Science," *Journal of Academic Librarianship*, 3 (1977): 20–22.

Riggs, Donald E. *Strategic Planning for Library Managers*. Phoenix, AZ: Oryx Press, 1984.

Robertson, S.E. "The Parametric Description of Retrieval Tests," *Journal of Documentation*, 25 (1969): 93–107.

Rossi, Peter H. and Howard E. Freeman. *Evaluation: A Systematic Approach*. 3rd edition. Beverly Hills, CA: Sage, 1985.

Rubin, Richard. *Inhouse Use of Materials in Public Libraries*. Urbana, IL: University of Illinois, Graduate School of Library and Information Science, 1986.

Sanders, Nancy P., Edward T. O'Neill, and Stuart L. Weibel. "Automated Collection Analysis Using the OCLC and RLG Bibliographic Databases," *College & Research Libraries*, 49 (July 1988): 305–314.

Siegel, Sidney. *Nonparametric Statistics for the Behavioral Sciences*. New York: McGraw-Hill Book Co., 1956.

Slonim, Morris James. *Sampling in a Nutshell*. New York: Simon and Schuster, 1960.

Smith, Dana E. "Create: Customized Reference Statistics Programs," *American Libraries*, 15 (March 1984): 179.

Spiegel, Murray R. *Theory and Problems of Statistics*. New York: Schaum Pub. Co., 1961.

Stakenas, James A. and Nancy P. Merrick. "Application of SPSS to Management of Computer-Assisted Instruction Usage Statistics," *Bulletin of the Medical Library Association*, 70 (April 1982): 231–233.

"StatPac Gold—Statistical Analysis Package for the IBM: Manual." Minneapolis, MN: Walonick Associates, Inc., 1988.

Strain, Paula M. "Evaluation by the Numbers," *Special Libraries*, 73 (July 1982): 165–172.

Swisher, Robert and Charles R. McClure. *Research for Decision Making: Methods for Librarians*. Chicago, IL: American Library Association, 1984.

Tate, Elizabeth L. "Telling the Tale with Tables," *The Journal of Academic Librarianship*, 14 (1989): 348–352.

Taylor, Bernard and John R. Sparkes. *Corporate Strategy and Planning*. New York: Wiley, 1977.

Taylor, Joyce and Tracey Viegas. "A Mathematical Approach to Branch Library Operations: A Case Study," *Special Libraries*, 79 (Fall 1988): 322–327.

Tekfi, Chaffai. "Readability Formulas: An Overview," *Journal of Documentation*, 43 (September 1987): 257–269.

Toifel, Ronald C. and Wesley D. Davis. "Investigating Library Study Skills of Children in the Public Schools," *Journal of Academic Librarianship*, 9 (September 1983): 211–215.

Tolle, John E. *Current Utilization of Online Catalogs: Transaction Log Analysis*. Dublin, OH: OCLC, 1983.

Townley, Charles T. "Using SPSS to Analyze Book Collection Data," *Drexel Library Quarterly*, 17 (Winter 1981): 87–119.

Tufte, Edward R. *The Visual Display of Quantitative Information.* Cheshire, CT: Graphics Press, 1983.

"The Usefulness of Fill Rates: Research and Debate," *Public Libraries*, 27 (Spring 1988): 15.

Van House, Nancy. "In Defense of Fill Rates," *Public Libraries*, 27 (Spring 1988): 25–27.

————, Mary Jo Lynch, Charles R. McClure, Douglas L. Zweizig, and Eleanor Jo Rodger. *Output Measures for Public Libraries.* 2nd edition. Chicago, IL: American Library Association, 1987.

Wallace, Danny P. "The Use of Statistical Methods in Library and Information Science," *Journal of the American Society for Information Science*, 36 (November 1985): 402–410.

Weiss, Robert S. *Statistics in Social Research.* New York: Wiley, 1968.

Wells, Margaret R. and Randolph S. Gadikian. "BISTATS: Using dBASEIII to Compile Library Instruction Statistics," *Research Strategies*, 5 (Fall 1987): 180–185.

White, Howard D. "Measurement at the Reference Desk," *Drexel Library Quarterly*, 17 (Winter 1981): 3–35.

Wiegand, Wayne A. and Dorothy Steffens. "Members of the Club: A Look at One Hundred ALA Presidents." Occasional Papers No. 182. Urbana, IL: University of Illinois, Graduate School of Library and Information Science, April 1988.

Wilson, Pauline. *Stereotype and Status: Librarians in the United States.* Westport, CT: Greenwood Press, 1982.

Wong, William S. and David S. Zubatsky. "The Tenure Rate of University Library Directors: A 1983 Survey," *College & Research Libraries*, 46 (January 1985): 69–77.

Wren, Daniel A. *The Evolution of Management Thought.* New York: Ronald Press, 1972.

Yin, Robert K. *Case Study Research: Design and Methods.* Beverly Hills, CA: Sage, 1984.

Zweizig, Douglas L. "Reviews," *Library Quarterly*, 58 (October 1988): 403–404.

Author Index

Subject Index

A

ABI/INFORM, 149, 153–154, 157
Action Research, *see* Research
ALA Survey of Librarian Salaries, 49
Analysis of Covariance, 132, *see also* Analysis
   of Variance
Analysis of Variance (ANOVA), 24, 123–125,
   127–133, 141
   calculation, 128–129, 131
   examples—hypothetical, 130–131
   examples—literature, 125
   formula, 129
   see also Analysis of Covariance, Multivari-
      ate Analysis of Variance, One-way
      Analysis of Variance, Two-way Analy-
      sis of Variance
Analytical Databases, 32–33, *see also* Reflex
ANCOVA, *see* Analysis of Covariance
ANOVA, *see* Analysis of Variance
Applied Research, *see* Research
Area Chart, *see* Frequency Polygons
Averages, *see* Measures of Central Tendency

B

Bar Charts, 31, 64–68, 71
   examples—literature, 67–68
Basic Research, *see* Research
Binomial Distribution, 54–56, 154
BRS, 143, 148

C

CHART-MASTER, 64
Chi-square Test of Independence, 24, 40, 46,
   54, 89–91, 97–103, 105, 147–148,
   156–158
   calculation, 98–99, 101, 148, 157–158
   examples—hypothetical, 98–101, 147–148,
      156–158
   examples—literature, 91
   formula, 98
Ci2 System 100, 30

Citation Analysis, 19–20
Cluster Sampling, *see* Sampling
Confidence Level, 40–41, 79, 83, 111, 138–
   139
Correlation, 24, 89, 106–122, 133, 144
   types, 106–107
   see also Gamma, Kendall's tau, Pearson's *r*,
      Somer's *d*, Spearman's rho
Correlation Coefficient, 44, 58, 66, 94, 101,
   106–107, 110–112, 116, 122, 134,
   136, 138, 142
Correlation Matrix, 107, 109, 121–122, 141,
   156
   examples—hypothetical, 121
   examples—literature, 109
Cramer's *V*, 90–91, 102–105
   examples—literature, 91
   formula, 104
Current Index to Journals in Education, 149

D

Data Collection, 9–12, 18–22, 24–25, 29–30,
   40–44, 83–84, 123
Database Management Software, 12, 27, 31–
   32, 47
dBase III, 12
Decile, 49
Decision Making, 5, 7–15, 20–26, 31, 37, 46
   decision levels, 8
   research, 9–10, 20–21
   stages, 8
Decision Support Systems (DSS), 11–12, 25,
   184
Degrees of Freedom, 53, 94, 98–99, 101,
   128–129
Descriptive Statistics, 5–6, 12, 24, 32, 44,
   47–74, 87, 144, 172
   see also Decile, Dispersion, Mean, Mea-
      sures of Central Tendency, Median,
      Mode, Normal Curve, Percentiles and